Santa Clarita

Best Wishes

Jerry Reynolds

Photo Research by Teri Davis Greenberg

Produced in Cooperation with the Santa Clarita Valley Chamber of Commerce

World Of Communications, Inc.
Granada Hills, California

Santa Clarita
Valley of the Golden Dream

An Illustrated History
by Jerry Reynolds

World of Communications, Inc.
President/Editor-In-Chief: Jane Boeckmann
General Manager: Fred Braden
Project Coordinator: Olivia Boyd
Senior Editor: Teri Davis Greenberg
Staff for Santa Clarita: Valley of the Golden Dream

Library of Congress Cataloging-in-Publication Data
Reynolds, Gerald G.
Santa Clarita : valley of the golden dream : an illustrated history/by Jerry Reynolds;
Santa Clarita Valley Chamber of Commerce.
216 pp.; .22 x 24 cm.
Includes bibliographical references and index.
ISBN 0-89781-442-8 (acid-free paper)
1. Santa Clarita Valley (Calif.)—History. 2. Santa Clarita Valley (Calif.)—Description and travel—Views.
3. Santa Clarita Valley (Calif.)—Industries. I. Title.
F868.L8R49 1991
979.4'93—dc20   91-30060
CIP

© 1992 World of Communications, Inc.
All rights reserved
Published 1992
Printed in the United States of America
First Edition

Portions of the first six chapters of the text of this book were originally published, in slightly different form, in the *The Newhall Signal and Saugus Enterprise*.

The information in this publication has been carefully researched to ensure maximum accuracy. World of Communications, Inc., and the Santa Clarita Valley Chamber of Commerce cannot and do not guarantee either the correctness of all information furnished them or the complete absence of errors and omissions. Consequently, responsibility for same neither can be, nor is, assumed.

Contents

1 INTRODUCTION 7

1 INDIANS, SPANIARDS, AND CALIFORNIOS 9
Before 1850

The Mysterious Tataviam • Spain Marches • Mansions of God • The Asistencia • Revolution • The Santa Clara's Lord • The Del Valle Dynasty • Golden Dream • Twilight of the Dons • Manifest Destiny • King Cattle

2 GETTING AROUND AND SETTLING DOWN 27
1850s-1860s

Wiley's Windlass • Over the Pass • Camel Caravans • Lyon's Station • Nature Strikes Back • End of Solitude • Beale's Bonanza

3 BLACK GOLD AND THE IRON HORSE 39
1860s-1870s

Rivers of Oil • Peaceful Pico Canyon Erupts • John Lang and the Bear • The Saga of Tiburcio Vásquez • The Life and Times of Henry M. Newhall • Judge Powell of the Soledad • Coming of the Iron Horse • Driving the Golden Spike

4 TOWN FOUNDINGS AND EARLY SETTLERS 55
1870s-Early 1900s

The Founding of Newhall • The Baron of Castaic • The Stills of Railroad Canyon • Life in Mentryville • Mining the Soledad • The Acton Chronicles • The Saugus-Surrey Saga • Needham of the St. John Tract • The Crown Valley Feud • The Rise and Fall of the Sterling • Mulholland's Magnificent Waterworks • Conquering the Hills of Castaic

5 HARD TIMES AND CELLULOID COWBOYS 83
Early 1900s-1929

The Thrill of It All • An Age of Progress • Requiem for St. Francis • Tales of the Twenties • The Great Saugus Train Robbery • Riders of the Silver Screen • A Melody of Slippery Gulch

6 NEW BEGINNINGS AND GROWING PAINS 103
1930s-Present

Troubled Times • The Battle of Mad Mountain • Farewell to the Simple Life • The Awakening Giant • Tract Homes and Shopping Centers • Halls of Ivy • A Great Place to Play • Sagebrush Reservoirs • The Great Rebellion • The Birth of a City

SANTA CLARITA VALLEY MILESTONES 129
A Chronology of Historical Highlights— A.D. 450-1991

7 PARTNERS IN PROGRESS 133
Histories of Santa Clarita Valley businesses, organizations, municipal agencies, educational institutions, health care facilities, professional associations, and professionals.

ACKNOWLEDGMENTS AND BIBLIOGRAPHY 212

INDEX 213

INTRODUCTION

Wedged into northern Los Angeles County and bounded by two great mountain ranges is an area known as the Upper Santa Clara River Valley.

Part of this basin is incorporated as the City of Santa Clarita, including Newhall, most parts of Saugus, Valencia, and some of Canyon Country. Outside of the boundaries, but long considered part of the Santa Clara, are Val Verde, Castaic, Castaic Junction, Gorman, Agua Dulce, and Acton; while located on the perimeter are Lebeck, Fort Tejon, Lake Hughes, and Lake Elizabeth.

Most of the 170,000 residents of this immense region seem to think that these communities were born only yesterday, hardly, if ever, giving a thought to the generations of Indians, explorers, soldiers, pioneers, farmers, ranchers, and shopkeepers who went before them.

The chronicle of the Santa Clarita is a rich one, indeed, for it is actually a microcosm of the bombastic saga of the American West. Yet, in many ways, the heritage of the area is unique. Here there are still traces of mammoth hunters dating back perhaps 28,000 years. Spanish lancers left their shadows upon the land as did padres and Mexican dons.

Gold was discovered here long before the "rush" to Northern California. Yankee dragoons clattered across the valley led by John C. Frémont and Edward F. Beale, pennants fluttering in the breeze. There were imprints left by the hooves of camels, tracks of high-sided freight wagons, and grand red coaches belonging to the Butterfield Overland Express. There were stage stops, oil wells, hard rock mines, and empires of cattle. Yet, curiously, we memorialize H.M. Newhall, a businessman, and Tiburcio Vásquez, an outlaw.

These pages will introduce you to men with names now associated with places. You will get to know the Lyon Brothers, Sanford and Cyrus, whose name is now that of an avenue, and Henry Clay Wiley, a man who ran a stage stop, whose name has been given to a canyon and a road.

While the Del Valle tract recalls the masters of Rancho San Francisco, Pico Canyon honors a Mexican general. Nickels Street in Acton, Lloyd Houghton in Newhall, and Castaic's Tapia Canyon preserve the memory of valley pioneers.

These people and others caused events to happen that still affect and illuminate our times. The Santa Clarita can boast of the oldest-existing oil refinery in the world, until recently, the longest-producing oil well, and the greatest water delivery system. It was also the site of the second-largest disaster in California and a range war/feud that took 23 lives.

Like all histories, this story has no end. It is constantly changing and progressing. Yet, this is the way it was in the last decade of the twentieth century.

Cowboy by Jerry Reynolds depicts a wrangler surveying the beautiful terrain of Towsley Canyon.

1

Indians, Spaniards, and Californios

Before 1850

The Mysterious Tataviam

About the time that the Roman Empire was crumbling away in Europe, a mass migration of people began across the upper Great Plains of America.

Fierce and warlike, they managed to push the Chumash beyond Piru Creek and the Yumans toward the Colorado River. These newcomers, arriving about A.D. 450, spoke Tacic, or the Uto-Aztedan language of the Shoshone Indians.

Later Spaniards would call them Serranos or Mountain People. These Serranos occupied the San Gabriel Mountains, settled along the Mojave River, where they were known as Vanyuma, and wandered into the Antelope Valley to become Kitanemuks. The invasion was completed by A.D. 500 with the takeover of the Upper Santa Clara River Valley.

Their cousins, the Kitanemuks, always called them Tataviam, meaning Dwellers of Sunny Slopes.

The Tataviam settled down into some 25 semi-permanent villages with strange-sounding names. Nuhubit was located south of what is now downtown Newhall; Kamulus stood at the site of the present Camulos Ranch; Piru-U-Bit was on the banks of Piru Creek; Tochonanga clustered west of Interstate 5; while Chaguibit was a metropolis of upwards of 500 souls residing at Castaic Junction.

They hunted small game such as rabbit and squirrel and exploited larger animals—deer, antelope, and mountain goat—which lived in abundance in the valley. They chewed or smoked tree tobacco and took yerba santa as a painkiller. Buckwheat was mixed with water and cooked to make a sort of gruel, while toyon berries were roasted and eaten.

Certainly the staple of the diet was acorns, which were leached of their bitter tannic acid and made into a sort of tortilla.

Home was a wickiup, which resembled an upside-down basket made of arched sycamore poles and thatched with grass. They also constructed dwellings partially underground with domed adobe roofs and raised platforms for sleeping.

The Tataviam wove excellent baskets, but made no pottery, even though clay was available. They were at the hub of a trading network that extended from the Channel Islands to Arizona's desert and northward into the San Joaquin Valley. Many imported items have been found in graves. No doubt asphaltum and fused shale were bartered over to the coast, while acorns and piñón nuts were sent inland.

The last of the Tataviam passed away on the Camulos Ranch in 1916. His name was Juan José Fustero. He recalled that his parents were born at the San Fernando Mission, while his grandparents came from Nuhubit (Newhall). He remembered a few ancestral phrases such as *hami kwa umi*

The Tataviam, most probably Serrano Shoshones, lived in wickiups constructed of arched sycamore poles thatched with grass as well as in underground dwellings. They wove excellent baskets, hunted small game, and ate roasted toyon berries, buckwheat gruel, and a type of tortilla made from acorns. Depicted here is a Tataviam village in Towsley Canyon. Drawing by Jerry Reynolds. Courtesy, Santa Clarita Valley Historical Society

Named after outlaw Tiburcio Vásquez, who used the area as his hideout during his 20-year reign of terror, Vasquez Rocks features an extensive display of Tataviam petroglyphs that date back some 1,500 years. Now a county park, Vasquez Rocks can be reached along Escondido Canyon Road in Saugus. Photo by Jerry Reynolds

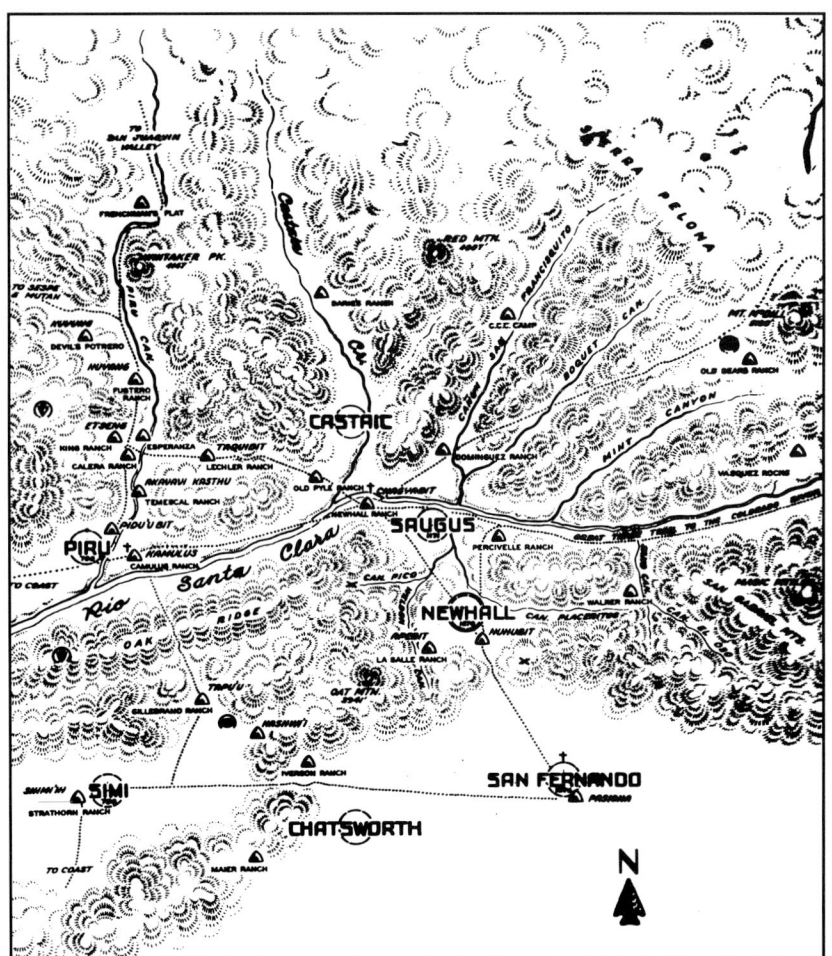

(Where are you going?); that a *Kika* was a chief; *Piiouku* (Piru), a tule reed; and *Islay* (Hasley), a berry.

The Tataviam left a wealth of information about themselves chiseled into and painted on rock overhangs or secreted deep in caves. Scattered about the Angeles National Forest or concentrated in several panels at Vasquez Rocks County Park are pictures of curious figures with rake-like hands resembling lizards. Some are outlines of human forms; others are abstract designs looking like zig-zags, hourglasses, grids, circles, or simply curvy lines.

Dominating the rock art are several circles with exterior projections resembling suns or moons. Unfortunately there is not a living person who can read them.

Also hidden away in caves were ceremonial items, none of which can compare to the treasure trove found at a place known as Bower's Cave. Discovered by local ranchers, McCoy and Everette Pyle, on May 2, 1884, the small cavern was crammed with large baskets, cleverly woven

LEFT: *On August 8, 1769, an expedition led by Don Gaspar de Portolá entered the Santa Clarita Valley through what is now known as the Santa Clara Divide at Elsmere Canyon. Portolá wore the officer's uniform of the First Battalion of the Second Regiment of Catalonian Volunteers. Drawing by Jerry Reynolds*

FACING PAGE, TOP: *At one time about two dozen semipermanent Tataviam Indian villages were located in the Santa Clarita Valley. Among these settlements were Nuhubit, which was south of today's downtown Newhall; Kamulus, located where the Camulos Ranch now stands; Piru-U-Bit, on the banks of Piru Creek; Tochonanga, west of what is now Interstate 5; and Chaguibit, which stood at what is known today as Castaic Junction. Map by Richard F. Van Valkenburgh, 1935. Courtesy, Santa Clarita Valley Historical Society*

FACING PAGE, BOTTOM: *Juan José Fustero (left), the last of the Santa Clarita Valley's Tataviam, posed with his family sometime in the first decade of the twentieth century. Fustero passed away on the Camulos Ranch in 1916. From the collection of Abigail Lechler Riley. Courtesy, Santa Clarita Valley Historical Society*

capes and headresses, crystals, and hundreds of other items. The collection was sold to Dr. Stephen Bowers, and most of it ended up in the Peabody Museum at Harvard University. It remains one of the most significant assemblages of Native-American crafts in North America.

SPAIN MARCHES

In the generations since their ancestors invaded the land, the Tataviam had become gentle, friendly, and trusting. If the probes of Cabrillo and Alarcón had been viewed with alarm—or at least curiosity—the arrival of a fully mounted troop of His Majesty's Catalonian Volunteers can only be compared in shock value to an alien spaceship suddenly landing in the middle of Lyon's Avenue today. Yet there was no panic or undue excitement, just quiet acceptance and cordial welcome.

It was the eighth day of August, 1769, when a strange cavalcade of soldiers appeared atop what is now called Santa Clara Divide Peak at Elsmere Canyon. Surveying the valley below through a telescope was the leader of the party, Don Gaspar de Portolá, who had been entrusted with the vital mission of bringing California into the imperial fold of Spain.

A month before, on July 16, Portolá and Father Junípero Serra had established a mission and presidio at San Diego. Serra remained there to nurse the struggling colony along while Governor Portolá headed north with 64 men to locate the Bay of Monterey.

Father Juan Crespí, the chief diarist of the Portolá Expedition, was a robust, intelligent Franciscan who wrote a faithful log of the journey from San Diego to Monterey. When the epic trek was over, he turned his journal over to Father-Presidente Junípero Serra, who had it published.

It is possible to read the narrative of the first European to visit the Santa Clarita Valley. Some excerpts follow:

It has a great deal of very good, grass-covered, flat soil . . . two large springs of water, each giving rise to a stream . . . running in among some trees. And so this place has two creeks and a river, a great deal of trees; cottonwoods, willows, sycamores and live-oaks; and pine trees which are to be seen in the mountains on the north side, and a great amount of lush plants of all sorts, with grapevines and rose patches. I named it for the lady St. Claire, SANTA CLARA, both that behind us and that which is still to come, trusting that in time it will become a very large mission, with a vast number of heathen folk, the finest that we have encountered so far.

ABOVE: *Don Antonio del Valle moved his family into the* asistencia *on the bluff overlooking the junction of Castaic Creek and the Santa Clara River, where he presided over his 48,829-acre Rancho San Francisco. When Don Antonio died in June of 1841, he left 16 bulls, 420 cows, 318 heifers, 576 calves, 1,008 sheep, 126 lambs, 128 mares, 86 horses, 70 colts, 75 square miles of land, and no will. Drawing by Jerry Reynolds*

RIGHT: *The Asistencia de San Francisco Javier at Chaguayabit (Castaic Junction) was established in 1804 on property belonging to the San Fernando Mission to stop homesteaders by "maintaining a presence" in the Santa Clarita Valley. Drawing by Jerry Reynolds*

LEFT: On March 9, 1842, after falling asleep under a massive oak tree in Live Oak Canyon, Juan Francisco de Gracia Lopez awoke and discovered gold in the roots of a wild onion he had dug up. Lopez' discovery set off California's first gold rush and later bestowed California Historic Landmark status on the Oak of the Golden Dream.

Father Junípero Serra, who headed the Franciscan order entrusted with the religious supervision of the Portolá Expedition, had the Crespí journal of the 1769 expedition published after extensive editing. Father Serra personally founded nine of the 21 California missions. From Cirker, Dictionary of American Portraits, *Dover, 1967*

After feasting on "delicious well-flavored sage," pinole gruel, "large well-flavored pine nuts and a sort of boiled almond" and other good things for two days, the Spaniards moved on in their quest for Monterey.

There were other explorers such as Captain Pedro Fages, who named Soledad Canyon and Agua Dulce in 1772, and the intrepid Father Francisco Garces, who recorded such Indian names as Islay (Hasley Canyon) and Kashtuk (Castaic) as the American Revolution was coming to a head a continent away in May of 1776.

Mansions of God

Father-Presidente of the California missions, Junípero Serra, passed on to his heavenly reward in 1784 and was succeeded by Father Fermín Francisco Lasuén. Lasuén noticed a tremendous gap between San Gabriel and San Buenaventura missions and many unconverted "heathens." One of his first acts was to dispatch an expedition to look for a suitable site for a new church.

Scarcely a year later (1785), Father Vicente de Santa María made his way up Río Santa Clara, stopping at a place called Triunfo, near Piru. Then he continued on to Chaguayabit (Castaic Junction), and struggled over the steep mountain pass down into what Father Crespí had named Santa Catalina de Bolonia de los Encinos or St. Catherine of Bologna of the Live Oaks.

Actually Chaguayabit or Triunfo would have been closer to being midway between San Gabriel and the sea. However, Father Lasuén decided upon "Los Encinos," the new mission to be named for St. Ferdinand, a king of Spain from 1217 to 1252.

The mission site was found to be occupied by one Don Francisco Reyes, a man of considerable political clout, inasmuch as he was then the *alcalde* (mayor) of the pueblo of Los Angeles. The padres proved that the land was, in fact, owned by San Gabriel, ousted Don Francisco, then moved into his small ranch house. On September 8, 1797, Father Lasuén was able to formally dedicate the Mission San Fernando Rey de España. The fathers lived in the old Reyes adobe until they could occupy the church complex.

Part of San Fernando's holdings was the Santa Clara River basin from Piru Creek on the west to "La Soledad," a rather vague boundary to the east. It was called "Rancho San Francisco." By 1800 long-horned cattle were grazing on the tall grass, pushing the native deer and antelope aside, while the gentle Tataviam were removed from their ancestral homeland to be "civilized" and taught "useful" trades such as brick making, household service, and cow punching.

Twenty-two years after it was established, San Fernando could claim 12,800 head of cattle, 7,800 sheep, 780 horses, and 144 mules; an impressive record indeed. It was doing a busy trade in hides and tallow and was famous for its leather work. There were 32,000 grapevines, 1,600 fruit trees, olives, dates, and field crops. A good portion of this was coming down from the Santa Clara, where a small granary had already been built.

The mission plan was to gather the Indians, teach them European culture, skills, and religion, then, when the natives were self sufficient (in other words, able to cope in a modern world), to restore the lands to them. Since this training period was cut short due to politics, it will never be known how successful it would have been.

The Asistencia

During the spring of 1804 the padres at Mission San Fernando learned that a Santa Barbara resident by the name of Francisco Ávila had laid claim to several thousand acres east of Piru Creek along the banks of Río Santa Clara to be known as Camulos.

They protested vigorously, notifying Governor José Arrillaga at Monterey that these lands belonged to the church. After due study, Governor Arrillaga acknowledged the mission's title and rescinded Ávila's grant. In order to forestall any more claim jumping, it was decided to "maintain a presence" in the Santa Clara.

According to church historian Zephyrin Engelhart, drawing upon official reports, "at the Rancho de San Francisco Javier or Chaguayabit a building was erected to provide for a granary and other necessary rooms."

The feast day of St. Francis Xavier was December 3, so we may assume that on that date in 1804 Father Pedro Muñoz and Father José de Miguel trudged up to the top of the little mesa overlooking Castaic Junction to set up a building on the very spot that Father Crespí had recommended 35 years earlier. It was 105 feet long by 17 feet wide with dirt floors and white-washed adobe walls 2 feet, 10 inches thick.

Sometime later a second structure was built, 107 feet, 4 inches long and 22 feet, 8 inches across with five rooms, the largest having a barred tile floor and an altar. This was to the north of the original building, right next to the precipice that dropped off to the valley floor below. Gated adobe walls ran between the two long, low buildings, both front and back, forming an enclosed courtyard. All of this construction rested solidly on rounded cobblestone foundations. Overall the front facade was 60 feet across.

Exactly when the granary was raised to the status of an asistencia, or submission, is not known. It probably happened when the new wing and tiled sacristy were authorized, but no one knows when that was. Sometime during this period a small milk house was built of adobe with a red-tiled roof. It sat down the hill from the main complex in a little canyon.

In order to keep cattle from wandering away, a bar was placed across La Puente in Elsmere Canyon in 1813, while a sturdy fence was erected along Piru Creek. A dam rose up Piru Canyon, and irrigation ditches brought water to crops in the western, or Camulos, section of the rancho.

During September of 1821 Father Ibarra wrote from San Fernando, "I just came from Rancho de San Francisco . . . Rabbits and hares and worms have done great damage to the crop." In spite of these depredations, a few weeks later 15 pack mules left the rancho loaded with 30 *fanagas* of corn bound for the troops at Santa Barbara. A *fanaga* equaled 100 pounds. So Asistencia de San Francisco must have been very prosperous, indeed.

While the padres and their Tataviam neophytes quietly tended to their cattle and crops at the lonely, isolated Asistencia de San Francisco, revolution was raging in New Spain. The outcome of the insurrection would have drastic effects, not only in the Santa Clara, but also for the whole of Alta California.

Revolution

After two years of warfare, an opportunist by the name of Augustin Iturbide succeeded in shaking off the senile grasp of old Spain on her Mexican provinces. On April 11, 1822, the capital city of Monterey swore allegiance to Iturbide, who now called himself Augustus I, Emperor of Mexico.

Less than a year later riders pounded up El Camino Real (The King's Highway) to inform his subjects that Augustus no longer ruled in Mexico City. He had been forced to abdicate in favor of a federal republic.

Almost immediately a group of California citizens began applying pressure on the Mexican congress to divide up mission properties as provided by law. These citizens, or Californios, as they liked to call themselves, believed that as soon as the lands reverted back to the Indians that these natives could easily be plied with liquor and persuaded to sign their rights away.

Finally, in August of 1833, the congress in Mexico City gave in, issuing an immediate general secularization law. Under its provisions the mission buildings would remain as church property, while the cattle, crops, and lands which had sustained them were confiscated. The priests objected; some of the people mounted revolts; while the supposed beneficiaries, the Indians, were bewildered.

Exactly a year later, Governor José Figueroa declared that the missions were to be reduced to the status of parish churches, with half of their property going to the natives, who were forbidden to sell it. Figueroa dispatched administrators to inventory clerical holdings and enforce the law.

During October of 1834, Lieutenant Antonio Seferino del Valle arrived at the gates of Mission San Fernando Rey armed with the authority of the governor to preside over the dismantling of the church—for an annual salary of $800.

Del Valle's great-grandfather, Juan del Valle, had come from Valencia, Spain, in 1642, settling in Columbia. Eventually he moved to Mexico, building considerable wealth and influence.

The lieutenant was born at Composilla in 1788, son of Antonio and María del Valle. He later married María Josepha Carillo and had two children, Ignacio and María. When his wife died, Antonio joined the San Blas Company, was commissioned a lieutenant, and shipped off to Monterey in 1819. The children were left in the care of a relative.

Monterey had just been raided by Argentine pirates and warmly welcomed the arrival of the good ship *San Carlos* bearing troops to shore up coastal defenses. It was not very long before the residents began to feel that they were better off in the hands of buccaneers than those of their own defenders. The San Blas Company was made up of a ragtag bunch of thieves and convicts causing so much trouble that the citizens petitioned for their removal.

At that moment the Indians at Santa Ynez revolted (February of 1824). A flame was ignited and spread to five other missions, threatening to engulf the whole Mexican establishment.

Lieutenant Del Valle was dispatched to the San Joaquin Valley along with his troops to round up neophytes making a stand in "the tulares." He was successful in his military operations and, in June, arrived at the Santa Clara del Sur with a long train of renegades in tow. He marched down the river to Ventura, then north to the presidio at Santa Barbara, where his prisoners were incarcerated.

Returning a hero to Monterey, it was not long before he was embroiled in political intrigue and various affairs with charming young ladies. Convicted of insubordination, Antonio spent six months of 1825 behind bars. At this low point in his career, Del Valle wrote to his son Ignacio to join him.

This was another mistake.

The Santa Clara's Lord

Antonio Seferino del Valle had not seen his son Ignacio for six years when the lad of 17 stepped off of the ship at Monterey on July 27, 1825.

It was not long, however, before differences of opinion between the two began to show themselves. Once again the residents were howling for the exile of Lieutenant Del Valle's San Blas Company.

That same year one of the periodic power plays broke out into warfare between Governor Manuel Victoria, holding out in Monterey, while General Echeandía came storming up from San Diego. In one crucial battle two lieutenants Del Valle faced each other, father and son, the younger man winning. Never again would they speak to each other.

Antonio was 46 years old when he was assigned to inventory the property of Mission San Fernando. He counted only 541 Indian neophytes, a large decrease, indeed. Among his recommendations was that a corporal be installed at the Asistencia de San Francisco to guard against the stealing of cattle and horses by Christian Indians.

During the rather quiet and productive period in his life, Antonio del Valle fell in love with Jacoba Feliz, a lady about the age of his own son, and they were married. After performing the ceremony, Father Ibarra, dissatisfied with life at a secularized mission, left for Sonora, never to return.

By 1838 Jacoba Feliz del Valle had borne two healthy children and was expecting a third. Her husband decided that the time had come to settle down. He resigned his commission in the army and petitioned Governor Juan B. Alvarado for a grant of land described as:

bounded on the west by the Arroyo Piru, which comes down from the mountains on the north and runs into the River called Santa Clara, and a line extended across . . . to a large oak tree (Roble) . . . upon the top of a hill and standing alone . . . A line drawn from said tree East through the hills until it reaches the door (La Puerta) or bar which is in the high road from San Fernando to San Francisco . . . And thence . . . to the Arroyo Taburga on the East, following said arroyo in a Northerly direction until it empties into the River St. Claire.

A *diseño*, or map, was drawn by Pablo de la Guerra of Santa Barbara at Antonio's request, claiming 11 square leagues or 48,829 acres known as Rancho San Francisco. One citizen protested that the land should go to the Indians, writing the governor that Del Valle "was nothing but a dried-up little piece of vanity."

Ignoring the opposition, Alvarado sat down at his desk in Santa Barbara on January 22, 1839, and, with his signature, made Antonio del Valle virtual lord and master of the Upper Santa Clara River Valley. The new ranchero became a part of that little clique of fewer than 400 people who owned land in old California.

After a traditional ceremony that went with the taking possession of a land grant, Don Antonio moved his family into the Asistencia on the bluff overlooking the junction of Castaic Creek and the Santa Clara River.

Antonio had scarcely two years to enjoy his rancho, for he died on June 21, 1841, leaving 16 bulls, 420 cows, 318 heifers, 576 calves, 1,008 sheep, 126 lambs, 128 mares, 86 horses, 70 colts, 75 square miles of land, and no will. Four months later Doña Jacoba gave birth to María Concepcion, making a total of eight children and a widow to battle over the estate.

THE DEL VALLE DYNASTY

On his deathbed, Don Antonio del Valle had decided that something had to be done to patch up relations with his eldest son.

Dr. Nicholas Den, the family physician, was sent for and entrusted with a personal message that he carried to Santa Barbara, where young Ignacio was in residence. If the son would settle down and marry, it said, Don Antonio would give him a half-interest in a house at Santa Barbara, 300 head of cattle, and the "place extending from the portesuelo of San Francisco towards the west," in other words, the land between Piru Creek and Blue Cut on the present Ventura County line. Poor Dr. Den went back without a response for the 53-year-old ranchero, who promptly passed away intestate.

Back in Santa Barbara, Ignacio del Valle was playing the role of a California Don Juan. He was heavily involved with María del Carmen Rodríguez and the lovely Manuelita Ortega, while living with María Los Angeles Carrillo in her father's home. Señorita Carrillo gave birth to a son, Juventino, but it would be half a year before the parents got married.

Seven months after Don Antonio died, on January 1, 1842, Ignacio and María Carrillo exchanged wedding vows before Bishop Narciso Duran. The couple then hustled down to Los Angeles, presenting the old Don's missive to his son as evidence of his title to the western portion of Rancho San Francisco.

The grieving widow, Doña Jacoba Feliz del Valle, still swathed in black, was suddenly faced with the prospect of losing half of her inheritance

After the death of Antonio del Valle, a bitter legal battle ensued between Antonio's widow, Jacoba, and his son, Ignacio (pictured here), over the inheritance of the Rancho San Francisco. A judge settled the dispute by splitting the property among Ignacio, Doña Jacoba, and her children. Ignacio's new rancho included a four-room adobe dwelling called Camulos. Courtesy, Santa Clarita Valley Historical Society

When Ignacio del Valle moved into the Rancho Camulos adobe in 1861, he had it enlarged from four rooms to 20. Before then he lived on the Plaza in Los Angeles and visited the house briefly four or five times a year. Pictured here is the inner court and garden of the house, which can still be seen near Piru. Courtesy, Ventura County Historical Museum

and livelihood. There were four sons and two daughters to care for. She needed a strong arm to lean upon; besides, women in old California had little or no rights. She countered her stepson's move by marrying José Salazar, her *mayordomo*, or ranch foreman.

Jose Francisco de Gracia Lopez, born at Mission San Gabriel on March 9, 1802, attended college in Mexico, where he took a course in mineralogy. He was still acting as ranch manager for his niece when she married Captain Jose Salazar, who was in charge of 50 Sonoran miners called Gambusinos. Lopez leased a section of Rancho San Francisco, pasturing his own cattle there.

On the morning of his 40th birthday, when Lopez set out to inspect the herds, his wife, Maria Antonia, asked him to gather some herbs for the evening meal.

At about noontime, Don Francisco was deep in Canon de los Encinos (Live Oak Canyon), picking a spot under an ancient oak tree for lunch and a siesta.

After his nap, Lopez dug up some wild onions with his knife and was surprised to discover gold clinging to their roots.

Joined by Manuel Cota and Domingo Bermudez, the trio feverishly dug along the banks of the stream, arriving home late that night.

The next morning, Lopez, Bermudez and Cota headed off to Los Angeles, along with his brother, Pedro Lopez, who was mayordomo of the San Fernando Mission. The gold was deposited with Yankee merchant Abel Stearns as he had the only safe south of the Tehachapis. Stearns sent a sample of the gold to the U.S. Mint, where it was reported to have a "fineness of 926-1000" with a

value of $19 an ounce.

Captain Salazar, meanwhile, dispatched his Sonoran miners into Live Oak Canyon (which was renamed Placerita Canyon), where 2,000 ounces of gold were removed in the next few months. Lopez sent a sample of gold to Governor Santiago Arguello along with a petition for a mining claim.

He was turned down because the location was on private property. The governor, however, had some jewelry made for his wife out of some of the gold, and forwarded the rest to Mexico City where it was eventually made into coins.

Don Ignacio del Valle was appointed "Magistrate of the Mines" by the governor. Del Valle kept accurate records for tax purposes and sorted out often conflicting claims. For the privilege of prospecting on his property, he charged the miners $8.

By 1843, the canyon was swarming with gold seekers, numbering 150 to 200 men and a few women. Lopez, like Sutter a few years later, was eased out of his claim, but made a second discovery in Santa Feliciana Canyon in the spring of that year. Lopez was granted Rancho Temescal, but it did not prevent him from being invaded, again, by Salazar's Gambusinos. One of them, in fact, picked up a nine pound nugget in the stream.

A second rancho, Los Alamos y Agua Caliente was granted to Lopez on October 2, 1843, near present day Pyramid Lake. If he found gold there, he kept it to himself.

With the Yankee invasion of 1847, the Gambusinos prudently hightailed it back to Sonora, forgetting the Placerita and Santa Feliciana mines. Between 1,250 and 1,300 pounds of gold came out of Placerita in the five-year period from 1842 to 1847.

While there had been rumors of other gold strikes prior to 1842, Lopez made the first authenticated find, started the first gold rush in California and made the first attempt at a mining claim. Del Valle was the first person to make mining laws in the state.

Today the site of this momentous adventure is marked only by a gnarled and twisted tree known as The Oak of the Golden Dream.

Twilight of the Dons

Frenchman Francois Chari, a sailor who jumped ship, became a citizen, changed his name to Francisco, and went to work herding cattle for Chico Lopez near Lake Hughes. Lopez pastured his beeves in Cañada de los Robles (Oak Canyon), to which Francisco Chari took a liking. In 1843 he established Rancho Del Buque (Ship Ranch), which would later be misspelled as Bouquet Canyon, changing the meaning from a "boat" to "flowers."

Aristocratic Californios would not soil their hands by grubbing about in the muck and mire, so it was the Sonorans again who did most of the work. One exception was José Salazar, Doña

Jacoba's second husband, who placered $4,300 in a year. Even more lucky was José Espinosa, who plucked up a six-pound, four-ounce lump of gold in Las Palomas Canyon.

According to Richard Henry Dana, it was not uncommon for Yankees to carry gold back to New England. This practice may have sparked an interest in California. As early as 1835 President Andrew Jackson attempted to buy San Francisco from Mexico for one-half million dollars. The offer was politely but firmly refused. Ten years later James Knox Polk was elected President on the strength of promises to reduce tariffs, establish an independent treasury, settle the Oregon boundary dispute with England, and, most importantly, "to secure the admission of California."

Francisco Chari, an ex-sailor from France whose birth name was Francois Chari, established Rancho del Buque (Ship Ranch) in Oak Canyon in 1843. Later the name of the canyon was misspelled as "Bouquet," thus changing the meaning from a "ship" to "flowers." Chari had discovered the canyon area while herding cattle for Chico Lopez. Drawing by Jerry Reynolds

One of Polk's first acts as President was to offer Mexico $40 million for her province. When that failed, he ordered a program of infiltration, encouraging pioneers to settle in the region.

Unknowingly, Mexico made the process simple. People such as Abel Stearns, William Wolfskill, and John Temple migrated, converted to Catholicism, became citizens, married the daughters of rancheros, and became a small army of Fifth Columnists under the direction of the President's personal agent at Monterey, Thomas O. Larkin. Their purpose was to foment revolt, and they did not have to try very hard.

Most of the leading citizens, including Vallejo, Pío Pico, and Ignacio del Valle, concluded that California would be better off under American rule than Mexican. They probably would have handed the state over to the U.S. without a shot being fired had it not been for the bungling of bureaucrats and the untimely arrival of an aggressive, egocentric, ambitious captain of topographical engineers—John Charles Frémont.

Manifest Destiny

John Charles Frémont would leave his name attached to mountains, towns, and even the pass between the Santa Clarita and San Fernando valleys. During a series of greatly publicized expeditions, he mapped the Missouri River, the Oregon Trail, and the northern Sierras. The press touted him as "The Pathfinder," even though Kit Carson was his guide and found most of the paths.

On May 13, 1846, President Polk had his war with Mexico declared official by the Congress, at which time Brevet Major Frémont and 62 members of his "map-making" expedition were dashing into Mexican California from Oregon. He had already clashed with Mexican officials and had been asked to leave the country. Dispatches from his father-in-law, Senator Thomas Hart Benton, and the President brought Frémont rushing down to Sutter's Fort in the Sacramento Valley in time to bolster up the Bear Flag Revolt.

Most Californios were dissatisfied with Mexican rule and had been convinced by Thomas O. Larkin, President Polk's consul at Monterey, that they would be better off under Yankee rule. The

RIGHT: On the evening of January 9, 1847, John C. Frémont and his 100-man "buckskin battalion" arrived at Castaic Junction, where they camped at the ranch of Don José Salazar. The next day Frémont and his men crossed over "a range of elevated hills" between the Santa Clarita Valley and the "plain of San Fernando." Subsequently known as Fremont Pass, the area is now called Elsmere Canyon. Courtesy, The Bancroft Library, University of California, Berkeley

The Capitulation of Cahuenga on January 13, 1847, marked the end of the Mexican War in California as Andrés Pico handed over his sword to John C. Frémont. Drawing by Jerry Reynolds

grandees were willing to hand over the province peacefully until Frémont fortified Hawk's Peak in the Gavilan Mountains, the Bear Flaggers kidnapped the venerated Mariano Vallejo, and one Archibald Gillespie antagonized Los Angeles by his high-handed methods.

War broke out, climaxed by General Andrés Pico defeating General Kearny at the Battle of San Pascual, northeast of San Diego. Meanwhile Frémont and his 100-man "buckskin battalion" marched southward along the coast, arriving at Castaic Junction on the evening of January 9, 1847.

Edwin Bryant, a member of the battalion, wrote:

we encamped this afternoon at a rancho situated on the edge of a fertile and finely watered plain of considerable extent, where we found corn, wheat, and frijoles in great abundance. The rancho was owned by an aged Californian of commanding and respectable appearance.

The "aged Californian" must have been the 45-year-old Don José Salazar, the man who had married the widow of Antonio del Valle.

"On January 10," young Bryant continued, "crossing the plain we encamped, about 2 p.m. in the mouth of a cañada, through which we ascended over a difficult pass in a range of elevated hills between us and the plain of San Fernando." The old "Pass of San Bernardo" or Fremont Pass is now known as Elsmere Canyon.

Three days later Andrés Pico met with Frémont's forces at the home of María Jesus Lopez de Feliz, handing over his sword and ending the war in California. Known as the Capitulation of Cahuenga, to Frémont's credit, it was, indeed, "peace with honor."

The Treaty of Guadalupe Hidalgo, signed May 30, 1848, ceded Texas, New Mexico, Arizona, and California to the U.S.

For two years after the Capitulation of Cahuenga the affairs of California were directed by a series of military governors, one of whom was John Charles Frémont. He was appointed by Commodore Stockton and promptly relieved by his own army superior, General Kearny.

Not recognizing Kearny's right to fire him, Frémont continued in office anyway. Kearny had him loaded with chains and court-martialed. President Polk pardoned Frémont, who, just as soon as he was restored to command, resigned to become a U.S. senator from California and later the first presidential candidate on the Republican ticket.

While all of this wrangling was going on, a carpenter by the name of James W. Marshall was hammering away on a sawmill on the American River. It was January 24, 1848, just nine days before the Treaty of Guadalupe Hidalgo officially made California a territory of the United States.

It was cold, dreary, and pouring rain that day at John Sutter's mill, but the nugget of gold that Marshall found would light the way for a veritable avalanche of humanity pouring in from all over the world.

King Cattle

While the rest of the world seemed to be flocking into the northern mines in a mad quest for sudden riches, the native-born Californios generally stayed home and tended to their cattle.

The cattle—black-and-white descendants of the small, tough, Spanish breed's great, brooding beasts—were born and bred on the range, half wild, and armed with an impressive spread of horns. Descended from sturdy Andalusian stock that landed at Vera Cruz in 1521, over the next 300 years they had evolved into 800-pound animals that could live on sagebrush, go for days without water, and beat the tar out of grizzly bears. Lean, mean, and raw-boned, they provided meat for the dinner table and a source of income for the dons, who traded hides and tallow for a couple of Yankee dollars. In Los Angeles one of the popular diversions of the day was to toss a bull and a bear into a pit and watch them fight to the death.

William Blunt Couts brought news of the gold seekers' craving for fresh meat up north and with his brother, Cave Johnson Couts, formulated a plan to deliver beef to an eager market.

This lithographic cartoon titled Pork and Beans in the Gold Diggins *satirizes a situation that helped the Couts brothers reap a fortune during the 1849 Gold Rush, when food and other provisions became more scarce and more valuable than the gold the miners were seeking. The Couts discovered that after eating about everything in sight, the miners would pay any price for a steak. So, the brothers began selling cattle for the unheard-of high price of $75 a head. Courtesy, Amon Carter Museum, Fort Worth*

Vaqueros worked on Santa Clarita Valley ranches tending to the cattle and assisting with cattle drives. This Frederic Remington oil painting titled A Vaquero *dates from 1890. Courtesy, Amon Carter Museum, Fort Worth*

During the spring of 1849 William and Cave Couts set out with a herd of some 700 head on consignment from Juan Bandini (Cave's father-in-law) and Juan Temple, the latter already renowned as the richest man in California.

According to William Couts, "it was an awful job," but they managed to get the cattle up the coast to San Jose where they were offered $14 each. Cave dickered with the buyers, finally getting $20, or about 10 times what they would have brought in the days of the hide-and-tallow trade.

Returning to Los Angeles, the brothers astounded the populace with their astronomical profits. While the grandees might not lower themselves to grovel for gold, they certainly didn't mind trading cows for the stuff.

The next year 2,500 head were driven north over present-day Newhall Pass down to the banks of the Santa Clara. Some went over to Ventura then up to San Francisco, while others took a route suggested by Ignacio del Valle through the San Joaquin Valley. Crafty Don Ignacio would not only realize a great profit, but also charge grazing fees on his rancho in the Santa Clarita and also El Tejon.

By this time the hundreds of thousands of miners had eaten up just about everything except the redwood trees and would pay any price for a steak. Well, the Couts brothers "stuck it to 'em" for $75 a head.

2

GETTING AROUND AND SETTLING DOWN

1850s-1860s

WILEY'S WINDLASS

As the Couts brothers were busily driving cattle northward to feed the hordes of hungry gold seekers, a constitutional convention was called at Monterey on September 1, 1849. Among the 48 delegates, 11 were Californios or property-owning Spanish-Mexicans. Their views were so radically different from those of the Yankees that splitting the territory into two separate states was seriously considered. A compromise was finally hammered out and sent to the U.S. Congress.

The application for admission to the Union dropped like a bombshell into the collective laps of senators and representatives, for California submitted an anti-slave constitution that would upset the carefully planned balance of power between Northern and Southern states.

A great debate was set off among towering giants of the U.S. Senate—men such as Henry Clay, John C. Calhoun, and Daniel Webster. At last the historical Compromise of 1850 allowed "The Golden State" into the Union in exchange for a strong fugitive-slave law. On September 9, President Millard Fillmore signed the bill making California the 31st star in the U.S. flag. The South was placated and Civil War delayed for a decade.

Meanwhile, Hispanic dons were cashing in on their newfound wealth extracted from frenzied gold diggers. They thought nothing of laying out $2,000 for a hand-tooled saddle trimmed with silver or electrum bridles. Golden spurs of immense proportions jangled from boot heels. Caballeros spent $500 to $1,000 for a suit of clothes and wrapped their women in yards of silks and satins.

Adobe homes were expanded to include Brussels tapestries and massive Victorian furnishings, and Persian carpets lay on packed-earth floors that later might be tiled with baked clay.

The long cattle drives that brought all of this wealth to the southland were not without their problems. In the spring of 1852 Cave Couts wrote to Abel Stearns:

The nest of thieves in the Santa Clara did all they knew how to make me loose [sic] a lot, but not all. By believing all they told me to be false and threatening a couple pretty closely, I escaped . . . I learned that they got about 100 head of Forester, 50 from Jose Antonio Arguello, 70 of Machados, all of Castros, and others in proportion.

On July 12 the Couts brothers arrived at San Jose to find 15,000 cattle milling around, the grass burned, and, to make life more unpleasant, vast swarms of mosquitoes. Rustlers, flooded streams, withered grass, and clouds of choking dust were forgotten when the animals were sold. Expenses would run about five dollars per head, including paying off the vaqueros, leaving a net profit of $70

Before 1852 getting over the mountain pass between the San Fernando and Santa Clarita valleys was an arduous task. Entrepreneur Henry Clay Wiley, new part-owner of a hotel-restaurant-saloon, saw an opportunity to make more money by offering to lower wagons and animals down the precipitous incline for a fee. Wiley installed and operated this massive windlass at the top of the hill. Here, a wagon is shown being lowered into the Santa Clarita Valley. Courtesy, Santa Clarita Valley Historical Society

RIGHT: *To indicate ownership, calves were marked on the hip with a red-hot branding iron. Each iron was registered with the proper officials and no two rancheros were permitted to use similar brands. Sketch by E. Vischer/The Bancroft Library, University of California, Berkeley*

BELOW: *With the price of cattle up tremendously during the Gold Rush, rancheros thought nothing of spending $2,000 for a hand-tooled, silver-trimmed saddle or buying gold spurs for their boots. This richly adorned ranchero displays his expensively outfitted steed. Courtesy, California Historical Society, San Francisco*

for each steer. Not bad for a month's work and a 400-mile-long journey.

The most arduous part of the trip was getting over the mountain pass between the San Fernando and Santa Clarita valleys. Along with the cattle came an increase in freighting out of Los Angeles and problems with the pass. Late in 1852 Henry Clay Wiley arrived on the scene, setting up a substantial wood frame hotel-restaurant-saloon in partnership with Ignacio del Valle. At the top of the hill Wiley installed a massive windlass that could actually lower animals and wagons down the precipitous declivity—for a fee, of course. After swinging between heaven and earth for several minutes at the end of a length of rope, even the most dedicated teetotaler probably ordered up a dose of "nerve tonic" at Wiley Station.

Over the Pass

During the summer of 1854 two events occurred that had a tremendous impact on the development of the Santa Clarita.

In July gold was discovered on the Kern River; men were taking $10 to $25 a day out of the ground. One miner wrote to the *Los Angeles Star*, "There is no doubt of there being plenty of gold here, the only difficulty is that we have no provisions."

Provisions? This key word was not lost on Angeleno businessmen, who had visions of El Pueblo becoming as great a supply center as San Francisco was for the northern mines. In the mad scramble and corporate back stabbing that followed, the merchants found suddenly that the only road north was neatly tied up by a beardless youth of 24 who went around town in shirtsleeves, bright suspenders, clodhopper shoes, and pants five or six inches too short. In spite of his country-yokel appearance, Phineas Banning had the largest freighting operation in Southern California, with 500 mules, 40 wagons, and 15 stagecoaches. When Fort Tejon (Badger) was established on Grapevine Pass on August 10, it was found that Banning already had an Army contract to provide the forwarding business neatly folded in his vault. In fact, a flinty-eyed gunman by the name of Gabriel Allen was bossing a crew of Banning's at work improving the road over Fremont Pass, up San Francisquito Canyon to Lake Elizabeth, through Pine Canyon—where a sawmill was being set up—then around Quail Lake to the cavalry outpost. Gabe, as he was generally known, was a veteran of the war with Mexico and later a county supervisor, who had a reputation as a shootist. Gabe Allen frequently used Indians for target practice and was arrested once by Sheriff Getman for picking off a roofer from the top of a building in order to test his marksmanship.

In December of 1854 Phineas Banning mounted the box of a towering red and yellow Concord coach to make the first run over the new route, although his foreman, Allen, insisted that the trail was not ready yet. Among the nine passengers who made that epic journey was Major Horace Bell, who left this wonderfully graphic description in *Reminiscences of a Ranger*:

The horses could not put the grade with all of the riders, so they were forced to get out and walk to the top. The question among his (Banning's) nine wondering passengers who had toiled up the mountain on foot was how the stage could descend . . . He cracks his whip, tightens his lines, whistles to his trembling mustangs, urges them to the brink of the precipice and they are going down!!! Rackety, clatter, bang. Sometimes the horses ahead of the stage and sometimes the stage ahead of the horses—all, however, going down, down, with a CRASH.

Finally the conglomeration of chains, harness, coach, mustangs and Banning were found in an inextricable mass of confusion—contusions, cracks and breaks . . . piled in a thicket of chaparral at the foot of the mountain. "Didn't I tell you?" said Banning, "A beautiful descent, far less difficult than I anticipated."

However, Banning sent a courier in hot haste, urging Don David Alexander to send 50 men immediately to repair parts of the road which he had, in his descent, knocked out of joint.

Gabe Allen and David Alexander did a little rerouting, cutting a 30-foot-deep cleft through what is now called Newhall Pass, effectively bypassing Henry C. Wiley's windlass and depot. Wagons rolled generally up the route of present-day Interstate 5 to San Francisquito Canyon, where an adobe station known as Moore's awaited thirsty and hungry travelers. It was later called Hollandsville, when Moore took off to pan for gold further up the arroyo. The next stop was at Elizabeth Lake, then on to Fort Tejon.

Camel Caravans

On the tenth day of August in 1854, Company "A," First United States Dragoons, arrived high up on Grapevine Pass under the command of First Lieutenant Thomas F. Castor. Tired, dusty, and bedraggled after a two-month march across the searing desert, they were, however, invigorated by the cool breezes at the refreshing altitude of 4,500 feet above sea level.

Lieutenant Castor wasted no time in laying out

Cave Johnson Couts, the son-in-law of wealthy cattleman and landowner Juan Bandini, went into the cattle business with his brother, William, in the spring of 1849. The Couts brothers reaped astronomical profits due to the enormous demand for fresh meat from the hundreds of thousands of gold miners who had streamed into California. Courtesy, Santa Clarita Valley Historical Society

barracks, officer's quarters, storehouses, and parade grounds for Fort Tejon.

The post, which was established to stop cattle rustling and protect the Indians, became the western terminus of supply trains composed of camels. The saga of the quixotic camel corps is an interesting one.

While exploring Death Valley with Kit Carson, Lieutenant Edward F. Beale got the idea of using dromedaries in the trackless Southwest. He suggested it to Secretary of War Jefferson Davis, who, at the time, was toying with the notion of a relay line of balloons across the desert. (So camels did not sound so farfetched.)

Colonel David D. Porter was dispatched to Egypt and Arabia with $30,000 in his pocket to buy the beasts. On May 13, 1856, Colonel Porter landed at Indianola, Texas, with the first contingent of 33; another 44 followed later. Some of them were sent to San Antonio, while 25 others made the trip to Fort Tejon under the command of Beale, now a colonel. A couple of experienced camel drivers came from Arabia—Hadji Ali (his name was quickly changed by the soldiers to Hi Jolly) and Greek George Allen.

The *Los Angeles Star* reported on January 27, 1858, that "Colonel Beale and about fourteen camels stalked into town last Friday week and gave our streets quite an Oriental aspect."

In a letter sent to the Secretary of War, Beale was lavish with his praise:

At times I thought it impossible they could stand the test to which they have been put, but they seem to have risen equal to every trial . . . With heavy packs, they have crossed mountains, ascended and descended precipitous places, (and) have traversed nearly double the distance passed over by our mules and wagons.

While Beale was enthusiastic, no one else seemed to be. The troopers found out, to their sorrow, that camels could inflict nasty bites, spit with deadly accuracy, and be far more cantankerous than a Missouri mule. Horses and cows panicked at the sight and smell of the ungainly beasts, while their roar, which was likened to that of a Bengal tiger, kept man and animal awake half the night.

With the outbreak of the Civil War in 1861, supply lines across the Southwest were cut by Confederates and the camel corps was put out of business. They were used locally between Tejon and Los Angeles until the fort was abandoned on September 11, 1864. Some were sold to zoos, others turned loose in the mountains. The last auction of camels was held at Camp Verde in 1866. For years afterwards there were rumors of camels wandering the Tehachapis or drinking deeply from the banks of the Santa Clara.

Camel Corp officers atop their animals must have been an incongruous sight in Southern California. The camel experiment, which began in the mid-1850s, was conducted to test the usefulness of camels as pack-train animals. Though the Civil War effectively ended the Camel Corps by causing the cutting of supply lines across the Southwest, locally the camels were used until September of 1864, when Fort Tejon was abandoned. Courtesy, Santa Clarita Valley Historical Society

Lyon's Station

In September of 1855 the ink was blotted on a deed signing Wiley's Station over to twin brothers who hailed from Machias, Maine—Sanford and Cyrus Lyon.

Born on November 20, 1831, the boys had shipped out "around the Horn," and arrived in Los Angeles during the Gold Rush of 1849. Sanford took a job as clerk for Alexander and Mellus, living in David W. Alexander's home, while brother Cyrus, being of a more adventurous spirit, became something of a gunman.

Los Angeles at that time was a collection of squat adobe huts with a few substantial homes on the Plaza. Curs lay on the dusty streets, while giant rats prowled the back alleys, providing target practice for the citizens. When they got tired of shooting strays, they blew each other away. Killings were so common that the papers stopped reporting them. There was a day in 1853, however, when no one was murdered; that made banner headlines.

Don Ignacio del Valle, mayor of the town, was fed up with the lawlessness, so he formed the California Rangers. Headed by a Major Horace Bell and three captains, W.W. Jenkins, William Reader, and Cyrus Lyon, the Rangers and various vigilantes soon bludgeoned or shot every "low element" with total disregard for constitutional rights or "due process." Within two years the force was abandoned since the reasons for its existence were either dead, incarcerated, or had moved to a more favorable environment.

Meanwhile, far away in New York, John Butterfield resigned from the board of directors of Wells Fargo and Co., formed American Express as a rival concern, and established his famed Butterfield Overland Stage, which set a land speed record of only 21 days from St. Louis to San Francisco. The Los Angeles Board of Supervisors appropriated $8,000 to improve the road between San Fernando and Fort Tejon as a part of the Great Southern or Ox-Bow route pioneered by Texas cattlemen. At 1 p.m. on October 7, 1858, the first of Butterfield's coaches rolled into the town. It was greeted by a 100-gun salute.

The next day the stage struggled over Fremont Pass, stopped at Lyon's Station to change horses and get a warm meal for the passengers, and rolled up San Francisquito Canyon bound for the "City by the Bay."

By 1868 Lyon's Station consisted of a large, frame building housing a store, post office, stage depot, and tavern. Behind that was the family cottage, hidden among stately oaks, while up the hill were some board-and-batten residences for 20 folks who worked for Lyon. A cemetery was established there, where names such as Rivera, Whitney, and even Lyon were eventually inscribed on the headstones. Across the road that would one day be known as Sierra Highway loomed a red New England-style barn surrounded by corrals and sheep pens with cattle roaming over the steep hills. Today the place goes by the name of Eternal Valley.

Sanford married a lady 12 years younger than he, Anna T., always known simply as Annie. They settled down at the station. Later Sanford was involved in gold mines, oil, farming, and other ventures, while brother Cyrus remained, for the most part, in Los Angeles.

Sanford Lyon and his twin brother Cyrus, who had both come to Los Angeles in 1849 from Maine, bought Wiley's Station in 1855. Lyon's Station, as it was subsequently named, grew from a small eating establishment and rest stop that catered to Butterfield Overland stages to a large, frame building that housed a store, post office, stage depot, and tavern. After marrying a woman named Annie and settling down at the station, Sanford became involved in gold mines, oil, farming, and other ventures. Courtesy, Santa Clarita Valley Historical Society

Igacio del Valle's children— (from left) Josépha, Ignacio, Jr., Ysabel, Reginaldo, and Ulpiano—retained ownership of Rancho Camulos until financial reversals forced them to sell the property in 1924. Courtesy, Ventura County Museum of History and Art

Nature Strikes Back

A drought in 1856 resulted in the death of at least 10,000 head of cattle in Los Angeles County alone, forcing the rancheros to take out mortgages on their vast estates. An interest rate of 4 percent per month was considered reasonable in those days. However, before the rains finally came, some of the dons were forced to sell their holdings at ruinous prices.

The next year brought bountiful precipitation, tall, luscious, green grass on the range, and the birth of many calves. The crisis passed, so the Californios carried on with their old ways of expensive clothing, roundups, and rodeos.

At 8:13 in the morning of January 9, 1857, the San Andreas fault snapped, sending shockwaves through the southland. Centered at Fort Tejon, the quake was probably every bit as strong as the one felt at San Francisco 49 years later (8.3 on the Richter scale).

Throughout the previous night, beginning at 11:30, there had been tremblings and an unusual occurrence of four foreshocks in which the ground opened up in places and hills seemed to explode in massive clouds of dust.

At Tejon barracks were tossed around like childrens' toys during the main event. On the adjoining Rancho La Liebre, Edward F. Beale had placed a round sheep corral right across the unknown rift zone. On the morning of the 9th it had shifted into an "S" shape to the amazement of the owner and the terror of the woollies, who ran for days.

The old Asistencia at Castaic Junction was severely damaged. Curved roof tiles fell through wooden beams to the floor. Adobe walls separated, some bricks smashing furniture as they hurled downward, sending the panicked family outside for safety.

When at last the earth settled down, José Salazar at the Asistencia surveyed the damage and decided that it would be best to move into the sturdy little milk house below the crest of the hill. This living arrangement was thought, originally, to be only temporary until the Hacienda (old Asistencia) could be repaired. Rancho San Francisco was already mortgaged to the hilt, however, so no funds would be made available for restoration. At last the principal creditor, William Wolfskill, was forced to foreclose. Wolfskill generously worked out a plan with Don Ignacio del Valle in which all debts owed by the Salazars were paid off, while Ignacio was deeded 5/11ths of the rancho or that section known as Camulos. By 1861 the Salazars were out of the picture, while Don Ignacio was free of the burden of their debts. He had already sold Rancho Tejon to General Beale in order to satisfy creditors of his in-laws.

The final, crushing blow came to the California rancheros just as the *Monitor* and *Merrimac* were engaged in the first sea battle between ironclad warships in the Civil War.

A three-year drought began in 1862, drying up streams and springs, while causing the grass to wilt under an incessant sun. Cattle died by the thousands, filling the air with the stench of death while littering the countryside with rotting carcasses. Statewide loss was estimated at 41 percent, but in Los Angeles, the "Queen of the Cow Counties," grim statistics chronicled a staggering decline. By the time Lee met Grant at Appomattox in 1865, the Los Angeles herds had been reduced from 70,000 head to fewer than 20,000 bony beasts—a loss of more than 71 percent.

It was the death knell of a way of life. Prime beef was worth only two dollars, harking back to the days of the hide-and-tallow trade. "California banknotes" started a way of life and ended it. The drama had gone full circle.

END OF SOLITUDE

Soledad Canyon in 1860 was a grim and forbidding place of sulfurous pools of foul-smelling water, stark, crumpled hills, and deep, twisting arroyos. Through this bleak landscape skulked outlaws, renegade Indians, buzzards, and grizzly bears. Even the name, which means homesick or lonely, would not attract someone wishing to settle down and raise a family.

Yet, for some reason, Colonel Thomas Finley Mitchell staked a claim to 160 acres near present-day Sand Canyon and Lost Canyon roads, then hauled a wood-frame miner's shack in from Paper Mill Canyon near Acton as headquarters of a cattle ranch that grew to a thousand acres.

The colonel apparently pacified the fearsome Piute Indians, who used to come raiding down the Soledad, by hanging a side of beef in a tree for them. He even offered a bed and breakfast to desperadoes such as Tiburcio Vásquez, and reportedly purchased a few trinkets from Tiburcio just to keep on his good side.

Only a year later, in 1861, the Civil War broke out with increased demands for gold, silver, copper, and lead to aid the Union cause. All of these minerals and more were found deep in Soledad Canyon, causing a rush to riches and, naturally, an increase of traffic past the Mitchell cabin.

A conglomeration of log cabins and tents moved up and down the canyon with each new strike. Called Soledad City wherever it was plunked down, it provided such basic needs as faro tables, rye whiskey, and ladies of the evening. A portable grocery was operated by James O'Reilly, a flaming-haired Irishman of medium build, pug nose, and happy-go-lucky air about him.

O'Reilly's black felt hat was clamped to the back of his head, and as he shuffled from place to place he was always slovenly looking. Luckily his clientele was none too fastidious, for his merchandise could not be considered improved by age or hard usage. Jim developed the New York and Parnell mines.

The post office in those days was a barrel into which outgoing mail was shoved and then carried to Los Angeles by anyone going that way. Travelers returning dropped incoming mail into the same barrel. Miners sorted through it from time to time, checking on word from the outside world. Located on the edge of the Thompson Smith Ranch facing Mint Canyon, the mail barrel was called Thompsons Corner.

Postal authorities rejected the name Soledad City for a formal post office, feeling it would be confused with the Soledad in Monterey County. O'Reilly proposed the name Ravenna for merchant and saloon keeper Manuel Ravenna,

The Telegraph Stage, partially owned by Henry Mayo Newhall, made regular mail delivery possible and provided transportation for those residing in Ravenna and Soledad City. Lightweight coaches such as this one were called "mud wagons" because they could travel over the worst of roads. Courtesy, Santa Clarita Valley Historical Society

On June 12, 1868, Soledad City was officially renamed Ravenna after merchant and saloon keeper Manuel Ravenna. This view of the Ravenna Depot dates from about 1900. Unfortunately the town has long since disappeared. Courtesy, Santa Clarita Valley Historical Society

who also made a tidy profit by bringing the city ice, which was wrapped in blankets and placed atop Wells-Fargo coaches. Everyone agreed on Ravenna, so it became official on June 12, 1868.

Ore from the mines was crushed by a massive stone wheel known as an *arrastra*, which was a slow, laborious process. Later a two-stamp mill powered by steam was set up close to the claims of James Gleason. Ravenna was the shipping point from which minerals were hauled in tall-sided freight wagons drawn by teams of oxen or as many as 20 mules down to San Pedro. The Telegraph Stage, owned partly by a fellow named Henry M. Newhall, pushed its way out to Ravenna and wherever Soledad City happened to be located at the moment, bringing passengers and a regular mail run.

Meanwhile, Thomas F. Mitchell hied himself back down to San Bernardino, marrying 17-year-old Martha Catherine Taylor on January 19, 1865. For his bride, who could not be expected to live in a clapboard shanty, he erected an adobe home, 45 by 60 feet, roofed with redwood shingles. Here were born six children, Mary, Thomas F., Jr., Frank A., Francis Ann, John Wesley, and Minnie Ivey.

Meanwhile, things had not been going too well for Jim O'Reilly. He lost his mines, his wife, and, finally, his mind. This man, who had been instrumental in forming the Cedar Mining District (one of the first in Southern California), was found dead in a squalid cabin.

Soledad City and Ravenna are now long gone, and, sadly, nothing of Jim O'Reilly's remains to remind the valley's residents of the man.

In September of 1863 A.A. Hudson and Oliver P. Robbins built the toll house that stood at the end of Beale's Cut. Tolls ranged from 25 cents for a horse and rider to $2 for teams of 12 or more horses. Courtesy, Santa Clarita Valley Historical Society

BEALE'S BONANZA

Probably the most famous landmark in the Santa Clarita Valley is a narrow slit through Fremont Pass called Beale's Cut. From 1863 to 1910 it was the only way to get out of Los Angeles and up to the San Joaquin Valley.

During the winter of 1862-1863, road improvements over the pass had been started by General Andrés Pico but washed out by flooding. General Edward Fitzgerald Beale, former scout for General Kearny, Superintendent of Indian Affairs, and Surveyor-General of California and Nevada, dashed down to the Los Angeles Board of Supervisors, took over Pico's franchise, and got $5,000 to do the work. He then called out the troops from Fort Tejon to actually dig a 90-foot-deep slash through the mountain barrier with picks and shovels. Then, on September 19, 1863, Beale advanced

Edward Fitzgerald Beale, who served as courier for Commodore Robert F. Stockton, Indian agent for all of California and Nevada, promoter of the 38th parallel route as the best and shortest railroad route to California, and instigator of the Camel Corps experiment, has also left his mark on the Santa Clarita Valley in the form of Beale's Cut. In addition, General Beale owned nearly 300,000 acres in the valley, including ranchos La Liebre, Tejon, Los Alamos y Agua Caliente, and Castac. From Cirker, Dictionary of American Portraits, Dover, *1967*

Juan Bautista Suraco (center), a native of Genoa, Italy, married Dominga Garla, a Californio, and settled in Bouquet Canyon. On the left is Charles Suraco and on the right is Joseph Antonio Suraco. From the Collection of Charles "Sonny" Suraco. Courtesy, Santa Clarita Valley Historical Society

$2,000 to A.A. Hudson and Oliver P. Robbins to build a toll house, the loan to be repaid at 2 percent interest from gate receipts, of which they got to keep one third of the total, with the lion's share going to the general.

For the next 21 years, until it reverted to the county, in order to pass through Beale's Cut, a horse and rider anted up a quarter, while teams of 12 or more paid two dollars. A horse and wagon forfeited 50 cents, teams of six or seven horses, $1.50, loose animals were charged a dime each, while at the bottom of the scale were sheep, at only three cents each. General Beale, by the way, had 100,000 head of woollies at the time.

Back in 1855, in order to settle a boundary dispute, General Beale had purchased Rancho La Liebre for three cents an acre. In time he acquired ranchos Tejon, Los Alamos y Agua Caliente, and Castac, a total of 297,000 acres.

The general married Mary Edwards, who was the financial genius behind his empire, built her an adobe hacienda that still stands at the west end of the Antelope Valley, and had one son, Truxtun.

In 1866 Beale bought Rancho Castac, (named Kashtuk, meaning "eyes," by the Indians) from José Covarrubias. The general changed the spelling to Castaic, and from his pond drained a creek teaming with native trout down to the junction with the Rio Santa Clara.

Juan Cordova married an Indian woman, settling Castaic Canyon in 1835. He was later a scout for Frémont. In May of 1867, Juan José Lopez settled on 120 acres, building an adobe house on the site of the now abandoned Trueblood Rest Stop.

In 1864 Private James Gorman was mustered out of the army at Fort Tejon and promptly homesteaded several hundred acres that became a regular stage stop. The town of Gorman still serves tourists, and it is owned by the Ralphs family, which has an interest in a large chain of grocery stores.

At the present time five generations of the Ruiz family have lived in San Francisquito Canyon. Farther up resided the Arujos. Their son Pablo became a renowned mule skinner, delivering supplies for the old Los Angeles aqueduct system.

Bautista Suraco, a native of Genoa, Italy, married a Californio and settled down in Bouquet Canyon. L. Ruiz enlarged the old F. Chari adobe home in 1872, where the Suracos lived. Members of the family are buried near the property.

Out in Sand Canyon a Captain Cunio staked a claim to a couple of thousand acres, becoming the first non-Indian resident of that hunk of now very high-priced real estate. Not far away lived Remi Nadeau, who made a fortune with his freight wagons supplying the miners of the Soledad. Nadeau's home was enclosed by a deer park that, in later years, became something of a tourist attraction. Now it is called North Oaks.

A lone wagon makes the approach to Beale's Cut in 1872. Upon orders from General Edward F. Beale, troops from Fort Tejon dug this 90-foot-deep slash through the mountain with picks and shovels and, thus, opened up a new transportation route for those entering or leaving the Santa Clarita Valley. Courtesy, Santa Clarita Valley Historical Society

3

BLACK GOLD AND THE IRON HORSE

1860s-1870s

RIVERS OF OIL

Along the southern rim of the Santa Clarita, in canyons called Placerita, Elsmere, Wiley, Towsley, and Pico, petroleum has oozed from rocky fissures for eons. Indians and Spaniards skimmed these pools, using the black, gooey substance for medicinal purposes and for waterproofing baskets. Other than that, oil did not seem much good for anything.

In 1855 General Andrés Pico began hauling "asphaltum" down from the canyon that now bears his name to Rancho San Fernando. Four years later the world's first oil well, in Titusville, Pennsylvania, gave birth to what would one day become the world's gigantic oil industry.

A Los Angeles chemist by the name of Dr. Vincent Gelcich began sampling the seepages in the canyons of the Santa Clarita, recommending that his friends invest in the area. Henry Clay Wiley, expressman and merchant, skimmed the pools in Wiley Canyon. Sanford Lyon invaded what is now Lyons Canyon, while other draws were named for a Dr. Rice, Christopher Leaming, and Darius Towsley. Dr. Gelcich became the biggest investor with his Santa Clara Oil Company, centered in Pico Canyon.

With the help of a Harvard University professor, General Edward Fitzgerald Beale inventoried 100 claims in Pico Canyon and then decided to gobble them up.

Beale quickly joined forces with his old foe from the Battle of San Pasquale, General Andrés Pico, to form the countywide Los Angeles Asphaltum and Petroleum Mining District, along with Dr. Gelcich and others. On June 24, 1865, three months after the creation of this district, the group set up the San Fernando Mining District. In essence, the first board was created to sort out often-conflicting claims, while the second existed to buy up those patents that the first board ruled invalid.

The first thing that was done was to grant to Andrés Pico the naphtha springs claim in Pico Canyon. This was done by back dating the claim to January 24, 1865, three months before the formation of the Los Angeles Asphaltum and Petroleum Mining District. Then the claim of Wiley was approved. (Wiley was, by the way, General Pico's son-in-law.)

Through the agency of Christopher Leaming, Beale, and his partners—Colonel Robert S. "Bobby" Baker, Wiley, Pico, and others—moved in on what was called the Mammoth Claim, which was held by 91 grantors. On August 7 the ink was blotted on a deed in exchange for $300. Beale and his associates now controlled everything between the Santa Clarita and San Fernando valleys.

Crude oil was skimmed from the pools, poured into leather sacks, slung on the backs of mules, and then hauled downstream to the port of

The first engine steamed through the San Fernando Tunnel on August 12, 1876, prompting the following statement by John Gifford at Lyon's Station: "The iron horse poked its head through the San Fernando Tunnel this evening at six o'clock and neighed long and loud his hearty greeting to the citizens of the Santa Clara Valley." Courtesy, California Historical Society, Los Angeles History Center Photographic Collections

Ventura. There coastal steamers picked up the cargo and sailed north to San Francisco, also carrying cattle, grain, passengers, or whatever else could be crammed on board. Since the Industrial Revolution had not yet made its appearance in California, oil was used to grease wagon wheels and for other lubrication chores, but was mainly refined into kerosene, the really big seller.

Late in the year the first Star Oil Company was founded by Beale, Baker, Pico, Lyon, and Juan and Francisco Forester in order to build a refinery that used a process developed by Dr. Gelcich.

PEACEFUL PICO CANYON ERUPTS

On January 8, 1869, Henry Clay Wiley, Sanford Lyon, and William W. Jenkins began drilling a hole in Pico Canyon by the primitive spring-pole method. By physically jerking a long beam up and down they averaged some three feet per day. At a depth of 50 feet, 9 barrels of green oil rushed up the casing.

Before long, spring-poles were growing like weeds in the canyons between San Fernando and the Santa Clarita. Smelling a profit, that oily triumvirate of Edward Beale, Colonel Baker, and Andrés Pico formed the Los Angeles Petroleum Refining Co. as a subsidiary of Star Oil and began construction of a small, two-still refinery at Lyon's Station. It was built by Captain W.S. Smith to the specifications of Dr. Vincent Gelcich and completed in April 1874. Unable to produce smoke-free kerosene, the refinery folded up, as did Star Oil, beset by financial troubles.

During this same year the Pennsylvania oil fields began to fall off in production, causing experienced drillers and managers to drift toward the west. One of the first arrivals was Demetrius G. Scofield, tall, slender and just 30 years old. Scofield was amazed at production obtained by skimming and spring-poles, realizing that a

FAR RIGHT: General Andrés Pico, who had fought against General Edward F. Beale in the Battle of San Pasquale, went into partnership with Beale and others to form the Los Angeles Asphaltum and Petroleum Mining District and, in 1865, the first Star Oil Company. Ten years before, Pico had begun hauling "asphaltum" to Rancho San Fernando from the canyon that now bears his name. Courtesy, Santa Clarita Valley Historical Society

RIGHT: Dr. Vincent Gelcich, a Los Angeles chemist, was one of the first promoters of California oil. After collecting petroleum samples from various locations in the Los Angeles area, including from Pico Canyon, Gelcich encouraged his friends— Sanford Lyon, Henry Clay Wiley, Christopher Leaming, and Darius Towsley—to stake claims in the Santa Susana Mountains. Gelcich's Santa Clara Oil Company in Pico Canyon made him the largest operator. Courtesy, Santa Clarita Valley Historical Society

modern operation would result in a bonanza. Sending back to Titusville for some eastern expertise, Scofield helped to form California Star Oil Works (CSO) on July 8, 1876, with headquarters in San Francisco. CSO then began buying up property owned by the nearly bankrupt original California Star.

John A. Scott, who owned a profitable Pennsylvania refinery, discovered "white oil" in Placerita Canyon so clear that a newspaper could be read through it. Bottles of the stuff were displayed at the great Centennial exhibit in Philadelphia in July.

Meanwhile Scofield was in desperate need of an experienced driller, whom he found right under his nose, so to speak. This driller was a Frenchman named Charles Alexander Menetrier. He was born in 1846, and at the age of 7 he was brought to America by his parents. Here he developed a fascination for things mechanical. He became a driller, sinking 42 successful wells at Titusville before landing in San Francisco during November 1873. The family name had been changed to Mentry, and Alex, as he liked to be called, settled on 180 acres in Placerita, exploring the surrounding hills for oil.

Demetrius Scofield was well aware of Mentry's formidable reputation when he employed him as superintendent of the Pico lease. Alex Mentry rigged up a three-pole derrick, making a drill from an old railroad axle, and kicked the Lyon-Jenkins-Wiley hole down to 120 feet. The flow was increased to 12 barrels per day—not exactly a bonanza, but promising. Two more wells were bored, yielding meager results. Then it happened!

On September 26, 1876, Mentry brought in CSO Number 4—a gusher of 50 barrels a day rushing up and out of a casing a bit less than six inches in diameter, literally exploding into the clear blue sky above the canyon.

Thus was born the oil industry of California. More wells were sunk. The little town of Pico Springs changed its name to Mentryville, sustaining a hundred families. General Beale was not entirely out of the picture as he still collected a toll on all of those wagons creaking through his cut. D.G. Scofield did all right, later becoming the first president of Standard Oil of California.

CSO 4 was, until recently, producing that emerald green petroleum deep in the canyon. Surrounded now by plaques proclaiming it a landmark, it was the oldest-operating oil well in the world until it was shut down in September of 1990.

ABOVE: Alex Mentry, came to California from Titusville, Pennsylvania, in November 1873. In 1876 he became superintendent of California Star Oil Works (CSO) and that summer brought in the first commercially successful oil well west of Pennsylvania— CSO Number 4. Mentry radically changed the methods of oil production and drilling and revolutionized the entire oil industry in the West for the next quarter century. From the collection of F.J. Legasse. Courtesy, Santa Clarita Valley Historical Society

LEFT: This 1877 photograph by pioneer photographer Carleton Watkins shows California Star Oil's Number 4 well. The well, which once produced between 30 and 50 barrels of oil a day, not only signalled the birth of the California oil industry, but also was the world's oldest operating oil well until it was shut down in September of 1990 after 114 years of production. Courtesy, Santa Clarita Valley Historical Society

John Lang and family posed for this group portrait about 1880. Lang, who lived in Soledad Canyon, established the Sulphur Springs School District with Thomas Mitchell, built the first Sulphur Springs School with Cyrus Lyon, and, in 1873, killed a ferocious grizzly known as Monarch of the Mountains. Courtesy, Santa Clarita Valley Historical Society

JOHN LANG AND THE BEAR

In 1971 Southern Pacific Railroad demolished Lang Station, the last remnant of a community, ranch, and health spa that dominated the history of Soledad Canyon for 100 years.

The depot was named for John Lang, who arrived in California from New York in 1854. He met with moderate success panning for gold in the Mother Lode Country and chasing silver rainbows near the Comstock before marrying and settling down in San Francisco. The damp air was bad for his wife's health, so they moved to the drier climate of Los Angeles, where Lang farmed some 35 acres in 1870. According to Harris Newmark, he was known as "Lang No. Two," as there were no fewer than four John Langs in the area at the time.

During the spring of 1871 "Number Two" bought from the railroad 160 acres of Soledad Canyon about a mile east of Colonel Thomas Mitchell's spread. In time this would grow to be a 1,200-acre dairy.

Together with his neighbor, Thomas Mitchell, Lang established the Sulphur Springs School District during September 1872. It is the second-oldest school district in Los Angeles County. For half of the year, 17 children were taught by Martha Mitchell at her adobe—two Langs, three Mitchells, three Mannings, two Suracos, three Smiths, two Cuneos, an Erwin, and a Lorbeer. For the other half of the year the students trudged over to the Langs. By 1886 there were far too many students enrolled to keep shuffling them from one house to the other. Mitchell donated a site, while Lang and Cyrus Lyon built the first Sulphur Springs School.

The district and later schoolhouse were named for a number of foul-smelling sulfurous wells that bubbled up in the region. During 1873 Lang tapped 10 of these white springs, piping the waters down to a two-story, nearly 1,300-square-foot resort hotel. Pools were created for health seekers to languish in and "take the cure."

At the same time, renowned Los Angeles freighter Remi Nadeau began his run up to the Cerro Gordo silver mines in Inyo County. Nadeau contracted with Lang to provide a station stop for the 100 men and 80 teams that were involved in the long haul. Warm meals and soft beds—perhaps even a splash in a spa—were luxuries to men accustomed to camping out and cooking over open fires. In those days Owens Lake was really a lake, and freight was loaded onto a paddle-wheeler called the *Bessie Brady* and ferried across the waters. After that it was only 18 miles up to the silver mines. Back the straining teams would come, as many as 20 mules, pulling high-sided blue wagons groaning under a load of high-grade ore, bound for a stopover at Lang Station (as it came to be known). The station was probably more profitable than the spa.

There were numerous stories about ferocious grizzly bears told and retold around the state from the days when bulls and bears were goaded into battle by Mexicans in downtown Los Angeles to Peter LeBeck being eaten alive up on Grapevine Pass to Grizzly Adams roaming the Tehachapis around Fort Tejon with his pet. The most celebrated at the time was known as the Monarch of the Mountains. Ol' Monarch wandered down out of the San Gabriels into the Soledad, dining on everything and everyone in sight. He is credited with munching up seven men and 100 head of cattle before July 7, 1873,

FAR LEFT: Thomas and Martha Mitchell were instrumental in the education of the valley's pioneer children. In September 1872 Mitchell, along with John Lang, established the Sulphur Springs School District (now the second-oldest school district in Los Angeles County), and Martha Mitchell taught the area's 17 children in her adobe home until a proper schoolhouse could be built. Before settling near present-day Sand and Lost Canyon roads, Mitchell had served with distinction as a colonel in the Texas Mounted Volunteers and had panned the American River for gold. From the collection of Charles Mitchell. Courtesy, Santa Clarita Valley Historical Society

LEFT: Although California once supported a population of 10,000 grizzly bears, by 1924 nearly all the bears had disappeared from the state due, in part, to hunters, ranchers, and homesteaders shooting, trapping, and poisoning them. After the Monarch of the Mountains had reportedly killed seven men and 100 head of cattle, John Lang shot and killed the bear on the banks of the Santa Clara River. This lithograph by J.W. Audubon titled Grizzly Bear *dates from 1848. Courtesy, Amon Carter Museum, Fort Worth*

Tiburcio Vásquez, who came from a wealthy, respectable, religious family, turned into one of the most sought-after outlaws in the history of the Los Angeles area. He and his gang rustled cattle and stole horses, robbed freight wagons, stagecoaches, travelers, and isolated ranches, and ransacked the towns of Tres Pinos, Kingston, and Firebaugh, which resulted in the death of three men. After finally being captured in 1874, nearly 10 months after taking over Tres Pinos and killing a hotel keeper, Vásquez was hanged on March 19, 1875. Vasquez Rocks, one of Tiburcio's hideouts, was named for the outlaw. Courtesy, Santa Clarita Valley Historical Society

when he was killed on the banks of the Santa Clara by John Lang and his big Henry rifle.

Lang claimed that the bear weighed 2,350 pounds, which would make it, by far, the largest bruin ever bagged anywhere in the world. The record Kodiak weighed only 1,670 pounds. The skin of the grizzly was sold and ended up in Liverpool, England.

THE SAGA OF TIBURCIO VÁSQUEZ

He stood 5 feet, 6 inches tall, weighed 135 pounds, and had a light complexion, thin moustache, and goatee. He was courtly in his manners, inordinately proud of his handwriting, fairly well read, and considered something of a gentleman.

On the other hand, Tiburcio Vásquez held the state in a literal reign of terror that lasted for 20 years, robbing stages, running off cattle, and capping his career by completely taking over two towns, plundering them at will. In between "jobs" he rested at a weird jumble of rocks that now makes up a county park named after him.

Vásquez was born on August 11, 1835, in a Monterey home that still stands. His family was wealthy, respected, honorable, and religious. At the age of 18 he was involved in a rumpus over a girl in which a constable was killed. Not trusting Yankee justice, he took off for Pacheco Pass, where he fell in with Anastacio Garcia, who took him under his wing and taught Vásquez the fine art of outlawry. Garcia had learned the trade from Joaquín Murietta.

Tiburcio started out by rustling cattle and robbing freight wagons. It is related that in 1855 he ran off a herd of horses from Rancho Camulos and was caught trying to sell them to a relative of the owner, Ignacio del Valle. Del Valle was also the judge who sentenced Vásquez to a long term in the hoosegow. Feeling somewhat restricted in his activities, Vásquez went over the wall one night, committed a few more petty thefts, was confined again, then released to ponder his past. Learning from his mistakes, the outlaw perfected the hit-and-run tactics of modern guerrilla warfare that would earn him the title of "The Scourge of California."

Vásquez put together a gang to rob freighters, stagecoaches, travelers, and isolated ranches up and down the state. When things got too hot, members of the band would be sent their separate ways. After a few months, when the law gave up the chase, a new group would be formed and the cycle repeated. This went on for years.

Vásquez had three brothers. One of them, Francisco, lived at Elizabeth Lake, while another, Claudio, resided in Soledad City. Sometime during 1871, while vacationing with his relatives, El Bandido discovered a perfect rock fortress near Agua Dulce Springs. He used it as a hideout off and on for three years under the alias of Ricardo Cantuga, mayordomo of Rancho Posa de Chane. Locals, such as Suraco, Mitchell, and Lang, believed that he was a horse buyer.

During August 1873 Vásquez and his men descended on the town of Tres Pinos, taking it over and looting it. During the operation three men were killed. After hiding out for five months, the gang raided Kingston, tied up the citizens, then removed everything not nailed down. The State was outraged. Governor Newton Booth offered a reward of $8,000 for Vásquez.

Tiburcio had a weakness for women that was legendary. He admitted to fathering one illegitimate son and had many liaisons, the most famous with a young lady in Los Angeles known only as La Coneja—"The Rabbit." He took Abdon Leiva into his doughty band simply because he had a playful wife named Rosaria. When Leiva deduced what was going on, he surrendered to Undersheriff William Jenkins at Lyon's Station, turning State's evidence against his former boss.

Tiburcio Vásquez had been the object of the greatest manhunt in the history of California. Not only were local peace officers gunning for him,

These men belonged to one of the numerous posses organized to search for Tiburcio Vásquez during 1873 and 1874. Courtesy, Santa Clarita Valley Historical Society

but there was also a sort of super posse put together by Governor Booth and led by the renowned sheriff of Alameda County, Henry (Harry) N. Morse. For 27 days, riding 1,000 miles, Harry Morse relentlessly pursued Vásquez at the head of his eight-man select troop of deputies.

Meanwhile, Sheriff William ("Billy") Rowland of Los Angeles found out that Vásquez had crossed into Los Angeles County. To make a long story short, Billy Rowland would not recognize Harry Morse's authority in his territory, and sent out his own troops. When this failed he relied on spies to ferret out the outlaw. Vásquez had his counterspies to keep him appraised of Rowland's movements. This game of cat-and-mouse went on until May 14, 1874, when the desperado was captured at the home of "Greek" George Allen, where Allen's wife was entertaining Vásquez.

Los Angeles went wild at the arrival of "The Scourge" stretched out in an ox cart on bloodstained hay. After being tossed into a cell, Vásquez was brought a bottle of whisky, which he cheerfully accepted, and, with the first gulp, toasted the President of the United States. Gushing ladies presented him with bouquets of flowers. A photographer set up his camera, took some pictures, and hawked them on the streets for a quarter each. "The Life of Vásquez" played to standing-room-only audiences at the Merced Theatre, the principal actor being coached by Tiburcio, who even loaned him his clothes. Everyone wanted the outlaw to play himself, but at that Rowland drew the line.

Tiburcio Vásquez was transferred to San Jose, where he was convicted of murdering a hotel keeper at the Tres Pinos "outrage." He was hanged at 1:35 p.m., March 19, 1875, his last word being "Pronto."

The number-two man in the Vásquez organization had been Cleovaro Chavez. For three years they rode together, becoming a perfect team and perpetrating increasingly bolder crimes. Chavez was about two years younger than his "Captain" and considerably taller. He was 5 feet, 11 inches in height, very muscular, and weighed a good 200 pounds.

Chavez took off for Mexico as soon as the Captain was captured, but returned to Hollister to demand the release of Vásquez. Otherwise, he said, he would "unleash a reign of terror the likes of which have not been seen since the days of Murietta."

True to his word, as soon as Tiburcio was hanged, Cleovaro put together a gang that raided the back country in the best Vásquez tradition.

Late in October Chavez broke up his guerrilla band. He headed into Arizona Territory, taking a job breaking horses 60 miles north of Yuma on the Colorado River. There, on November 25, 1875, two bounty hunters caught up with him, nearly cutting in half with shotgun blasts the unarmed successor to Vásquez. He went down with 17 buckshot in his stomach. For this noble deed, the adventurers collected a $2,000 reward.

Henry Mayo Newhall, born in Saugus, Massachusetts, in 1825, first came to California during the Gold Rush of 1849. Finding no success in the gold fields, Newhall moved to San Francisco, where he brought his wife, started a family, and built a successful business empire. Between 1872 and 1875, he purchased five old land grant ranchos, including the Rancho San Francisco (later called the Newhall Ranch) in the Santa Clarita Valley. Soon, for one dollar, the clever Newhall deeded over a right of way to Southern Pacific to lay tracks. Then, for another dollar, he sold the S.P.R.R. a site for a depot and town to be called Newhall. By 1878 the town of Newhall was the largest community in the valley. From the collection of Ruth Newhall. Courtesy, Santa Clarita Valley Historical Society

THE LIFE AND TIMES OF HENRY M. NEWHALL

The Rancho San Francisco, sprawling from beyond Bouquet Junction to the waters of Piru Creek, had seen several owners since the Del Valles sold out to William Wolfskill. Thomas R. Bard, acting as agent for the Philadelphia and California Petroleum Company, purchased it, and as oil production was nonexistent, sold the property to a pair of Santa Barbara lawyers, Charles Fernald and Jarrett T. Richards for $33,000. During May 1874 they placed the following advertisement in the Ventura newspaper:

*RANCHO SAN FRANCISCO
Contains 48,000 acres and is situated on the River Santa Clara. The lines of the Southern Pacific and the Atlantic and Pacific Railroads are surveyed through portions of this rancho. It contains
a large quantity of*

ARABLE BOTTOM LANDS

Is well watered and timbered, on the line of travel between Los Angeles and Cerro Gordon and other interior mining districts and is a first rate property for colonists and small farmers.

*Prices of arable land
$6.00 to $12.00 per acre*

At those outrageous prices no one would buy the estate, which went up for sheriff's sale when the partners defaulted on their payments.

On January 15, 1875, the ink was blotted on a deed in which most of the Santa Clarita Valley was exchanged for $90,000, or about $1.84 per acre. The new owner was a 50-year-old businessman from San Francisco by the name of Henry Mayo Newhall.

He was born in Saugus, Massachusetts, on May 13, 1825, where his ancestors had settled 200 years earlier. Newhall acquired the skills of an auctioneer, but at the age of 25 took off for the California gold fields to make his fortune. After a few futile months in the mines, he was so poor he had to sell his clothes in order to get down to San Francisco, where he fell back on his old trade of buying and selling shiploads of merchandise. He built a two-story, New England-style brick home in the fashionable South Park district of Rincon Hill. There, during the fall of 1852, he brought out his bride, Sarah Ann White. They had three sons—Henry Gregory, William Mayo, and Edwin White Newhall—before Sarah died in childbirth six years later. He promptly married her sister, Margaret Jane, and from this union came two more sons, Walter Scott (1860) and George Almer (1862).

Newhall busily expanded his business empire, branching out into wholesaling, insurance, real estate, and railroads. While Newhall was presiding over the construction of the first line out of the Bay City, Southern Pacific stepped in, bought him out for more than a million dollars, then installed him as a vice president of the company. With these profits in hand, Henry M., between the years 1872 through 1875, purchased five old land grant ranchos, totaling 114,271 acres, scattered between Los Angeles and Monterey.

A year after he acquired Rancho San Francisco, Henry Mayo Newhall, for the princely sum of one dollar, deeded over a right of way to Southern Pacific to lay tracks. Another buck got Southern Pacific the site for a depot and town to be called Newhall.

Late in 1878 Henry and his eldest son, Henry Gregory, set up headquarters in a frame house, hiring a motley crew of Mexicans, Indians, and Chinese to plant corn, flax, and alfalfa, while plowing 500 acres for cultivation. It was the beginning of the Newhall Land and Farming Company.

Judge Powell of the Soledad

Shortly after Tiburcio Vásquez was hanged, and while Cleovaro Chavez was still plundering the countryside, it was decided by the L.A. County Board of Supervisors to bring law and order to the Santa Clarita. Therefore, on May 8, 1875, The Soledad Judicial District was established and the first justice appointed. The task of taming the valley fell to a 35-year-old Irish immigrant by the name of John F. Powell, a man who had pursued an interesting and exciting life.

Born in Galway, Ireland, on December 17, 1839, he was brought to Charleston, Massachusetts, by his parents at the tender age of 15 months. He was commissioned a lieutenant in the U.S. Navy during July 1859, assigned to the USS *Constellation*, and packed off to suppress the slave trade in Africa. In between hunting lions and other big game, Lieutenant Powell met Dr. David Livingston, who led him to a camp filled with 705 slaves. The liberation of these poor blacks was an accomplishment that he took pride in to his dying day.

Leaving the Navy, Powell became an Army officer during the Civil War, leading the 5th Massachusetts Infantry into seven battles. Then he was placed in command of Goat Island in San Francisco Bay until discharged on December 1, 1869. He and his brother set up a sheep ranch at Big Rock in the Antelope Valley, where his fair dealings and treaties with marauding Indian tribes brought him to the attention of the board of supervisors.

For nearly 40 years Judge Powell presided over an immense territory that sprawled from the Sierra Pelona to Piru Creek, becoming famous for settling most of his cases out of court. Never did he have one of his decisions overturned by a higher court.

He came to a land peopled by outcasts from

Los Angeles for the most part, the "solid citizens" being a few ranchers, miners, or oil drillers. The only thing really approaching a community were the 20 or so families of Lyon Station, Mentryville in Pico Canyon, and Soledad City, who moved with each new gold strike.

Within two years the railroad came, bringing depots called Acton, Lang, Honby, Humphrys, and Newhall. Towns grew around Acton and Newhall, complete with general stores and those absolutely indispensable establishments—saloons. Bars were built long before churches or schools.

The judge relaxed by going off on hunting trips for days at a time, tracking down deer,

Judge John F. Powell was appointed the first justice of the Soledad Judicial District in 1875. Serving the courts for nearly 40 years, he presided over a far-flung jurisdiction. Powell was famous for settling cases out of court and for never having his decisions overturned by a higher court. The judge passed away in his Newhall home at the age of 87. From the collection of F.J. Legasse. Courtesy, Santa Clarita Valley Historical Society

LEFT: *Judge John F. Powell, wife Dora, their children, and friends enjoy the fresh air in the yard of the Powell's Newhall home on Main Street (Railroad Avenue) in 1888. Powell tended one of the largest orchards in the West. Courtesy, Santa Clarita Valley Historical Society*

FACING PAGE: *The first Newhall School was built for the staggering cost of $3,500 in 1887. Judge Powell, who took an interest in civic activities, contributed financially to the construction of the schoolhouse. Courtesy, Santa Clarita Valley Historical Society*

pronghorn antelope, coyote, or grizzly bear. He once bagged a rare white wolf up in Bouquet Canyon, which he had made into a rug that sold for $125. Powell held the record for the largest mountain lion in the state. It was very old with loose teeth and few claws left, but measured 12 feet, 6 inches from nose to end of tail.

Powell met and married Dora Lake, starting a new career of child raising. Her sister, Flora May, was later wed to Alex Mentry, the superintendent of the California Star Oil fields in Pico. The brothers-in-law became fast friends and even business partners. In 1896 they staked out a gold claim in Seco Canyon and built a small dam. After they sold out, the dam collapsed.

As Newhall was the largest community in the valley, the judge moved his court there sometime in 1878 and set out fruit trees. Before long he was tending one of the largest orchards in the West. Deeply interested in civic activities, John Powell contributed to building the school in 1887 (it cost a staggering $3,500) and the Community Presbyterian Church.

At the age of 87, Judge John F. Powell quietly passed away in his sleep at the Newhall home that he built. It could truly be said that out of a wilderness he had created a garden.

COMING OF THE IRON HORSE

The gentle folks down in Los Angeles realized that if their scruffy-looking pueblo was ever to attain the status of a city it would have to be connected to the rest of the world by the railroad, and that meant dealing with Charles Crocker, Leland Stanford, and the Southern Pacific.

Southern Pacific drove a hard bargain in which the citizens voted to buy up all rights of way—including Phineas Banning's 21-mile line to San Pedro—and then hand them over to the giant conglomerate.

Twin ribbons of steel began to snake their way out of Oakland down through the San Joaquin Valley, then over the Tehachapi Mountains, where a famed loop brought engines chugging underneath their own cabooses.

On March 22, 1875, a small army of Chinese laborers stood at the base of the San Gabriel Mountains, picks and shovels in hand. They had put down track from Los Angeles northward across the wide expanse of the San Fernando Valley up to this seemingly impenetrable barrier. A swarthy, heavily built man stepped forward. This was Frank Frates, a native of the Azores Islands and superintendent of construction. Frates gave a signal, and the hillside erupted in a cloud of smoke and dust from a blast of Hercules powder. Calling out, "fall to," the boss stepped back as 330 laborers began attacking the hillside. Over on the other side another crew, under the direction of John T. Gifford, started to dig southward from Lyon's Station.

Almost immediately it was found that under the arid and desolate surface, these hills were saturated with water and oil. Steam-driven pumps had to be brought, which often broke down when they got clogged with sand.

For a dollar a day the Chinese labored through a gooey muck that stuck to shovels like pudding, caked onto boots in great balls, and turned the deepening hell hole into a steambath. They drilled. Others placed explosives. Then all ran for their lives before the charges went off. Frates sank three incline shafts for ventilation, which helped a little. Frequently the shaft caved in, causing more problems and fears that the project would have to be abandoned.

A year after the digging began a reporter observed:

If a portion of the roof of the tunnel falls, injuring some and dangerously frightening others of the men, or if the pumps or hoisting engines or machinery of any of the inclines give way, stopping work and allowing water to accumulate rapidly; if a landslide occurs . . . Mr. Frates is always promptly on hand, night or day, and by his skill and energy, soon has the work going ahead again.

There were times when Stanford, Crocker, and probably even Frank Frates had serious doubts if the tunnel would ever be finished. Angelenos worried that the route would be abandoned and consequently their town would be bypassed. Then, on the night of July 14, 1876, the two crews of laborers met at last, face-to-face. After a year and a half, $2 million, and uncounted casualties, the work was finished. John Gifford tapped out a message from Lyon's Station that read "Daylight shines through the San Fernando Tunnel."

It was a remarkable achievement. At 6,940 feet it was the third-longest tunnel in the United States and stood fourth in the world. The northern and southern bores had been off only half an inch in the two grades. The arched ceiling rose 22 feet above the floor, which was 16 1/2 feet across.

Before the railroad connected the Santa Clarita Valley with Northern California, it took about 49 hours and cost $20 to travel the 306 miles to Gilroy by stagecoach. This schedule of the Coast Stage Line dates from May of 1871. Courtesy, Santa Clarita Valley Historical Society

GILROY and LOS ANGELES.
COAST STAGE LINE.

W. G. ROBERTS, Agent, office 208 Montgomery street, San Francisco.
General Agent, W. BUCKLEY, San Jose, California.
Local Agents: JOS. KNOWLTON, Jr., Gilroy; WM. BALCH, San Juan; CHRIS. HAMEL, Natividad; L. C. Bostick, Plato Ranch; CHAS. KNOWLTON, Paso Robles Springs; J. C. ORTEGA, San Luis Obispo; ELI RUNDELL, Santa Barbara; J. WOOLFSON, San Buenaventura; GEO. M. FALL, Los Angeles.
Stage leaves Gilroy daily at 12 M. Stage leaves Los Angeles daily at 6 A. M.

From Gilroy To Los Angeles.			TOWNS May 18th, 1871.	See Page.	From Los Angeles To Gilroy.		
Fare.	Hours	Miles.			Miles.	Hours	Fare.
$ 0.00	0	0	Dep........Gilroy.........Arr.	161	366	58	
1.50	2	12	........San Juan........		354		
2.50	4	24	........Natividad........		342		
4.00	6	38	........Uttz Station........		328		
5.50	8	52	........Salinas River........		314		
8.50	11	76	........Last Chance........		290		
10.00	13	92	........San Antonio........		274		
12.00	15	107	........Plato Ranch........		259		
14.00	17	121	........Nacimento........		245		
15.00	19	136	......Paso Robles Hot Springs.....		230		
16.00	22	150	........San Margarita........		216		
16.00	25	164	........San Luis Obispo........	174	202	36	
17.50	28	180	........Arroyo Grande........		186		
17.50	31	196	........Zury Station........		170		
17.50	33	214	........Foxens........		152		
17.50	35	228	........Ballard's........		138		
17.50	37	243	........San Marcus........		123		
17.20	40	257	........McCaffey's........		109		
17.50	41	265	........Santa Barbara........	174	101	15	
18.00	44	280	........Rincon........		86		
18.00	47	293	........San Buenaventura........		73	11	
20.00	49	306	........Santa Clara Valley........		60		
20.00	51	320	........Sime........		46		
20.00	53	333	........Mountain Station........		33	5	
20.00	56	350	........El Cino........		16	2	
20.00	58	366	Arr........Los Angeles.....Dep.	164	0	0	

Connections.

At Gilroy, connects with cars of S. F. & S. J. R. R. for San Francisco.
At San Juan, connects with stages for Watsonville and Santa Cruz, New Idria, Castroville, Salinas City, and Monterey.
At San Luis Obispo, connects with stage for San Simeon.
At Los Angeles, connects with stages for San Diego, Fort Yuma and Tucson, San Bernardino, La Paz and Clear Creek.

GILROY and SULPHUR SPRINGS.
CAVANA'S STAGE LINE.

Stages leave Gilroy daily at 12.30 P. M.; arrive at Canada de Los Assos at 2.30 P. M.; distance 8 miles; fare $1.00; arrive at Hot Sulphur Springs at 3.30 P. M.; distance 15 miles; through fare $2.00. Returning, leave Hot Springs at 8 A. M.; arrive at Gilroy at 11 A. M. Connect at Gilroy with stages for Santa Cruz, Watsonville and Monterey, and cars for San Francisco.

The San Fernando Tunnel, nearly 7,000 feet long, was the third-longest tunnel in the country when it was completed on July 14, 1876. This remarkable feat of engineering made possible the connection of Northern and Southern California by rail. Courtesy, California Historical Society, Ticor Title Insurance

Men working on the San Fernando Tunnel take a breather from their labors to be photographed. This circa 1876 view of the job site shows the "Tunnel" Post Office in the background. From the collection of Zona Ake. Courtesy, Santa Clarita Valley Historical Society

The first engine steamed through on August 12, providing another poetic message from Mr. Gifford. "The iron horse poked its head through the San Fernando Tunnel this evening at six o'clock and neighed long and loud his hearty greeting to the citizens of the Santa Clara Valley."

Driving the Golden Spike

Shortly after the mighty San Fernando Tunnel was finished, Southern Pacific Railroad announced that on July 27, 1876, Tunnel No. 19 in Soledad Canyon holed through at 223 feet. The work crews were now moving across the wide, smooth Santa Clara River plain at a rate of two-and-a-half to three miles per day.

At a furious pace some 1,500 Chinese hammered their way down the canyon, the ringing of sledges slamming into iron spikes echoing off of the dry walls of the arroyo. A like number of laborers had already rounded the bend at Bouquet Junction and were headed for a historic meeting with their colleagues at John Lang's ranch.

Toward the end of August, Lang's Hotel received a distinguished guest. The president of Southern Pacific, Charles Crocker, arrived in order to person-

Among the dignitaries gathered at Lang Station on September 5, 1876, for the completion of the Southern Pacific Railroad were John G. Downey, ex-governor of California; Prudent Beaudry, mayor of Los Angeles, Isaac W. Hellman, banker; Robert M. Whitney, judge, and Mary Barnes Whitney; Phineas Banning, freighter; Charles Crocker, Southern Pacific president; B.D. Wilson, rancher, and Margaret H. Wilson; Romualdo Pacheco, governor; E.J. "Luckey" Baldwin, financier; David D. Colton, vice president of the Southern Pacific; Leland Stanford, Southern Pacific; Harris Newmark, Los Angeles merchant; and Major Benjamin C. Truman, editor of the Los Angeles Star. *Before driving the golden spike, Charles Crocker announced to the crowd: "Gentlemen, I am no public speaker, but I can drive a spike." Drawing by Jerry Reynolds*

ally oversee the final days of construction.

By September the northern and southern gangs were in sight of each other and on the evening of the 4th stood only 1,050 feet apart on the dusty, wind-blown roadway. The very air was charged with excitement, and two tents were set up by the Atlantic and Pacific Telegraph in order to flash the news around the world at the exact moment the final spike was driven. Tomorrow would be Crocker's day at center stage, and he would be more than equal to the occasion.

It was high noon on September 5, 1876. Engine Number 25, decked out with fruit branches, flowers, and American flags, ground to a squealing halt a few feet west of the hotel. On board were 335 prominent Angelenos, including Mayor Prudent Baudry and ex-Governor John G. Downey. Also on hand was General Phineas Banning, the man who pioneered the stage and freighting business up San Francisquito Canyon 22 years before.

Crocker greeted them all warmly then threw back his head in thunderous laughter when B.D. Wilson remarked that the land "was fit only for the production of horned toads and scorpions."

An hour later Engine No. 38 steamed into view, bringing the 50-man contingent down from San Francisco. It too was draped with flags and carried Mayor Bryant, Leland Stanford, and Collis P. Huntington. Almost immediately a brass band made the desolate hillsides resound with a lively tune. As the dignitaries shook hands and exchanged greetings, the assembled crowd wildly cheered, and even the normally reserved Chinese shouted as if caught up in the spirit of the event.

The small army of Orientals then lined up on either side of the unfinished roadbed. They were dressed in wide-brimmed basket hats, blue-denim jackets and pants, with cotton sandals on their feet. At a signal from Crocker they began laying iron with gusto. The band played, and a rousing cheer went up when the two teams met and there was only one last nail to drive home.

As the dust settled, Charles Crocker was handed a silver mallet and a golden spike fashioned by a Los Angeles jeweler from San Gabriel Mountain ore. After brief remarks the portly railroader concluded by saying, "Gentlemen, I am no public speaker, but I can drive a spike." He then proved it by hammering it home with six blows.

The band played; there were more cheers; hats were thrown skyward as the locomotives shrieked in jubilation. California was, at last, bound together by twin ribbons of steel.

Slightly after 2 p.m. the great event was over and the engines were chugging back down Soledad Canyon. The night brought a magnificent banquet at the Union Hall in downtown Los Angeles for 190 invited male guests, none of whom had ever laid a rail or driven a spike—with the exception of Mr. Crocker.

Charles Crocker, president of the Southern Pacific Railroad, drove the golden spike that united, by rail, the Santa Clarita Valley and the rest of Southern California with the northern portion of the state. Crocker stayed at Lang's Hotel while personally overseeing the final days of track construction. From Cirker, Dictionary of American Portraits, *Dover, 1967*

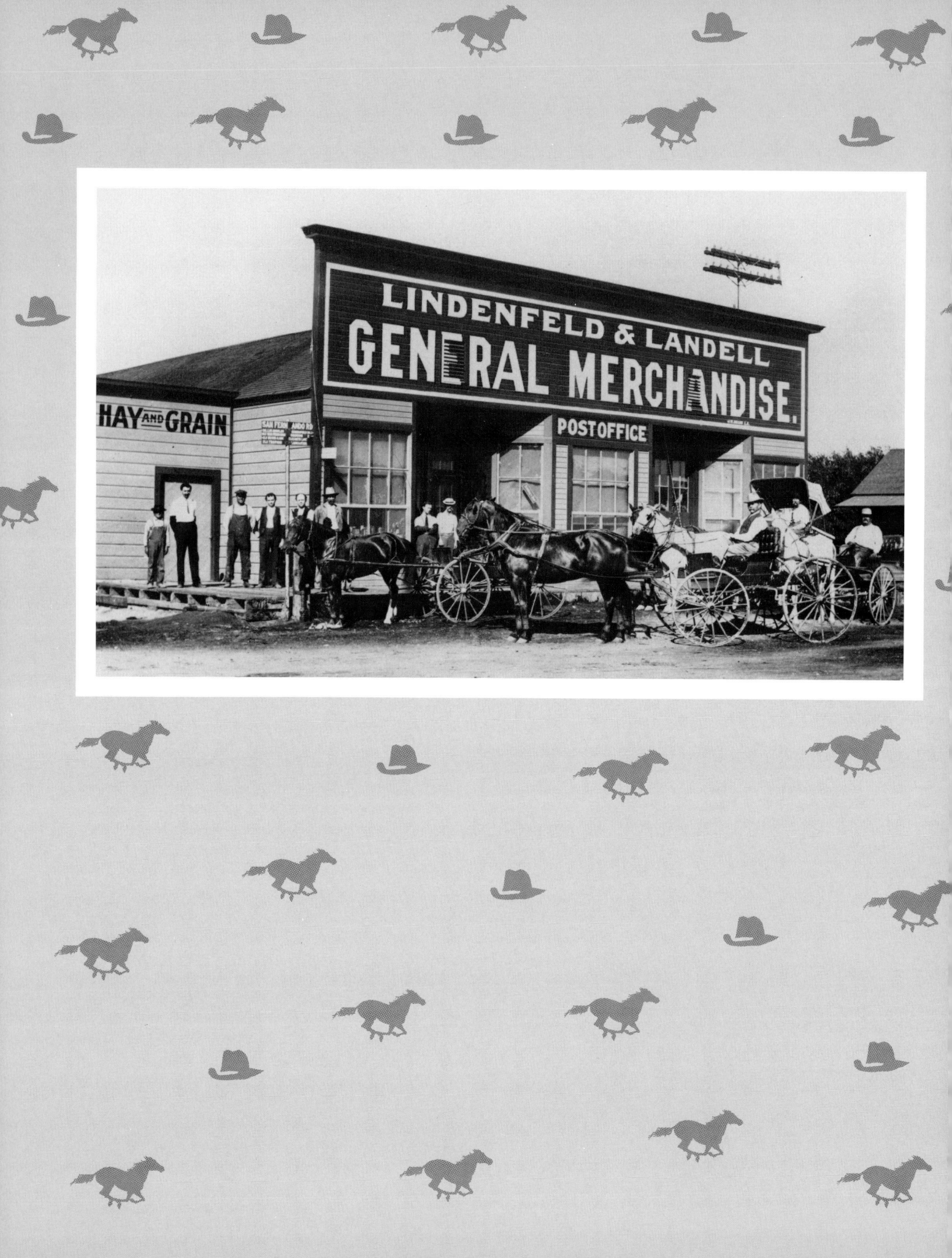

4

TOWN FOUNDINGS AND EARLY SETTLERS

1870s-Early 1900s

THE FOUNDING OF NEWHALL

On September 6, 1876, the day after the golden spike was driven at Lang Station in Soledad Canyon, Newhall Depot opened its doors for business. It was not located at the present townsite, but, rather, up at the junction of what are now called Bouquet Canyon Road and Magic Mountain Parkway.

Presiding over this small, box-like structure painted yellow with brown trim was John T. Gifford, a 29-year-old native of Genesse County, New York.

Gifford was married to an English woman, Sarah Beckworth, had been a crew chief overseeing the digging of the San Fernando Tunnel, and, perhaps because of his colorful telegraph messages sent from Lyon's Station, was appointed Southern Pacific's first agent at Newhall. It was a mixed blessing as quarters were not provided and there was no town, so John and Sarah set up housekeeping in a boxcar parked on a siding.

The town of Newhall was laid out on October 13 by Western Development, a real estate subsidiary of Southern Pacific. The first lot was sold to George Campton, who built a general store. This was followed by the Campton residence, Mrs. Harper's four-room boardinghouse (with dining area), and Wilson's Saloon.

Unfortunately, this was a time of drought, with levels of the wells dropping dramatically. Not only people, but also great steam engines needed the precious liquid, so, on January 15, 1878, it was decided to relocate the depot and town three miles southward to 6th and Railroad avenues. The move was completed and everyone was reestablished by the 16th day of February.

Later that year Henry M. Newhall began construction of his Southern Hotel at San Fernando Road and Market Street. The two-story Victorian structure became "one of the finest and best appointed establishments outside of San Francisco," according to one guest.

John and Sarah Gifford finally got a real home of their own after laying out $125 for two city lots and erecting a board-and-batt bungalow, the remains of which are now located under the parking lot of Anawalt Lumber Company.

By 1882 Henry M. Newhall could look with some pride on "his" little town. Businesses were sprawling up and down Railroad Avenue; residences were being built; the trains arrived on time; and there was considerable shipping from local ranches, farms, and mines. Arriving at his Rancho San Francisco, Newhall called for a horse to be saddled and went off for a leisurely canter across the rolling, oak-studded hills. Somewhere along the way the animal stumbled, pitching its rider headlong into the spring grass.

Newhall was taken to his home in San Francisco, where he died on March 13 at the age of 56.

Lindenfeld and Landell bought the Railroad Avenue general store from George Campton along with the post office. Gift of Mr. R. Lindenfeld, Fillmore, California. Courtesy, Santa Clarita Valley Historical Society

RIGHT: George Campton, born in July of 1839, hailed from the British West Indies and immigrated to the U.S. during the Civil War. In 1876 he married a 19-year-old native Californian named Gregeria and established the first general store in the fledgling community of Newhall in October of that year. Courtesy, Santa Clarita Valley Historical Society

Henry M. Newhall's Southern Hotel offered guests "well appointed, spacious accommodations," a dining room, a reading room, and a "genteel bar." D.W. Fields had a general store in the corner and managed the hotel for Newhall, while D.W. Boynton ran the bar. Built in 1878, the structure only stood about 10 years, for it burned to the ground on October 1, 1888. If the hotel was still standing, Market Street would run right through its center, Newhall Avenue would angle off behind it, and San Fernando Road would run in front. Courtesy, Santa Clarita Valley Historical Society

LEFT: By the time this photograph of Newhall's dirt main street was taken in the 1890s, Campton's store (third building from the right) had competition from general merchant James M. Gulley (left). Courtesy, Santa Clarita Valley Historical Society

George Campton's general store opened for business in 1876 near Bouquet Junction. A year and a half later, when Newhall was relocated to its present site, he and the whole town moved to 8th and Spruce (now San Fernando Road). Courtesy, Santa Clarita Valley Historical Society

A 1908 Fourth of July picnic in Newhall Park on the Newhall Ranch brought together some of the Santa Clarita Valley's young people. Pictured left to right are Lillie Mayhue, Valentine Biscailuz, Mae Culver, Frank Swall, Marguerite Culver, Joe Moore, Eva Banks, and Jim Freer. From the collection of Betty H. Mayhue Pember. Courtesy, Santa Clarita Valley Historical Society

Rather than quibble over Newhall's six California ranches and other holdings, the widow and five sons banded together, incorporating Newhall Land and Farming on June 1, 1883. The eldest son, Henry Gregory, then just 30 years old, took over active management of Rancho San Francisco, which would from that time to the present be known as the Newhall Ranch.

THE BARON OF CASTAIC

One of the most colorful characters to ever gallop across the dusty Santa Clara plain was William Willoby ("Wirt") Jenkins, who pursued an interesting career both inside and outside of the law.

Born October 12, 1833, on a farm near Circleville, Ohio, he later accompanied his family to the goldfields of California. By the time he was 18 years old, "Wirt" had learned the fine art of gunslinging while holding off attempts at claim jumping on the American River. Two years later he drifted into old Los Angeles, where his prowess with a six-shooter came to the notice of Alcalde (Mayor) Don Ignacio del Valle.

Don Ignacio was having some law-enforcement problems in the town. Several of his sheriffs had either left suddenly or were killed, so he formed the California Rangers, a group very much like San Francisco's Vigilantes.

Horace Bell was appointed major with Cyrus Lyon, William Reader, and Bill Jenkins as captains. Within two years, by 1855, it was safe to walk the streets again.

In 1869 Jenkins helped spring-pole the first oil well in Pico Canyon with Sanford Lyon and H.C. Wiley and, later, as undersheriff, accepted the surrender of Abdon Leiva, which led to the conviction of Tiburcio Vásquez. He had staked a claim on Castaic Creek during 1872, but did not settle on it until 1878, when he married Olive Rhoades. Two daughters, June and Anita Ruby, were born on the Lazy Z.

Jenkins held a claim to Alcatraz Island dating back through Governor Downey to John Charles Frémont. As he pursued his interests in federal court, Horace Bell started calling him "The Baron of Alcatraz and Casteca" in his newspaper. Unfortunately for Jenkins, he never did get Alcatraz.

Not to be discouraged, the aging ranger outfitted a boat with wheels in order to "sail" government surveyors over a few parched acres that he claimed were swamplands. Some of this property was held by the Carmichaels and Roses, who took exception to the obvious land grab and started a feud that raged over the Castaic Hills for years, complete with night riders, running gun battles, house burnings, and 21 people dead.

Forest Ranger Robert E. Clark arrived in 1905, meeting with Bill Jenkins, whom he described as "a great knife thrower, always wore a vest with a throwing knife in a holster under it. He generally rode in a buggy and (had) his six-shooter on the seat beside him." Clark managed to bring an end to the feud, for which Theodore Roosevelt rewarded him with a brace of pistols.

The final act in the drama occurred during the spring of 1916, when Bill Jenkins moved some cattle up into Charlie Canyon. There was Billy Rose already encamped with his herd. An altercation broke out; shots were fired; and Jenkins rolled from his saddle, dropping to the ground with a thud.

All that marks the Lazy Z today are Stonegate tract homes along Lake Hughes Road where it intersects with the Ridge Route.

LEFT: This portrait of Olive Rhoades Jenkins dates from about 1885, seven years after she married W.W. "Bill" Jenkins. The Jenkins' had two children, daughters June and Anita Ruby, and lived along Castaic Creek on the Lazy Z horse ranch. From the collection of Anita Ruby Kellogg. Courtesy, Santa Clarita Valley Historical Society

LEFT: William Willoby Jenkins, who was nearly six feet tall and rail thin, stands out as one of the valley's most colorful characters. Jenkins was a gunslinger during the Gold Rush of 1849, a captain of the California Rangers, the undersheriff who helped convict Tiburcio Vásquez by accepting the surrender of Vásquez' partner in crime, and a major player in a long-lasting feud with the Carmichael and Rose families that involved Jenkins' attempt to claim their land as his own. The feud ended in the spring of 1916 when Billy Rose shot and killed Jenkins. From the collection of Anita Ruby Kellogg. Courtesy, Santa Clarita Valley Historical Society

The Stills of Railroad Canyon

The directors of Star Oil Company decided that the best place for a refinery would be at Lyon's Station since it sat on the north-south freight and stage routes and was the probable location for the future railroad. Star contracted Captain W.S. Smith to build a 15-barrel still, which was completed in April 1874. The operation was not profitable, so a second 20-barrel tank was constructed in order to increase production. This only increased the financial problems, so Lyons Refinery, along with Star Oil, promptly went bankrupt.

Meanwhile, during the year of 1875, a crafty man by the name of Andrew Kazlinski set up a rival stage stop in Railroad Canyon, which seemed like a rather out-of-the-way place to do business. Before long, however, the railroad was laying tracks right through the front yard of Andrew's Station, as it was called, and oil men from the east were swarming all over the valley, intent on building a newer, larger refinery.

On July 8, 1876, California Star Oil Company (CSO) was born in San Francisco, taking over the old defunct Star Oil Company and buying up the leases in Pico and other canyons, including Elsmere. The company's general manager, Demetrius G. Scofield, sent back to Titusville, Pennsylvania, for a highly successful refiner by the name of Denton Cyrus Scott.

Assisted by a driller named W.E. Youle and a fellow named Wood, D.C. Scott moved the two old stills from Lyon's to Andrew's Station, so that by the end of July they were producing 24 to 40 barrels of refined product per day. It was the first practical refinery in California.

Demetrius Scofield was so impressed that he headed east in January of 1877, returning with a big 120-barrel cooker. A fourth still was added late in 1879 with a capacity of 150 barrels.

On March 1, 1877, the following advertisement appeared in the *Los Angeles Evening Express*:

Why consumers should use kerosene oil manufactured by the California Star Oil Works Company: First it is to patronize home manufactures; second, it has no equal as an illuminating oil; third, it is entirely safe and will not explode. It is put in a first-class package and will not leak and it gives a light equal to gas. Hereafter there will be no delay in filling orders promptly. All orders should be addressed "California Star Oil Works Co., Andrew's Station, Los Angeles County," and will receive prompt attention.

When the town of Newhall moved down to its present location, CSO built a cottage on what is now Pine Street (March 1878) to accommodate visiting dignitaries. A Chinese house boy was also provided. A second cottage existed up the hill behind the refinery.

Oil was processed up until 1884, when refining facilities were centered at Alameda Point. The Newhall Refinery disintegrated until it was reborn in 1930 as "The Pioneer." Today it is the oldest-existing refinery in the world.

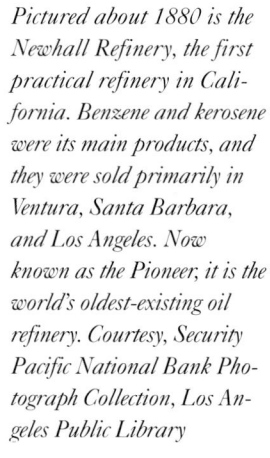

Pictured about 1880 is the Newhall Refinery, the first practical refinery in California. Benzene and kerosene were its main products, and they were sold primarily in Ventura, Santa Barbara, and Los Angeles. Now known as the Pioneer, it is the world's oldest-existing oil refinery. Courtesy, Security Pacific National Bank Photograph Collection, Los Angeles Public Library

The Gavin and Powell families visited the Mentry Ranch in Placerita Canyon, where this group photo was taken. Nellie, Pat, and Grace Gavin stand at left, while Dora Lake Powell and John F. Powell and their children—Francis, Florence, and Alfred (Fred)—stand at right. From the collection of F.J. Lagasse. Courtesy, Santa Clarita Valley Historical Society

LIFE IN MENTRYVILLE

There was a cluster of homes out in the canyon known as Pico Springs or Pico Camp before 1876. After 1876, however, the settlement came to be known as Mentryville, named for Charles Alexander Mentry, the man who brought in CSO 4. Three years later Alex married a New York girl, Flora May Lake, eventually producing three sons and a daughter: Arthur, Ray, Guy, and Irene.

Meanwhile, up in San Francisco, several businessmen formed the Pacific Coast Oil Company (PCO) and began gobbling up small petroleum claims. Among the directors were Demetrius G. Scofield of CSO and Charles Felton. Felton had made his money during the California Gold Rush, had an impressive home in Menlo Park, and would one day became a U.S. senator. After seven months of "wheeling and dealing," PCO was finally incorporated on September 10, 1879. By this time California Star was a wholly owned subsidiary, still employing Alex Mentry as superintendent of the Pico Field.

Mentryville, at best, was an oil boom town with cottages scattered among the derricks in no organized pattern. By 1880 there were about 100 families living there in redwood board-and-batt structures built on leased land. When the head of the household moved, he either took his home with him or sold it to his replacement.

New arrivals stayed in a couple of bunkhouses

ABOVE: This photo of Pico Canyon (Mentryville) depicts a boom town complete with a main "drag" and Alex Mentry's two-story, 13-room, gas-heated and gas-illuminated Victorian mansion that everyone referred to as "The Big House." Courtesy, Santa Clarita Valley Historical Society

or boardinghouses until they secured a place of their own. Bachelors slept in a sort of tent city.

Farther down the canyon was located a large machine shop, a blacksmith, boiler sheds, and store houses. Without stores or shops of any kind, residents had to travel down to Newhall for foodstuffs and personal items. Finally, in 1897, Anthony Cochems started a bakery, supplying bread, cakes, and other "goodies" for the community.

Twice daily the Telegraph Stage creaked and rocked into the town from Andrew's Station or Newhall, bringing passengers, mail, and contraband liquor. Alcohol was forbidden, yet it is reported that the coach drivers carried some under the seat to be sold to residents who, no doubt, kept a few bottles in their first aid kits as protection against snake bites.

Lyman Stewart and Wallace Hardison drilled seven dry holes in the canyon on a lease agreement with PCO. Their eighth produced 75 barrels a day at 1,620 feet at a place called Christian Hill (named this because of Stewart's aversion to profanity). That same year, 1883, they built a warehouse in Newhall, but finally went bankrupt. Discouraged, the partners moved over to Santa Paula, becoming immensely successful with Union Oil Company, which they founded in 1890.

To get an education the children were packed off to San Fernando until October 1885, when the Felton School opened its doors. After school hours, dances and meetings were held within its walls.

Mentryville may very well be the first town completely heated and lighted by gas, which seems natural since it sat in the middle of an oil field. Even the tennis courts, croquet field, and horseshoe area were illuminated by natural gas.

Common laborers were paid two and one-half dollars per day while experienced drillers got four dollars by working 12-hour days. (This might not seem like much by today's standards, but bear in mind, in 1880 a nickel would get you a loaf of bread or a pitcher of beer, while blue jeans by Levi Strauss sold for a whole dollar.)

For those oil workers in Mentryville who had not yet built their own homes, there was the town's boardinghouse, which was usually crowded. Pictured in front of the boardinghouse are members of the Powell, Prall, and Mentry families. From the collection of Laverne Mentry. Courtesy, Santa Clarita Valley Historical Society

By 1893 Mentryville, in Pico Canyon, had developed into an oil boom town, and the "Pico Boys" gathered for this group portrait. Among the notables pictured are Ed Pardee (standing in center, wearing constable's star) and Charles Pardee (sitting in the middle row, with Ed's hand on his shoulder). Charles Pardee, who had been an experienced oil man in Titusville, Pennsylvania, was among the first Easterners to arrive in Pico Canyon. Ed Pardee eventually left Pico Canyon to become owner of the Newhall Livery Stable. From the collection of F.J. Legasse. Courtesy, Santa Clarita Valley Historical Society

FACING PAGE: Henry T. Gage, governor of California from 1899 to 1903, owned some of the most well-known and productive gold mines in the Santa Clarita Valley. His holdings included the Red Rover, the Emma, the Puritan, and the New York (later renamed the Governor by Gage's sons). Courtesy, State of California, Department of Parks and Recreation

This steam-powered, two-stamp mill was used in the Cedar Mining District during the 1880s. Courtesy, Santa Clarita Valley Historical Society

Mining the Soledad

By 1870 the Cedar Mining District came into being with several gold, silver, and mercury mines in the desolate canyons to the north of Acton. One of them, the New York (now known as the Governor), would become the greatest producer of gold in Los Angeles County.

The saga of the New York began in 1881, when 29-year-old Henry T. Gage arrived in Los Angeles from New York. A lawyer by profession, he was elected to the post of city attorney and, in 1888, was a delegate to the Republican National Convention, seconding the nomination of Levi P. Morton as Vice President. On January 5, 1899, he was sworn in as governor of California, becoming a political ally of Theodore Roosevelt.

During Henry Gage's flamboyant career he came to own some of the most famous and productive gold mines in the Soledad. Into his collection went the Red Rover, the Emma, the Puritan, and the fabulous New York. In three years, from 1895 to 1897, the New York produced $1.5 million. Closed shortly thereafter, the mine was reopened by Gage's sons in 1932 and renamed the Governor. The main shaft was pushed down 1,000 feet. It finally closed in 1942 when the vein petered out. It has been reopened a third time and is still producing a meager amount of paydirt.

The superintendent of Gage's Puritan Mine had a most unusual and precocious daughter known as Lou Henry. She was sent to Stanford University when it opened in 1891, becoming the first female graduate. While there she met and married a young geology student from Iowa, who, 30 years later, became President of the United States. He was Herbert Clark Hoover, and as he coped with the Depression, Lou Henry Hoover filled the White House with books and art works. The remarkable lady spoke five languages and relaxed by reading sociology and economics.

Hoover had been a mining expert who developed claims in Australia, Burma, China (the newlyweds were caught up in the 1900 Boxer Rebellion), and Russia. They frequently visited Lou's parents at Acton where, it is claimed, Herbert Hoover relaxed by fishing for native trout in the Santa Clara River. Mrs. Hoover was a member of the Acton Church, and even when she could not attend services she sent donations.

ABOVE: Henry T. Gage's mining interests were developing the Red Rover gold mine in Acton around 1890. These miners use candle power inside the Red Rover to illuminate a fissure vein for the camera. Left to right are Robert Clark, Joe Eckles, and Ed Brough. In the back is Frank Ericksen. From the collection of Clara Wright. Courtesy, Santa Clarita Valley Historical Society

THE ACTON CHRONICLES

The opening of the first Cedar Mining District in 1870 brought in a lot of miners and prospectors who, if nothing else, worked up a powerful thirst. Recognizing a need, John F. Duehren made the monumental decision that a lot more money could be had from selling liquid refreshments than by wielding a pick and shovel. Consequently, he built a small board-and-batt establishment known as the 49er Saloon, which became an instant success.

Six years later crews of the Southern Pacific Railroad put down tracks just south of the 49er, which certainly increased Duehren's business. By October 1876 the Southern Pacific depot was established, bearing the name of Acton. Supposedly it was named by Henry M. Newhall for the small community near his birthplace in Massachusetts.

Duehren built a large, two-story house for his family. (The house still stands.) He was the only full-time resident of Acton until October 11, 1887, when the Southern Pacific passenger train ground to a stop at the tiny station and out stepped a dynamic young man of 31 years, Rudolph Eugene Nickel.

Nickel, born on the German-Swiss border, immigrated to the United States and ended up on the plains of Kansas. There the railroad employed him as agent for the Acton Station, sending him west. By November he had constructed a general store with family living quarters above. He got the Soledad Post Office moved into his store and became the first Acton postmaster on January 24, 1888. His next venture was the Acton Hotel, completed in 1890, which hosted such celebrities as the governor of California, attorney Earl Rogers, the King of Spain, and two Presidents—Herbert C. Hoover and Theodore Roosevelt—before it burned down in 1942.

On July 15, 1891, Nickel published the first edition of the valley's first newspaper, *The Acton Rooster*, which crowed about local and international events on the 15th of each month for 22 years.

With $600 in capital, Nickel established the Acton Water Works on November 2, 1891, which was the first such agency in the Santa Clarita.

An ardent supporter of Governor Gage, Nickel was rewarded with an appointment as port warden

of San Francisco Harbor in March of 1900, moving off to Lorin, Alameda County, then to South Berkley. His interests in the local area, including *The Rooster*, were managed by Logan K. Rayburn, who arrived from Ventura to open a general store, run the Southern Pacific and Wells Fargo offices, and become mining recorder for the Cedar Mining District. Nickel gradually relinquished his newspaper, hotel, and water company and passed away in 1928.

The Soledad School was relocated to Acton in 1890. It was a big, brick structure costing the immense sum of $4,000. The district actually dated back to 1869 when a 12-foot by 16-foot adobe accommodated six pupils. A second board-and-batt structure opened in 1878 but was inundated in a flood 10 years later. This newest school, sheltering 45 students, was built on high ground as a precaution.

On Sunday, April 29, 1888, the Reverend F.W. Pattee preached the first sermon heard in the area, using one of the schoolhouse rooms. Nickel rescued the 1878 school from the pond in which it had been mired, moving it next to his hotel. This eventually became the present community church.

LEFT: You can practically hear Teddy Roosevelt shout "Bully!" in this 1903 photo taken at the train station during a stay in Acton. From the collection of Anita Ruby Kellogg. Courtesy, Santa Clarita Valley Historical Society

FACING PAGE, BOTTOM: Lou Henry Hoover is pictured in 1898 at the Puritan gold mine in Acton, where her father was the supervisor. This remarkable woman spoke five languages, went on to become the first female graduate of Stanford University, and later married Herbert Hoover, who became President of the United States in 1929. Lou and her husband frequently visited her parents in Acton. From the collection of Clara Wright. Courtesy, Santa Clarita Valley Historical Society

ABOVE: R.E. Nickel's Acton Hotel, a two-story, wood-frame Victorian structure, hosted several famous people, including Herbert Hoover and Theodore Roosevelt. Courtesy, Santa Clarita Valley Historical Society

RIGHT: In April 1891 this special flag-draped train carrying President Benjamin Harrison on a whistle-stop campaign for reelection pulled into the Saugus Train Station. Courtesy, Security Pacific National Bank Photograph Collection, Los Angeles Public Library

The Saugus-Surrey Saga

On September 1, 1887, a trainload of dignitaries arrived from Santa Barbara to dedicate the new spur line and the Saugus Station. There had been an earlier run on the 20th of August that derailed near Rancho Camulos.

Undeterred by the unfortunate incident 11 days before, David D. Colton, president of Southern Pacific, headed a party that included Governor Bartlett, mayors, and other officials.

The name of the new depot had been chosen by Henry Gregory Newhall for the little town in Massachusetts where his father, Henry Mayo Newhall, was born.

Henry G., then 34 years old, was the president of Newhall Land and Farming Company, which had given the railroad its right-of-way.

The first station master was Alexander Isaac Fraser, a Canadian, who married Margaret Forshner. His daughter, Christine, was born at the station on June 2, 1890. Meanwhile James A. Tolefree started a restaurant in the depot, while running another at Mojave.

On August 5, 1891, the Soledad Thompson's Corner Post Office was moved down to Saugus, but for some reason was called Surrey (a name that was to last for 24 years).

That same year brought President Benjamin Harrison on a whistle-stop campaign for reelection. On April 25, the special flag-draped train ground to a stop to take on water from the tower. President Harrison sported a bandaged hand that he had injured while moving from one car to another. A delegation from Santa Barbara met the President at Saugus, then they streamed down

ABOVE: Dick Wood, Martin Wood (mustache), Mrs. Richard Wood, and Mrs. Martin Wood posed next to their eatery, which occupied the north end of the Saugus Train Station. Originally named Tolefree's Saugus Eating House, the restaurant was bought by the Woods in 1898 and renamed the Saugus Cafe. In 1905 the Woods moved the cafe across the tracks. From the collection of Helen Wood Cone. Courtesy, Santa Clarita Valley Historical Society

LEFT: Students pose on the steps of the Saugus School in 1910. The Saugus School District was organized in 1908, and the first teacher was Margaret O'Connell. Courtesy, Santa Clarita Valley Historical Society

The proprietors and staff of the Surrey Inn pose in the dining room. Ore W. Bercaw opened the Surrey Inn in 1911, fours years before the Surrey Post Office became the Saugus Post Office. From the collection of Margaret Seltzer. Courtesy, Santa Clarita Valley Historical Society

toward Ventura, making brief stops at Fillmore and Santa Paula.

Richard R. and Martin Wood took over the station eatery in 1898, renaming it the Saugus Cafe. Martin also started a blacksmith shop that was later known as Wood's Garage. Richard moved the cafe across the tracks in 1905 to the spot where it still stands.

Ore W. Bercaw became station master in December 1906. A year later he built a general store near the cafe, then moved into the post office.

In rapid succession came the Ice House (1909), the Surrey Inn (1911), a garage, ice cream parlor, and Bercaw's residence. The post office became Saugus on September 4, 1915.

Though some quibbled over the name of the town, all agreed that a school was needed. Charles and Anita Kellogg (she was the daughter of Bill Jenkins, the Baron of Castaic), farmed the tract from present-day Magic Mountain Parkway up to Bouquet Junction and donated the land for a schoolhouse in 1907. The Bercaws, Woods, and Osborns put up $100 each and built a wooden, New England-style structure with belfry on top. Margaret O'Connell came down from San Jose to be the first teacher.

According to Helen Wood Cone, cowboys would come thundering into the little town on the backs of half-wild horses, raising all sorts of Cain. There was a day in 1899 when they shot up the Saugus Station as their way of greeting the northbound train.

Needham of the St. John Tract

From the time that it was founded in 1876, and, indeed, for the next 90 years, the metropolis of the Santa Clarita Valley was the community of Newhall.

By 1887 the town was all of two blocks long, with four saloons, a restaurant, two general stores, warehouses, the Southern Hotel, and railroad station fronting on what is now called Railroad Avenue. Ed Pardee, a muscular, barrel-shaped man, came down from the Pico oil fields to open up a livery stable that year, and the good citizens finally saw the need to build an elementary school.

It was a typical frontier village with dirt streets, boardwalks, and false-front buildings. High-sided freight wagons rumbled along, pulled by teams of 20 mules. Red-and-gold Concord coaches rattled and creaked over to Ventura on twice-weekly runs, jostling a jumble of farm wagons, buckboards, and surreys. At 1:20 in the afternoon residents could expect the great chugging, diamond-stacked engine of the Southern Pacific to pull in amid clouds of steam and sparks.

Bow-legged cowboys with wide chaps, jingling spurs, and Colt .45s stomped into Mike Powell's Palace Saloon for a little socializing, while vaqueros clad in wide sashes and silver-studded pantaloons cooled off at Nick Rivera's place. The Derrick Saloon, presided over by Joe Leighton, hosted oil workers and dusty miners. Dick Lifton served up digestible meals to farmers, beekeepers, and ladies swathed in yards of fabric.

The prosperity came with the railroad, which had also effectively bypassed the old Lyon's Station. Sanford and Cyrus Lyon sold out, and the property went through several owners until December 3, 1887, when it was purchased by a consortium headed by George B. Katzenstein of Sacramento, James Yarnell of Los Angeles, and John St. John, the governor of Kansas.

A two-block-long town that could support four bars must have been thunderstruck to find out that a bunch of wild-eyed prohibitionists had acquired 700 acres and were planning a "Dry Colony" in their midst.

Henry Clay Needham arrived to supervise the establishment of the St. John subdivision. A tall, slender fellow with bushy eyebrows and piercing gray eyes, Needham was a native of Kentucky, born June 8, 1851. He attended Elizabethtown College and then taught school in Missouri and Kansas, where he became active in the Prohibition Party. He and Governor St. John co-authored the famous Kansas Dry Law, which is still on the books. Here too, he met, courted, and wed Lillie Florence Taylor, a union that eventually produced five children.

Ed Pardee, who came from Pennsylvania to Pico Canyon (Mentryville) in 1883, soon moved to Newhall with his wife and baby and opened a livery stable. Courtesy, Santa Clarita Valley Historical Society

FAR LEFT: Pearl Pardee, shown here at age 16, came to Mentryville with her mother in 1884, where they joined Pearl's father Ed. Three years later the Pardees were living in Newhall. The old Pardee Home still stands at Market and Walnut. Courtesy, Santa Clarita Valley Historical Society

RIGHT: Henry Clay Needham, who came from Kansas to California in the late 1880s to establish a non-alcoholic colony in Newhall, stayed on to deal in hardware, lumber, land, mining, and oil. This oratorical spellbinder was to be the Prohibitionist candidate for President from California in 1920, but at the crucial moment was stricken with heat prostration, and the nod went instead to Aaron S. Watkins. Courtesy, Santa Clarita Valley Historical Society

Sales at the St. John tract were not exactly brisk, so Needham opened a lumberyard and hardware store in order to support his growing family. He branched out into oil (the Pearl and Zenith wells did poorly), farming, livestock, and mining. One of his first projects was to build a Good Templars Lodge on Pine Street. It was later sold to Ed Pardee, who moved it to Walnut and Market streets.

To the delight of the town's children, the schoolhouse, which was located way out on Ninth Street, burned down in 1890. A second one was erected, largely through the generosity of Needham, just in time for the fall term. He and M.W. Atwood of Pasadena developed the Happy Valley district, selling 10-acre chunks for $300 apiece. In 1891 he helped found the First Presbyterian Church.

Needham's powerful speaking voice and spellbinding oratory helped carry him in 1920 to the Prohibition National Convention as a candidate for President of the United States. At the crucial moment Needham fell ill with heat prostration, and the nomination went to Aaron S. Watkins.

FACING PAGE, BOTTOM: In 1908 Emil Chaix took over the operation of the appropriately named Derrick Saloon on Main Street. Then, about 1913, when a new highway replaced Main Street, Chaix moved to the southwest corner of 8th and Spruce and opened a grocery store. From the collection of Daryl Haskell. Courtesy, Santa Clarita Valley Historical Society

LEFT: The second Newhall School was built in 1890 at 9th Street and Newhall Avenue shortly after the first schoolhouse burned down. In 1914 this second schoolhouse suffered the same fate as the first. Courtesy, Santa Clarita Valley Historical Society

The Newhall livery stable opened by Ed Pardee in 1887 is pictured here in 1892. We can only guess why most eyes are focused on the man and horse at left. From the collection of Geraldine Pardee Bojarski. Courtesy, Santa Clarita Valley Historical Society

Not long after the turn of the century, Acton's main street became the scene of a duel between N.H. "Rosy" Melrose and William Broome. The duel, which was prompted by Melrose shooting Broome's dog after it attacked Melrose's canine, resulted in Broome's death. After three trials ended in hung juries, charges against Melrose were dismissed. Drawing by Jerry Reynolds

The Crown Valley Feud

A great many of the early settlers of Acton were of German descent from upstate New York. A leading citizen of this frugal, hard-working, well-behaved faction was William Broome. He was a farmer, church deacon, school board member, and unofficial mayor.

During the 1890s newcomers, mostly from the South, began arriving. Their leader turned out to be N.H. Melrose (called "Rosy" by his friends). Melrose was a big, fun-loving Kentuckian, addicted to practical jokes, besides being quick on the draw and deadly accurate. He easily ingratiated himself with county officials and on May 10, 1898, his wife, Flossie A. Melrose, became postmistress.

The trouble seems to have started when William Broome's dog, a snorting, snarling pit bull, attacked Melrose's good-natured Llewellyn, prompting Rosy to shoot the offending animal. Broome had him arrested, but at the trial the schoolteacher, Minnie Boucher, backed up the Kentuckian. Naturally the German element tried to get her fired. As Acton became an armed camp, the schoolmarm was transferred. On a winter day a few years after the turn of the century, Melrose and Broome faced each other on the dusty main street of Acton in the best tradition of the Old West. Guns roared, and William Broome dropped with five well-placed bullets in his body.

The trial was a sensation, with Earl Rogers (the most famous criminal lawyer of the time) as council for the defense, D.A. Fredericks accused of corruption as he was a close friend of Melrose, and then the exhumation of Broome's body with a news photographer on hand. Three trials ended in hung juries, so the D.A. dismissed the charges. Still, there was bad blood, and shots rang out in the night around Crown Valley for years to come.

The Rise and Fall of the Sterling

Perhaps the most famous of the valley's mines had nothing to do with precious metals, such as gold or silver, but, rather with a common commodity most people associate with hand soap. This is the story of borax, technically known as sodium tetraborate decahydrate, the Sterling mine, and a place called Tick Canyon.

Before the Civil War borax was imported for use in glassblowing and refining gold. In 1856 deposits were found north of San Francisco. Then the Borax Company of California was formed, beginning operations eight years later. Borax had become a hot item in industry as a flux in making iron and steel when, in 1881, one Francis M. "Borax" Smith discovered acres of the stuff in Nevada. Between 1883 and 1889, 20 million pounds of borax were hauled to the railhead at Mojave by the renowned 20-mule teams. Smith formed the Pacific Coast Borax Company in 1890, buying up everything in sight. One of his employees was a clerk in the Chicago office by the name of Thomas Thorkildson.

About 1897 Thorkildson decided that he would never get rich working for someone else, so he quit his cushy job and took off for California to prospect for sodium tetraborate decahydrate. He found it near Frazier Park; then, in a twist of fate, he hired his old boss, Steven Mather, to help him run the claim.

During the spring of 1905 two grizzled prospectors—Henry Shepard and Louis Ebbenger—trudged up Tick Canyon looking for gold. Instead they discovered a rich deposit of borax. Hightailing it up to Frazier, the men sold their claim to Thorkildson and Mather for $30,000. The Sterling Borax Works was formed, and the operation began producing by 1908.

A large mill was constructed to the north of what is now Davenport Road, while a narrow-gauge train line took a small "dinky"-type engine six miles down the canyon to Lang Station. There was no way for the locomotive to turn around, so after steaming forward down to the railhead, it would have to chug back up to the mill in reverse. It was built in 1905 by the Vulcan Company for Henry M. Whitney, who sold it to Thorkildson five years later. Ol' "Sterling Number 2" hauled borax for nearly 70 years until it was finally scrapped. Its final resting place is atop the dump at Ryan, Nevada.

The mining camp, located below Davenport, featured a boardinghouse, offices, company store, a dozen residences, corral, and warehouses. It was called Lang and really wasn't much to write home about. A string of board-and-batt houses, all looking the same, faced the railroad tracks, which ran down the "main street."

The Sterling, at best, was never what could be called a big producer, especially when compared to Teel's Marsh in Nevada and the works at Boron, California. At its peak, 18,000 to 20,000 tons of marketable borax came out of the ground in a year's time, resulting in an income of nearly a half-million dollars.

Into the picture came "Borax" Smith with an offer the partners couldn't resist. His new company, Borax Consolidated, bought the Sterling in 1911 for $1.8 million, but it ran it as a separate entity, retaining Thorkildson as president of the division with Mather as vice-president. Smith went bankrupt three years later, and his holding eventually became part of U.S. Borax, the company that still features 20-mule teams on its product.

Meanwhile, the mines of Tick Canyon petered out, so the equipment was transferred to Ryan, Nevada, in 1921. Within four years Lang was a ghost camp, having been destroyed by wind, rain, vandalism, and fire. Steven Mather went on to become the first director of the National Park Service. Thomas Thorkildson, born in Sturgeon Bay, Wisconsin, the son of a Norwegian lumberjack, "lived it up" in Los Angeles as the "Borax King" for a while until his money, like his mine, ran dry. He died in 1950 at the age of 81, confined to a La Crescenta nursing home. The "king" was, in the end, alone and penniless.

At the Sterling Borax Works' reduction plant, mine ore was sorted and screened. About 40 percent of the ore was diverted to the waste dumps, sacking the remainder for shipment to eastern refineries. The sacks were put on the loading platform and onto flatcars. Courtesy, Santa Clarita Valley Historical Society

Mulholland's Magnificent Waterworks

ABOVE: William Mulholland is considered the "Father of the Los Angeles municipal water system" for building the 238-mile-long Los Angeles-Owens River aqueduct. Under Mulholland's leadership, 5,000 men worked for five years on what the Department of Water and Power calls "the most difficult engineering project undertaken by any American city up to that time." Courtesy, Santa Clarita Valley Historical Society

During the summer of 1907 the population of Saugus took a sudden and dramatic upturn as a score of new buildings was thrown up along the north side of what is now called Magic Mountain Parkway. In San Francisquito Canyon, Tunnel Station Camp also seemed to pop up out of the ground.

The reason for all of this frenzied activity was that the flamboyant chief of the City of Los Angeles' Department of Water and Power, William Mulholland, was on the move, building the world's greatest aqueduct system. These were just two of 57 supply centers strung from the city to the Owens Valley. It was a curious mixture of mule teams hauling sections of pipes, steam shovels gouging out hillsides, dynamite, tractors, picks, and shovels.

Faced with increasing water supply problems for a population that exceeded 102,000, the city of Los Angeles had bought the Los Angeles Water Company, created the Los Angeles City Department of Water and Power (DWP), and installed Bill Mulholland as its chief engineer and general manager in 1902.

The Chief, as he was always called, set out to find a reliable supply of water for the town, gauging river flows from Piru to the Kern. Nothing seemed adequate to quench the growing thirst of

the mushrooming metropolis.

At the suggestion of former mayor Fred Eaton, the two men traveled to Owens Lake on a rickety buckboard drawn by a team of mules. Forty days later they were back home, elated by a dream that would soon become a reality.

Quietly the City of Los Angeles bought 307,000 acres of Inyo and Mono counties at very attractive prices, making sure that the deeds included mineral and water rights. In June of 1907 a $23-million bond issue passed, followed by those supply centers reaching from Saugus to Bishop.

Upwards of 4,000 men were employed toiling over rugged mountains, across sterile deserts, or burrowing through hillsides, such as the five-mile-long Elizabeth Lake Tunnel. The Chief, it

LEFT: *Spectators gathered along the sides of the newly completed Owens River aqueduct on November 5, 1913, anxiously awaiting the long-anticipated rush of water. Courtesy, California Historical Society, Ticor Title Insurance*

FACING PAGE, BOTTOM: *During aqueduct construction, mule trains such as this one hauled sections of pipe. Frank Lebrun was the driver. Courtesy, Security Pacific National Bank Photograph Collection, Los Angeles Public Library*

seemed, was everywhere. This barrel-chested apparition with a hard, square jaw and bristling moustache, always chomping on a black cigar and carrying a gold-headed cane, stalked the aqueduct, calling everyone by name.

Mulholland's moment of glory came on November 5, 1913, when he opened a gate valve high on a hillside between Sylmar and Newhall. As a crowd of 40,000 watched, the Owens Valley began to drain into a new man-made lake named for the Chief's assistant—Harvey Van Norman. "There it is," Mulholland called out. "Take it!"

The Owens Valley-Los Angeles Aqueduct was 225 miles long without a pump in the whole system. As an engineering feat, it was exceeded only by the Panama Canal. Power was added to the water on March 19, 1917, when the three turbines in San Francisquito Power House Number One began generating enough electricity to supply the whole city.

Back in 1917, Mulholland had purchased 235 acres in Hauser Canyon northeast of Agua Dulce. He soon developed a so-called model ranch where he raised a variety of grains and cattle. A 60-foot by 110-foot home was built, a barn, and two outbuildings of "native rock and city cement," according to local legend. Guests included General Harrison Gray Otis of *The Los Angeles Times*, Governor Hiram W. Johnson, and Will Rogers. But Bill Mulholland was not destined to lead the quiet, bucolic life.

FACING PAGE, TOP LEFT: George Washington Lechler, who came to California in search of gold in 1849, was a stagecoach driver who eventually settled in Castaic's Hasley Canyon in 1879 to farm and run cattle. From the collection of Abigail Lechler Riley. Courtesy, Santa Clarita Valley Historical Society

Conquering the Hills of Castaic

At the time that Southern Pacific established its depot at Castaic Junction in 1887, the residents north of the Santa Clara River could easily be tallied up on one's fingers and toes. Among them were the Lopez, Cordova, Jenkins, and Bella families.

Foremost among the rugged, independent settlers of the region was George Washington Lechler, who arrived in Los Angeles as a stagecoach driver in 1853. After a time in Bishop, he built a small adobe home deep in Hasley Canyon as headquarters for his ranch in 1879. Lechler was one of those 49ers who found being a reinsman for Butterfield and Wells-Fargo more profitable than digging for gold. He married Abigail J. Hazzard, which started a sort of dynasty that still runs cattle over the crest of the hills between modern Val Verde and Piru Lake. (Abigail's brother, Henry T. Hazzard, was a mayor of Los Angeles and has a street named for him in that city.)

Then there was big, raw-boned William C. Chormicle, described as always being "full of peppery antics. He wore two six-guns and usually carried a rifle in case any argument started at long range."

John Batist Daries settled below the Cordova spread about the time that the Civil War ended, while William Blackburn Rose drifted down from the San Joaquin in 1886 to homestead Charley Canyon. The arroyo was actually named for Charley Moore, a latecomer.

The Tapia family came from Mexico in 1820, landing in Monterey. They later moved to Los Angeles, where Jesus was born during 1861. Twenty-seven years later he settled into the canyon named, of all things, Tapia.

A panorama of Piru City shows a community of a few scattered structures surrounded by and filled with orchards. From the collection of Abigail Lechler Riley. Courtesy, Santa Clarita Valley Historical Society

ABOVE: May McDonald and Ethel Casey wait beside the railroad tracks at the Castaic depot in 1909. Southern Pacific Railroad had established its depot at Castaic Junction in 1887. Courtesy, Santa Clarita Valley Historical Society

LEFT: Abigail J. Hazzard married George Washington Lechler and settled on the Lechler ranch in Castaic. She was the sister of Henry Hazzard, a mayor of Los Angeles. From the collection of Abigail Lechler Riley. Courtesy, Santa Clarita Valley Historical Society

RIGHT: *The Cordova family, probably the oldest of the Castaic families, settled the area in 1835 and always worked as top hands on cattle ranches. The Cordova house is pictured about 1886 as are (back row, left to right) Mrs. Cook, Virginia Cordova, and Mrs. Urtasun, and (front row, left to right) Joe Olme, Dolores Cook, Fred Cook, Theodore Cook, and Simon Cordova. From the collection of A.B. Perkins. Courtesy, Santa Clarita Valley Historical Society*

FACING PAGE: *Lunch pails in hand, these Temescal School students take a break from their lessons. Pictured in 1899 are Hazel Lechler, Digna Garcia, Maudie Lechler, Lena Fustero, Abbie Lechler, and Francis Fustero. If the school was still standing, it would be covered by Piru Lake. From the collection of Abigail Lechler Riley. Courtesy, Santa Clarita Valley Historical Society*

With all of this immigration, a post office was set up at the junction on September 15, 1894, but discontinued the following August. A Castaican going down to Newhall would gather up all of the mail for everyone in the area and simply take it home with him. Somehow or another the ranchers, farmers, and beekeepers knew who had been to town last, dropping by to sort through the pile that was usually heaped up in a barn or some other outbuilding.

The good citizens did get together (in spite of feuds and range wars that were popular at the time) to organize the Castaic School District on March 25, 1889. Another learning establishment known as Live Oaks appeared in Hasley Canyon during 1915 but was united with Castaic in 1929.

Ever since the days of Phineas Banning, General Beale, and the Butterfield Overland stage, vehicles made their way out of Los Angeles, through San Francisquito Canyon, down the Grapevine Pass, and then into Bakersfield. The California Highway Commission was formed in 1911, and one of its first priorities was to build a simpler, more direct road through the La Liebre Mountains. That task fell to the man with the unlikely name of W. Lewis Clark.

Frustrated in several attempts to locate an easy way across the stony barrier, Clark, at last, blazed a trail right over the top from the mouth of Castaic Canyon to Gorman. It was called the Ridge Route.

After a year of toil, during which four-horse Fresno scrapers graded hilltops alongside chugging Caterpillar tractors to the tune of a staggering half-million dollars, the Tejon Route, as it was originally dubbed, opened to the motoring public late in November of 1915. The Auto Club did a little calculating, finding that in the 36 miles between Castaic and Gorman, there were 642 curves that added up to 97 complete circles. It did cut 60 miles off the old road, however.

Even before construction started in 1914, an enterprising businessman by the name of Sam Parsons purchased an acre of land from W.H. Cook fronting the stake line, then threw up a general store that catered to the needs of the workers. Afterwards, "Sam's Place" became a mecca for truckers and the beginning of a new town called Castaic.

5

HARD TIMES AND CELLULOID COWBOYS

Early 1900s-1929

THE THRILL OF IT ALL

William S. Hart stood on a knoll overlooking Newhall, clenching a dark sombrero tightly in his hands. A breeze caressed those familiar craggy features, now deeply etched by time, and ruffled a shock of silvery hair. It was 1939 and this veteran of some 100 Western films was facing the cameras for the last time. In a rich, booming, baritone voice charged with emotion, he said:

My friends, I loved the art of making motion pictures. It is as the breath of life to me. The rush of the wind as it cuts your face. The pounding hooves of the pursuing posse. Out there in front—a fallen tree trunk that spans a yawning chasm, and an old animal under you that takes it in the same low, ground-eating gallop. The harmless shots . . . the cloud of dust . . . Oh, the thrill of it all!

The trail that brought William Surrey Hart to that windswept hilltop in Newhall began in Newburgh, New York, on December 6, 1870. The family moved west, where the youth grew up playing with Sioux Indians, working horses, and herding cattle. "Stage struck" in 1891, he was packed off to England by his father to learn the craft of acting. Hart eventually starred in some Shakespearean plays. Returning to the U.S., he created the role of Messala in *Ben Hur*, was Cash Hawkins in *The Squaw Man*, and became *The Virginian*.

Early in 1914 Bill Hart wandered into a movie house after paying his nickel to view a Western "flick." He came out appalled. "It was awful," he later recalled. "The sheriff was a sort of cross between a Wisconsin woodchopper and a Gloucester fisherman." He quickly got in touch with an old friend in Hollywood by the name of Thomas Ince, offering his services as a consultant. Producer Ince countered the offer by hiring Hart at $25 per week to be a villain in *His Hour of Manhood*. The thespian moved to Hollywood.

Hart was obsessed with the idea of complete authenticity as he remembered it from the northern plains of his boyhood. He seemed to want to document the cowboys, dusty streets, false-front buildings, blue-coated cavalrymen, and Indians in flowing, feathered warbonnets. It would seem that the public agreed, for by 1919 "Two-Gun Bill" was one of the three biggest stars in Hollywood along with Doug Fairbanks and Mary Pickford. He grossed $4 million that year, commanded 60,000 people at a personal appearance, and even his horse, Fritz, had his own fan club, which included a Prince of Morocco.

Certainly one of the finest examples of horsemanship ever put on celluloid occurred in Hart's last film, *Tumbleweeds*. From the dust clouds kicked up by crowds of wagons dashing for free land in Oklahoma emerges the figure of a man on

William S. Hart displays a stern countenance in a Thomas Ince film titled Riddle Gawne. *Courtesy, Santa Clarita Valley Historical Society*

83

RIGHT: *Movie star, writer, and director of feature Westerns, William S. Hart is credited with being the first to emphasize realistic settings and authentic action.* Hell's Hinges, The Gunfighter, Silent Man, Wild Bill Hickok, *and* Tumbleweeds *were some of the films that made him the leading cowboy star of the day. Hart, pictured here in 1914 as his film career was just beginning, retired from films after completing* Tumbleweeds *(1925) and settled into life on his 254-acre Horseshoe Ranch in Newhall in 1928. Hart died on June 23, 1946, leaving his Newhall estate to Los Angeles County. Courtesy, Santa Clarita Valley Historical Society*

FACING PAGE, TOP: *Chief Iron Tail, one of the Sioux Indians used as a model for the U.S. "Buffalo" nickel, resided in Soledad Canyon. Buffalo Bill's Wild West Show featured the chief in its performances. From the collection of Margaret Louder. Courtesy, Santa Clarita Valley Historical Society*

a horse. Across the prairie they gallop, sweeping through the landscape swift as a gale of wind.

Hart got into a hassle with some movie moguls, who succeeded in banning *Tumbleweeds* from major showings. His popularity was being eroded by newcomers such as Tom Mix, so he retired in 1925 to Newhall.

Back in February 1921, Bill Hart had purchased the 254-acre Horseshoe Ranch from Babcock Smith. He used it as an outdoor movie set for the next four years, then began construction of a Spanish-style home high atop "La Loma De Los Vientos," or The Hill of the Winds. He moved in during 1928, surrounding himself with a magnificent collection of Western art and antiques, including 100 Navajo rugs, Sioux beadwork, an array of handguns, and original Russell, Remington, and Flagg paintings. The guest list included Robert Taylor, Barbara Stanwyck, Will Rogers, Charlie Russell, and Maurice Chevalier. He wrote books, penned his autobiography, and filmed that dramatic introduction to the reissue of his classic *Tumbleweeds*.

There were several romances in Hart's life, including a torrid affair with Norma Talmadge, yet he married 17-year-old Winifred Westover in 1921. The stormy relationship lasted just long enough to produce one son, William, Jr. The hostess of the Horseshoe was his sister, Mary Ellen, who died in 1943. William S. Hart died on June 23, 1946, leaving his estate to the County of Los Angeles.

An Age of Progress

The Los Angeles Aqueduct and the Ridge Route were designed to get water and motorists through the Santa Clarita Valley as quickly as possible with no benefit to local residents. However, both did provide a positive stimulation to growth, the likes of which had not been seen since the days of the coming of the railroad.

Mulholland's waterworks employed a number of people up in San Francisquito Canyon who tended the aqueduct and worked in two powerhouses. Bungalows were built in this isolated location, large enough to house whole families, who, naturally, shopped in Saugus or Newhall.

While the Ridge Route did not bring permanent residents, for the most part it did cut down on travel time to the great markets of Los Angeles. One could journey to town and back in a single day—amazing! Then there was the increasing

BELOW: This 1919 view of an unpaved San Fernando Road looking north features the brick Swall Hotel (now Newhall Pharmacy) and Doty's Garage, both opened in 1914. At the time the photo was taken, the speed limit was 15 miles per hour. Courtesy, Santa Clarita Valley Historical Society

RIGHT: Among Saugus' commercial establishments in 1920 were Renfro Drugs, the Saugus Cafe, and Wood's Garage. Others included the Conrad Store and Caswell's. From the collection of Helen Wood Cone. Courtesy, Santa Clarita Valley Historical Society

BELOW: Carl Sischo built Newhall's first "service station" in 1917, but sold it to King Collins about two years later. Courtesy, Santa Clarita Valley Historical Society

BELOW: Frances Delano Phillips, a widow who operated a rooming-house cafe as well as serving on the school board and PTA, was the first person in the Santa Clarita Valley to own an automobile. Phillips purchased her Cadillac in 1908 and is shown driving in Placerita Canyon the following year. Courtesy, Santa Clarita Valley Historical Society

horde of gentlemen clad in long, linen dusters with goggles over their eyes, piloting their chugging, spitting vehicles with names such as Marmon "41", Winton "Six," or Packard ("Ask the man who owns one"). They, their womenfolk, and children might get hungry along the way or need gasoline or automobile repairs. So began a series of what might be called "tourist traps."

Jesse Doty opened the Ford Garage facing San Fernando Road in Newhall in 1914. Doty, way ahead of his time, employed two attractive young ladies by the names of Margie Smith and Nell Bailey to act as "service station attendants." From a 100-gallon barrel in the back room, the women would draw gasoline in buckets to be funneled into waiting car tanks for 10 cents a gallon! (The price was outrageous, but what could one do; this was an isolated location.) Two years later Carl Sischo acquired the corner of 8th and San Fernando and opened the first real gas station in the valley.

Albert C. Swall, who arrived in Newhall from Tracy during 1890 at the age of 19, leased the

ABOVE: *By about 1925 automobiles had become commonplace in the valley, and a railroad crossing sign in Saugus warned motorists to "Look out for the cars." From the collection of Mary Wright. Courtesy, Santa Clarita Valley Historical Society*

meat department from James A. Gulley's general store. Incensed when the rent was raised, Swall moved over to present San Fernando Road. Soon other businesses followed, leaving Railroad Avenue nearly deserted. In 1914 he built the two-story brick Swall Hotel (now Newhall Pharmacy) complete with electric lights (to the general wonder of the local populace).

Swall also invested in Saugus, opening a general store about 1911. Martin Wood expanded his Saugus Cafe in 1916, while brother Richard switched from operating a blacksmith shop to running an auto repair shop known as Wood's Garage.

Next stop up the Ridge Route would have been Castaic, where Sam Parson managed to get a post office established in his general store on April 3, 1917. Two years later he sold out to Anthony H. Schuyler, who added a gas station to the shop. At the same time Burt Reynolds opened up the Evergreen Motel and campground next door.

On the way up there was the Ridge Road Garage, The Tumble Inn, Reservoir Summit, and that splendid establishment in the wilderness known as Sandberg. Local rancher Herman Sandberg provided excellent, guaranteed-fresh steaks at his hotel. Slot machines could also be found there and, in a long, low building out back (known as "The Crib"), feminine companionship was available for weary truckers and lonely salesmen.

As far as is known, the very first locally owned horseless carriage was purchased in 1908, not by some adventurous man, but, rather, by a charming, hard-working widow by the name of Frances Delano Phillips. After her husband Harry died, Frances opened a rooming house-cafe and served on the school board and PTA. When she bought her car, it was a Cadillac.

In 1920 Newhall's showpiece, the A.C. Swall Block, consisted of the Swall Hotel, the Meat Market, the Newhall Post Office, and the Newhall Pharmacy, which was the only drugstore between San Fernando and Palmdale. The men pictured are, left to right, August Ferrier, Ed Abbott, Philip Rivera, Robert Ball, and Albert Swall. Unfortunately, this two-story brick block, which stood on Market and Spruce (now San Fernando Road) since 1914, was destroyed in the 1971 earthquake. From the collection of A.B. Perkins. Courtesy, Santa Clarita Valley Historical Society

LEFT: In 1928 five young women went on a novel Fourth of July outing in Pico Canyon. Three of the revelers have been identified as LaVon Harker Zell (with the shotgun), Celina Chaix (behind LaVon), and Naomi Lamkin (behind the driver). Courtesy, Santa Clarita Valley Historical Society

FACING PAGE, BOTTOM: Albert Swall (left) poses with his father and brothers in 1899, a few years before becoming an early Santa Clarita Valley businessman. By about 1922 Albert Swall owned 90 percent of the valley's commercial buildings. From the collection of A.B. Perkins. Courtesy, Santa Clarita Valley Historical Society

FACING PAGE, TOP LEFT: Only one section of the St. Francis Dam remained standing after the collapse. Courtesy, Santa Clarita Valley Historical Society

BELOW: Construction of the concrete St. Francis Dam in San Francisquito Canyon lasted from August 1924 until its completion in May 1926. The dam stood nearly 200 feet high and each step measured five feet. Courtesy, Santa Clarita Valley Historical Society

Requiem for St. Francis

By 1924 the gentle farmers and ranchers of the Owens Valley were furious with the City of Los Angeles Department of Water and Power, and especially with its general manager, William Mulholland. The great aqueduct, which brought life, prosperity, and growth to the Los Angeles basin, meant only destruction to the residents of Lone Pine and Bishop. They watched water tables drop; Owens Lake was transformed into a wasteland; and crops withered under a merciless sun. They watched only for a while. Then they acted.

Masked men seized DWP employees, escorting them out of the valley. There were shots in the night and, in time, wholesale dynamiting of the water-delivery system. Mulholland armed his men, and a regular war in the best tradition of the Wild West broke out. The Chief decided that it would be wise to build a dam near his city, just in case there was an interruption of service.

So, it came to pass that the mighty forces of the DWP again descended upon the peaceful Santa Clarita Valley in order to create a reservoir in San Francisquito Canyon to be called the St. Francis. Begun in August 1924, the concrete dam rose to a height of 185 feet with a series of step-like offsets running up the front of it. Owens Valley water arrived on March 1, 1926, and two months later the dam was completed. The reservoir gradually covered 300 acres with 38,168 acre feet of water.

Almost immediately there was apprehension over leakage from the dam. A wing dike was built over the schist formation forming the west abutment. Finally, on March 12, 1928, Tony Harnischfeger, the dam keeper, became so alarmed that he put in an emergency call to his superiors in Los Angeles. William Mulholland and Harvey Van Norman arrived at the site around 10:30 in the morning, inspected the dam, then went home, saying that everything was in order (even though the downstream side was soaking wet).

That night, at precisely 11:57, half of the St. Francis Dam suddenly collapsed, hurling a wall of water down the canyon at 18 miles per hour. The massive concrete-and-steel Powerhouse No. 2 was swept away without a trace.

The ground shook with the force of an earthquake, while the moonlit night was filled with a roaring sound variously described as a rumbling freight train or onrushing tornado.

Striking the Santa Clara riverbed, this glistening monstrosity veered westward, lumbering across the plain like some prehistoric beast, demolishing and carrying away everything in its path. At Kemp, a railroad siding just beyond Castaic Junction, 150 Edison Company employees were sleeping in tents. Security officer Ed Lock looked up from his round to see flashes of light rising into the eastern sky. He had no way of knowing that these were transmission lines being downed by the flood. Then came a great roar and, before he knew it, the terrified man was staring at an avalanche of water towering 130 feet into the sky. Racing madly to awaken the construction camp, he was overtaken and drowned along with 84 of his fellow employees.

On the relentless tide went, downstream, inflicting death and destruction clear to Ventura, where, at 5:25 a.m., a mound of mud and debris

finally oozed into the sea. Behind it was a 54-mile-long swath of uprooted trees, damaged or destroyed homes, and at least 425 dead people. It was the second-greatest disaster in the state's history. The St. Francis Dam also brought down the mighty Mulholland, who retired to become a consultant on the Colorado River project.

Among the many stories of pathos and heroics that night, one is especially poignant. A morgue was set up in Newhall into which wandered that great Western star, William S. Hart. Overcome with grief at the sight of a small boy lying cold and stiff on a slab, Hart dressed him in a little cowboy suit with his own trembling hands, then paid the child's burial expenses.

ABOVE: The raging floodwaters traveled 54 miles to Ventura, uprooting trees, destroying houses and automobiles, and killing more than 425 people on the way. Here, locals named Carter, Mullen, Hyans, and Stonenburg examine a demolished auto. From the collection of Mildred Story O'Neill. Courtesy, Santa Clarita Valley Historical Society

LEFT: The desolate aftermath of the St. Francis dam disaster was looked upon with awe and disbelief by these survivors. Courtesy, Ventura County Library

Tales of the Twenties

As one age was beginning, along the banks of Piru Creek another came to an end. After three generations in the Santa Clarita Valley, the Del Valle family bid farewell to their beloved Camulos. The last great barbecue was held on August 10, 1924. It was attended by Adolfo Camerillo, representing the old dons, author Charles F. Lummis, artist Charles M. Russell, and William S. Hart, to name a few. The last of the "Lords" of the Santa Clara, Reginaldo Del Valle, was finally forced to sell his shrunken domain. As Lummis wrote, "this is the last stand of the patriarchal life of Spanish California, which has been so beautiful to the world for more than a century."

At the same time another somewhat diminished Mexican holding was placed on the market—the Villa Rancho at the junction of San Martin and Hasley canyons. Back in 1843 Francisco Lopez, the man who found gold in Placerita Canyon and was granted Rancho Temescal, plucked some nuggets from Santa Feliciana Creek, starting California's second gold rush to riches. José Espinoza carted off a nine-pound lump of gold in 1856, which was sold for $1,900, or about $16 per ounce. A boom town called Val Verde (Green Valley) came and went on the site of a 30-acre tract Eureka Villa Alline (the last heir) sold in 1925 to Sydney P. Dones. Perhaps as a take-off on the grand lady's name, Dones subdivided Eureka Villa and employed Arthur Provost as district manager to sell half-acre sites. By 1928 it was called Val Verde again, and it was a totally black community.

Certainly the largest hunk of real estate in the Santa Clarita Valley belongs to the federal government—the Angeles National Forest. It covers about one quarter of Los Angeles County or some 691,000 acres. Originally this was a part of the old Santa Barbara National Forest, created in 1900 and encompassing the Coast Range of mountains from Wrightwood to Big Sur. In September of 1925 it was divided into the Angeles and Los Padres, at which time the Saugus Ranger District was set up in Newhall, with N.E. Peterson appointed as district ranger.

The Great Saugus Train Robbery

A tall, slender Venturan by the name of Jenks Harris thought himself a worthy successor of Jesse James or, perhaps, Tiburcio Vásquez. Putting together a six-man gang, he swept down on the Fillmore State Bank in Piru, carting off $11,000 in currency. The loot was loaded into saddlebags, and the desperadoes headed into the wilds of Castaic Canyon on horseback.

This event did not occur in the 1870s or 1880s, but, rather, on December 17, 1925. Hot on their trail was intrepid Constable Jack Pilcher of Newhall, who cornered the gang in the Cienega region. A lengthy shootout followed in which sheriff's deputies reinforced the local constabulary, but the outlaws slipped away with the coming of night.

The following day, Harris was arrested while making some purchases at the general store of Anthony H. Schuyler in Castaic, while the rest of the boys were rounded up within a week.

The most spectacular local robbery occurred during the early evening of November 10, 1929. After pulling into the Saugus Station for water, a massive three-barreled steam locomotive of the 5000 series left at 7:40 p.m., rounding the bend at Bouquet Junction, then starting to gather speed as she headed out Soledad Canyon. Suddenly Engine No. 59 began to lurch violently back and forth. Then, after chewing up 600 yards of track, it crashed over on its side as a torrent of flaming red sparks flew from spinning drivers. The engineer barely escaped being scalded to death as his steamer slid to a halt behind the Saugus Speedway.

Somehow the passenger cars remained upright, although there was total panic aboard. Into this bedlam, from out of the clear night, stepped a 5-foot-6-inch man with an air of authority. Quickly he calmed the hysterical women and nervous men, got them back on the Pullmans, and, as soon as everyone settled down, robbed them of all their valuables at the point of a .38 caliber revolver. He then vanished into the inky darkness.

Next on the scene was Deputy Sheriff Jack Pember, who identified the gunman as Thomas E. Vernon, an itinerant cowboy who liked to call

FACING PAGE: These black World War I veterans, named Banks and Hammond, were residents of Val Verde when this photo was taken in the late 1920s. Originally called Eureka Villa, Val Verde was a completely black Santa Clarita Valley community developed on land owned by Sydney P. Dones. Courtesy, Santa Clarita Valley Historical Society

BELOW: On November 11, 1929, the day after the "Great Saugus Train Robbery," Southern Pacific officials and police examined the wreckage. Courtesy, Santa Clarita Valley Historical Society

ABOVE: Prohibition enforcement officers show off confiscated bootleg-alcohol storage barrels after a raid in Soledad Township. Jack Pilcher is leaning against the "Storage 45" barrel. Courtesy, Santa Clarita Valley Historical Society

RIGHT: Tom Averill, alias Tom Vernon, began calling himself "Buffalo" Tom in honor of William F. "Buffalo Bill" Cody. After serving time for committing several criminal acts, Vernon found work on a Saugus ranch. Then, after being disappointed in his efforts to secure a job with Southern Pacific, he decided to derail S.P. engine 59 and rob the passengers. Vernon was captured after another train derailment and robbery and sentenced to life in prison at Folsom. He was paroled 35 years later in 1964. Courtesy, Santa Clarita Valley Historical Society

himself "Buffalo" Tom. Pember found that Vernon had broken into the Saugus Yard tool shed, lifting a wrench and spike puller. He then yanked the bolts that held the rails together, settling down in the bushes to see what would develop.

After the robbery, which only netted $300, "Buffalo" Tom walked over the low ridge to Wood's Garage, where he hitched a ride down to L.A. with one Thomas Firth of Burbank. Vernon claimed that his nonexistent daughter was injured in a train wreck and paid Firth five dollars for a lift to the Children's Hospital.

Two weeks later he derailed another train near Cheyenne, Wyoming, and was plotting a third when he was captured at Pawnee, Oklahoma. On December 18, 1929, "Buffalo" Tom Vernon was sentenced to life in Folsom Prison. He was released 35 years later—a small, nervous, aged, gray-haired man—who died shortly therafter of "a social disease."

In the days of Prohibition, the sheriff's department had what was called a "Dry Squad," headed up by an officer with the familiar name of James Bond. He and Constable Jack Pilcher made quite a team, breaking up stills from one end of the valley to the other. The most elusive was a cooker mounted on the back of a flatbed truck in San Francisquito Canyon. When the lawmen came roaring up, the moonshiners simply drove all of the evidence up to Lake Elizabeth.

Riders of the Silver Screen

In December of 1913 Jesse L. Lasky and Cecil B. de Mille released a motion picture called *The Squaw Man* based on a stage play that had starred William S. Hart. *The Squaw Man* was unique for several reasons. It was a Western; it was the first American-made feature-length movie at five reels long; and it was not shot in New Jersey or New York, but, rather, in a barn set in a wilderness called Hollywood.

Within a very few years Hollywood became the motion picture capital of the world, while the Santa Clarita Valley, with its rugged scenery and old-fashioned towns, functioned as its "back lot." The area was especially suited as a backdrop to sweeping outdoor melodramas.

William S. Hart was using the streets of Newhall and Walker Ranch in Placerita Canyon as early as 1914 for location shots. Three years later Universal Studios hired John Ford to direct a series of films. His first effort was *Straight Shooting,* using Beale's Cut and other local landmarks as "sets," and starring two men who would loom large in the industry and settle down near Saugus—Harry Carey and Hoot Gibson.

Carey owned a ranch, trading post, and part-time movie set which, for a time, had its own post office in San Francisquito Canyon. His wife, the former Olive Golden, made her last film appearance in *The Searchers*, in which John Wayne, at the end of the story, stood framed in a doorway with his right arm lying across his chest to grasp the left one. The pose threw Olive Golden Carey into tears. It was the typical stance of Harry Carey and Wayne's tribute to the late star.

The Carey Ranch was destroyed during the St. Francis flood of 1928.

Roy Baker purchased a 40-acre tract east of Bouquet Junction during 1923, starting construction on a rodeo arena a year later. Hoot Gibson bought the ranch and stadium in 1930, putting on shows that attracted such stars as Tom Mix, John Wayne, and Clark Gable. In 1934 Gibson sold out to Paul Hill, who ran the Western Livestock yards and leased it to film companies for three years until a huge flood filled the home and arena with mud and debris. He was unable to make payments, and the bank repossessed the property, which was eventually taken over by a professor of economics at Occidental College, William Bonnelli. Today it is known as the Saugus Speedway.

When William S. Hart retired in 1925, his position as "King of the Cowboys" was quickly taken over by the son of a Pennsylvania coal miner by the name of Tom Mix. At an early age, he drifted West to be a cowboy, served in the Spanish-American War, then became a rodeo rider with Miller Brothers' 101 Ranch Show. He purchased his own ranch, which he called the 101, serving as consultant to a film called *Ranch Life in the Great South West* in 1911. This started his career in the most consistently satisfying and commercially successful series of small Westerns in the history of movies.

Dashing Errol Flynn as Robin Hood draws back his bow and takes aim in The Adventures of Robin Hood. *Various scenes in the picture were filmed in Placerita Canyon. From the collection of Betty H. Pember. Courtesy, Santa Clarita Valley Historical Society*

ABOVE: Newhall's Presbyterian Church doubled as a movie set. Courtesy, Security Pacific National Bank Photograph Collection, Los Angeles Public Library

RIGHT: The beautiful Olive Golden Carey, an actress and the wife of Harry Carey, made her last film appearance in The Searchers, starring John Wayne. From the collection of Anita Ruby Kellogg. Courtesy, Santa Clarita Valley Historical Society

Several outdoor sets called Mixville, consisting of false-front buildings and boardwalks, were established around Southern California. One of them ran along Newhall Avenue at Market Street, and Tom used the Pardee House (recently the telephone company office) as a dressing room and sort of retreat. There are, of course, persistent rumors of liaisons with young ladies of easy virtue and tales of him racing down San Fernando Road in sports cars of incredible speed. Mix, by the way, had five wives. He died in an auto accident in Arizona.

In the 1923 film, *Three Jumps Ahead* Tom Mix and his "Wonder Horse," Tony, appear to make a death-defying leap across Beale's Cut. One thing is sure, Tom and Tony did not do it. According to local rancher Andy Jauregui, who was a friend of Mix's, the whole scene was dubbed in. Yet stuntman Richard Talmadge claimed to his dying day (1982) that he made the jump atop a horse named Ranger.

The most famous studio in the Santa Clarita Valley was the great Monogram Western Town that came to be known as Gene Autry's Melody Ranch.

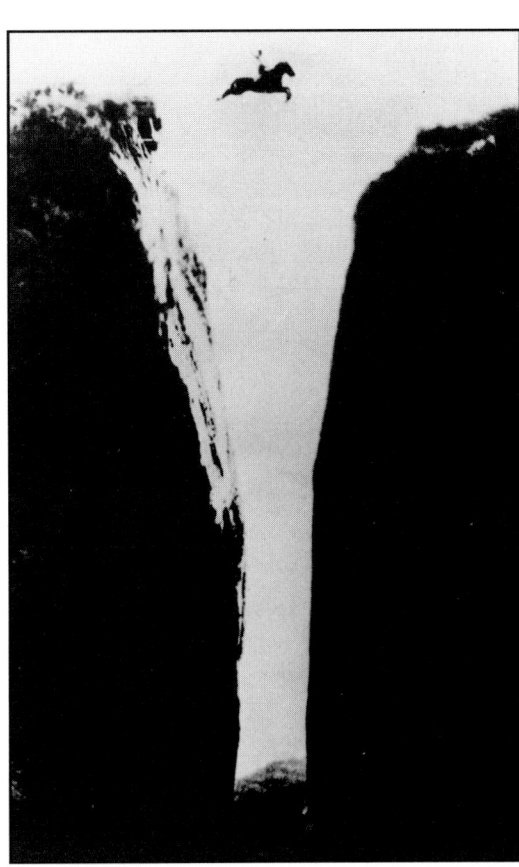

LEFT: Though Tom Mix and "Tony the Wonder Horse" appeared to make this death-defying leap across Beale's Cut in the 1923 film Three Jumps Ahead, *stuntman Richard Talmadge swore that he and his horse, Ranger, made the spectacular jump. Others claim it was dubbed in. Courtesy, Santa Clarita Valley Historical Society*

FAR LEFT: The popularity of cowboy star William S. Hart was eclipsed by that of Tom Mix during the early 1920s. Mix, shown here with guns drawn, was already a veteran performer in Wild West shows when he began starring in moving pictures. While filming in Newhall, Mix used the Pardee House as a dressing room/retreat. Unlike Hart, who insisted that his films reflect reality, Mix portrayed a virtuous, clean-living cowboy who triumphed over evil outlaws. By the time he retired from films in 1928, Mix had starred in about 100 feature Westerns. From the Windsor Archives

LEFT: The Harry Carey Ranch Store Trading Post was used as a part-time movie set before being destroyed by the St. Francis Dam disaster. From the collection of Anita Ruby Kellogg. Courtesy, Santa Clarita Valley Historical Society

A Melody of Slippery Gulch

The movies' first singing cowboy was not Gene Autry, Roy Rogers, or Tex Ritter, but, rather, the "Duke" himself, John Wayne. Although he only mouthed the words while Smith Ballew did the actual warbling, Wayne played Singin' Sandy in the early 1930s, a man who vocalized such memorable tunes as "Blood on the Saddle," just before he blew away the villain.

These and other epics, including a series called "The Three Mesquiteers," were shot in Soledad and Placerita canyons. Most of the Western classic *Stagecoach* was filmed in Monument Valley during 1939. However, there is one sequence where the great rocking Concord lurches through Beale's Cut on its way to a place called Lordsberg. As for Lordsberg, that was actually the old Monogram movie ranch located in Placerita Canyon.

The story began in 1922 when Ernie Hickson came to California, going to work as assistant technical director for Trem Carr of Monogram Pictures. Both men had a fascination for things Western, so it was only natural that they felt at home with the biggest producer of B Westerns in Hollywood. Carr owned the Rancho Placeritos near the Oak of the Golden Dream, and Hickson needed a place to put his ever-growing collection of nineteenth-century Americana, which included just about everything he could get his hands on, from spurs to whole buildings. So it came to pass in 1930 that an authentic Western town was born deep in Placerita Canyon, most of the structures imported from Nevada.

Although kept busy by many motion picture companies (especially Monogram and Republic), Trem Carr was forced to sell the Placeritos, and Hickson moved the whole town to the intersection of Placerita and Oak Creek. Placeritos, by the

RIGHT: In the early 1930s John Wayne played a character named Singin' Sandy in a series of "B" Westerns shot in Soledad and Placerita canyons, thus making him the first singing cowboy in films (even though he only mouthed the words to someone else's singing). Courtesy, Santa Clarita Valley Historical Society

Hidden away amid the foliage of Placerita Canyon is Golden Oak Ranch, a Western movie set owned by Disney Studios. Courtesy, Santa Clarita Valley Historical Society

way, was purchased by Disney Studios in 1959, where another Western town was built and is now known as Golden Oak Ranch.

During the 1930s and 1940s just about every celluloid cowboy one could name rode down the dusty streets of Ernie Hickson's "town." Here could be found the black-clad, silver-haired William Boyd, alias Hopalong Cassidy. Tall, slim Gary Cooper clumped down the boardwalk with silver spurs jingling at each step. Buck Jones, Ken Maynard, and Bob Steele shot it out with the bad guys on Main Street. The Latin figure of the Cisco Kid was represented in silver-trimmed bolero jacket by Gilbert Roland, Caesar Romero, and, later, Duncan Renaldo. Even Ronald Reagan was nearly lynched in a flick called *The Santa Fe Trail*.

Here were born the television Westerns "Sugarfoot," "The Life and Legend of Wyatt Earp," and the famous opening showdown for the long-running "Gunsmoke" series.

ABOVE AND LEFT: Among the celluloid cowboys to ride into Ernie Hickson's Western "town" at the intersection of Placerita Canyon and Oak Creek roads were William Boyd (above), better known as Hopalong Cassidy and Buck Jones (left). Photo of William Boyd from the collection of Mike Brown. Courtesy, Santa Clarita Valley Historical Society. Photo of Buck Jones from the Windsor Archives

FACING PAGE, TOP LEFT AND BELOW RIGHT: Singing cowboy Gene Autry bought Ernie Hickson's Western "town" in 1952 and renamed it Melody Ranch. Autry used the ranch as the setting for his weekly television shows. Main Street, complete with hotel, cafe, schoolhouse, and other nineteenth-century Western buildings is shown here. Photo of Gene Autry from the Windsor Archives. Photo of Melody Ranch Courtesy, Santa Clarita Valley Historical Society

FACING PAGE, TOP RIGHT: On August 28, 1962, a brush fire swept through Placerita Canyon, reducing Melody Ranch to ashes. Signal *editor Fred Trueblood, Jr., called the event "one grand, heartbreaking show by a fine old trouper," and when the fire was out he wrote: "as the last glowing embers died away, the curtain fell on its final act." Courtesy, Santa Clarita Valley Historical Society*

RIGHT: Duncan Renaldo starred in the television series "The Cisco Kid," which was filmed in Placerita Canyon. From the Windsor Archives

But there was another side to the renowned movie ranch. It was the scene for the annual roundup of the Los Angeles Westerners Corral, and from 1949 through 1951 it hosted Newhall's Old West Fourth of July Celebration. During those long weekends it was called "Slippery Gulch," and just about everything that goes, went. There was even a battery of slot machines for the enjoyment of the locals.

On January 22, 1952, Ernest Hickson died, and shortly thereafter the property was sold to Gene Autry. Renamed Melody Ranch, the ancient buildings and re-created Spanish mission and pueblo became the setting for Autry's weekly television shows until August 28, 1962. Then a raging brush fire roared down from the hills, engulfing the ranch and reducing those historic buildings to a pile of ashes.

Signal editor Fred Trueblood, Jr., wrote the epitaph. "The great illusion went up in a roaring inferno of fire and smoke, as did many of the frontier towns it modeled. It was one grand, heartbreaking show by a fine old trouper, and as the last glowing embers

died away, the curtain fell on its final act."

Over several years Autry and his second wife, Jackie, sold off parts of the 110-acre ranch and relocated many of the artifacts stored there to his Western Heritage Museum, which opened in Griffith Park in November of 1988. Finally the last 10 acres, the real heart and soul of Melody Ranch, which contained the few remaining structures, was placed on the market on November 16, 1990. It was quickly purchased by the Paul Veluzat family, operators of a film production business with movie locations in Newhall and Bouquet Canyon. By early 1991 restoration and construction of new sets were already underway as new film contracts were being signed. The historic Placeritos-Monogram-Melody Ranch rose from its ashes like the phoenix of legend.

6

NEW BEGINNINGS AND GROWING PAINS

1930s-Present

TROUBLED TIMES

During the 1930s another Santa Clarita Valley gold rush occurred. It kept local farmers supplying food and merchants dusting off rusty pans. Men flocked in from all over Southern California, turning over the spent gravel of the ancient placer diggings. The work was back-breaking, but results were fantastic. Anywhere from one to six dollars a day could be gleaned from Placerita, Piru, and Soledad canyons.

In 1933 Highway 99 was carved up the canyons, bypassing the 18-year-old Ridge Route, which was already antiquated. Tip's restaurant, established at Castaic Junction, provided a little sustenance and liquid refreshment to weary motorists.

Under the administration of Franklin D. Roosevelt, the Civilian Conservation Corps (CCC) came into being, employing young men between the ages of 18 to 25 in a variety of public works programs. Camps were established near Oak Flat, in Elizabeth Canyon, Bouquet, and Soledad. For $30 a month they built highways, fought fires, and, in 1936, erected the Spanish Revival-style Saugus Elementary School.

Two years later the Newhall Tunnel was cut away and replaced by a spacious asphalt thoroughfare known initially as Highway 6, then 14, and finally Sierra Highway.

All of this progress and domestic tranquility was shattered on a crystal-clear Sunday afternoon. Most residents were just sitting down to the traditional afternoon dinner when voices crackled over the Atwater-Kent or Console Zenith. It was unbelievable—the Japanese were bombing a place called Pearl Harbor:

Yesterday, December 7, 1941—a day that will live in infamy—the forces of the Japanese Empire suddenly and deliberately attacked our principal naval base on the island of Oahu in the Hawaiian chain.

Monday morning, at the request of President Franklin D. Roosevelt, the Congress of the United States declared war on Japan.

Suddenly searchlights pierced the night sky from surrounding mountain tops. The National Guard camped at Newhall School, while 18 air raid zone wardens met to draw up plans for evacuation and civil defense. As Christmas approached, parties were given for servicemen by William S. Hart at the French Village (a restaurant and motel), Ernest Hickson at the Monogram Ranch, and Harry Carey, who gave a carton of cigarettes to everyone whether they smoked or not.

The first local casualty was Sergeant Vern Ferguson of Castaic, who was killed in the Philippines on Christmas Eve. Roland Reidel and Olin Skirvin were captured on Wake Island. During March of 1942 a column of 148 cars and buses

On July 4, 1936, many of Newhall's old-timers gathered for a homecoming celebration. From the collection of Betty H. Pember. Courtesy, Santa Clarita Valley Historical Society

Location shooting for Universal Picture's Seven Sinners, *starring Marlene Dietrich, took place at the Saugus Air Field in 1938. The film was released in 1940. Courtesy, Santa Clarita Valley Historical Society*

Tip's restaurant at Castaic Junction was billed as "One of the finest restaurants in California" on this postcard dating from the 1940s. At the time, Tips touted its "thick steaks" and "thin pancakes." From the Windsor Archives

chugged up Mint Canyon under close military guard. These were the first Japanese-Americans on their way to Manzanar and internment "for the duration."

The old Halifax Powder Company was purchased by Bermite, which moved in with a large government munitions contract, employing 300 persons by July 16, 1943. Most of them came from elsewhere and were housed in cottages that rented for $36 per month with an option to buy.

Amid paper and soap drives, rationing of gas and food, residents learned that a fighting ship was to be named for their leading community. It was not a great battlewagon, but, rather, a 16,500-ton oil tanker. Nearly 70 years before, Sarah B. Gifford had come to live in a boxcar as the wife of the first railroad agent in Newhall. Now, at 4 p.m., December 6, 1944, she christened the USS *Newhall Hills* in the Sausalito yards of Marinship Corporation. Unfortunately, it was sunk by a torpedo powered by compressed air, virtually undetectable by radar, in Micronesia.

On April 5, 1945, a deeply troubled William S. Hart picked up the telephone and dialed the two-digit number of *The Signal*. Editor Trueblood answered. "Fred," the Western star said, "I have a premonition, a hunch—call it what you will—I can't explain it. Something is going to happen to Mr. Roosevelt."

Exactly one week later the President of the United States was dead.

Flags were lowered to half staff; businesses were closed; and people wept openly as if they had lost a dear friend or relative. The man who led the nation longer than anyone else was gone. Harry S Truman had a gigantic pair of shoes to fill.

In May Germany surrendered, but the war was not over. A silvery spheroid silently wafted over the mountains, dropping down into the Santa Clara riverbed near Saugus. Army experts found it to be a Japanese fire-bomb balloon, released in the Land of the Rising Sun to wander across the Pacific in order to burn down the forests of California and Oregon.

A more insidious device was dropped on Hiroshima and Nagasaki, vaporizing both Japanese towns and 120,000 citizens. On August 14, 1945, World War II ended, and the ecstatic citizens of Newhall went wild.

A sheriff's patrol car cruised down Spruce Street (now San Fernando Road) with red light flashing and siren screaming. It was followed by a parade of cars sounding horns, people dancing in the streets, and shredded paper blowing with each gust of wind. Soon the boys would be marching home to a hero's welcome. Discharged soldiers and sailors arrived just in time to find employment in a reborn oil industry.

THE BATTLE OF MAD MOUNTAIN

Mentryville, in Pico Canyon, was practically a ghost town. However, a number of petroleum prospectors had been rooting around the hills for years. One of them, Gene Sherman, was a brilliant, if controversial, geologist who convinced the Wilmington firm of O'Kane and Brain to drill Barnsdale No. 1 near Castaic. At a depth of 1,780 feet, on August 23, 1945, they did hit a meager supply of oil, about two barrels an hour. Abandoned, it is best recalled as the discovery well of the rather extensive Castaic Field.

On the Jenkins Ranch, then owned by Anita Ruby Jenkins Kellogg, two wells came in on the same day—Wednesday, March 1, 1952—a million-to-one shot that made national headlines.

Homer and Russell Havenstrite struck black gold near Beale's Cut in 1949, selling out to Royal Dutch. The usually staid citizens of Newhall suddenly began drilling into their own backyards— with no results.

Into this scene of frantic activity strode a short, heavyset man by the name of Milford Yant. He was no stranger to these parts, having sold postage stamp-sized oil leases in Placerita Canyon during the late 1930s. Somehow he had run afoul of the law and skipped off to Nevada only a step or two ahead of the sheriff.

Yant boldly bored a hole in the ground near Placerita and Sierra Highway on one of his old leases. And, though unbelievable, he struck oil.

Since the original grants had, by this time, been lost or destroyed, it became a no-mans land and scene of what was to become known as "The Battle of Mad Mountain."

Anyone who could beg, borrow, or steal a drill rig moved in and homesteaded the Yant territory. Wildcatters deliberately burrowed into other claims, squirting drilling mud into protestors' faces. There were shootings and battles between lumbering bulldozers slamming into each other. Local officials tried to sort out overlapping and conflicting claims. However, order was not restored until large companies moved in, buying out independents. To this day the place is referred to as "Confusion Hill."

A scene titled "Roundup on the Andy Jueregie Ranch" appeared in David O. Selznick's 1946 Duel in the Sun. *The film, which starred Gregory Peck, Jennifer Jones, Lionel Barrymore, Joseph Cotten, and Harry Carey, was partially shot on the Newhall Ranch. From the collection of Camille Jueregie. Courtesy, Santa Clarita Valley Historical Society*

ABOVE: *Before the Lebrun Ranch in San Francisquito Canyon was sold to the City of Los Angeles in 1922, it was the site of a gold-mining operation. Courtesy, Santa Clarita Valley Historical Society*

BELOW RIGHT AND FACING PAGE, BELOW LEFT: *Sisters Lillie Belle (right) and Opal Mayhue (facing page) were the daughters of William and Pallie Mayhue. From the collection of Betty H. Pember. Courtesy, Santa Clarita Valley Historical Society*

Farewell to the Simple Life

After World War II ended, urban sprawl hit Southern California. The San Fernando Valley was rapidly subdivided and paved over as new towns seemed to pop up out of bean fields and citrus groves. While there was some growth in the Santa Clarita Valley (the population nearly doubled from 4,000 in 1940 to 7,500 by the end of the decade), this was still the bastion of small farmers, cattlemen, and shopkeepers.

Hard-rock miners could be found leaning against the long bar of the 49er Saloon in Acton; oil men and beekeepers came to town at Newhall; while cowboys clumped into the Saugus Cafe wearing six-shooters strapped to their hips. Soon this would all be swept away in a frenzy of progress.

Since it is not possible to chronicle all of the pioneering families of the Santa Clarita Valley, three will have to serve as representative of a vanished way of life.

George Blum was a Swiss stonecutter who migrated to America, winding up in Chicago, where he met and married Magdalena, who hailed from a small village in Switzerland called Beggingen. As a honeymoon trip, they came to California, loved it, and settled in Los Angeles. In 1891 the Blums acquired a ranch in Aliso Canyon in Acton, where they raised grain and bees. Blum worked in the mines and still cut stone; he was the mason for the old Los Angeles County Court House. By 1908

LEFT: A 1949 aerial view of Castaic reveals an undeveloped, sparsely populated community and wide-open spaces. From the collection of Harold Furtsch. Courtesy, Santa Clarita Valley Historical Society

BELOW: William and Pallie Mayhue came to the Newhall area in 1893 and soon became productive members of the community. William worked in the Rice Canyon oil fields, farmed the area that would later become Valencia, and bought a general store, while Pallie ran a boardinghouse, tended oil wells, and raised two daughters. From the collection of Betty H. Pember. Courtesy, Santa Clarita Valley Historical Society

FACING PAGE, TOP: In 1953 the County Sheriff's Office was located in this building at 6th and San Fernando Road in Newhall. Courtesy, Santa Clarita Valley Historical Society

FACING PAGE, BOTTOM: The American theater, designed by S. Charles Lee, the foremost cinema architect in the nation, was built by William S. Hart in 1940. It was the valley's first movie theater. Courtesy, Santa Clarita Valley Historical Society

they could devote all of their time to the ranch and six children. Apple and pear trees were set out, then, in 1912, peaches. George, Sr., passed away in 1932, his wife living until 1951. Today the ranch covers some 2,000 acres and is probably best known for its colorful tulips.

On December 5, 1890, President Benjamin Harrison had signed a homestead grant awarding a sizable chunk of San Francisquito Canyon to Frank Lebrun. A typical American of mixed French-Spanish, Scotch-Irish descent, Frank married an Indian woman and began supplementing his income as a muleskinner of some renown. Just before the turn of the century, gold was discovered on the property and a complete mining operation was established. The ranch was sold to the City of Los Angeles in 1922, becoming the site of the ill-fated St. Francis Dam. By that time the gold was gone anyway.

The Mayhue family hailed from the Tennessee-Kentucky border country. They were close friends of the Needhams. William Mayhue was probably influenced by Henry Clay Needham to settle in the Newhall area, for he and his wife Pallie arrived in 1893, going to work in the Rice Canyon oil fields. Pallie Mayhue ran the boardinghouse and also tended oil wells when her husband was off on other chores. In between all of that, she managed to have two daughters, Lillie (named for Mrs. Needham) and Opal. She once recalled standing off a mountain lion who was stalking baby Opal, who was blithely sleeping under a tree at the time.

Moving down to 9th and Chestnut, William farmed the area that is now Valencia on a lease basis from Newhall Land. In 1906 he acquired a general store from Jim Gulley, whose tenant was Albert Swall. Mayhue raised the rent and Swall responded by moving out, setting up shop on Main Street (later Spruce, then San Fernando Road). Eventually this became the principal thoroughfare of Newhall—all because of a dispute over the rent. The store at Market and Railroad was converted to a dance hall known as Hap-A-Land, which was purchased around 1919 by Lloyd Houghton, who showed the good sense to marry Mayhue's daughter, Opal. In 1931 the Masons acquired the property and built a courthouse on the ground floor and a meeting hall above. Now a business office, it is still called Ye Olde Courthouse.

William Mayhue passed away in 1954 at the age of 90, his death marking the end of an era. Already a tract of homes was sprouting in Seco Canyon; William S. Hart High School was graduating scholars; and that slumbering giant, Newhall Land and Farming, was awakening from a long night of quiet dreams to hurl the valley into the realities of twentieth-century living.

A Thatcher Glass employee finishes bottles inside the San Fernando Road plant in 1955. Courtesy, Santa Clarita Valley Historical Society

The Awakening Giant

The first theater in the valley was built by William S. Hart in 1940. Designed by S. Charles Lee, the foremost cinema architect in the country, it was to be called "The Tumbleweed." When presented by Hart to the American Legion Post 507, the name was changed to "American." It still stands in Newhall.

Hart also contributed heavily to the first high school, for which Arthur B. Perkins suggested the name Santa Clarita, or Little St. Clare. This institution of higher learning opened for business only three months after the great Western star passed away, so it was named Hart High instead, in his memory.

The next year, 1947, the Bonelli family subdivided their Seco Canyon holdings, creating the first tract of 15 homes, called Rancho Santa Clarita. William Bonelli, Sr., prospered, then got

himself elected to the Board of Equalization. Unfortunately the last years of this kindly and gentle man who had been a college professor read like a Greek tragedy.

He became engaged in a political confrontation with the *Los Angeles Times*, in whose pages he was always referred to as "Big Bill" Bonelli, then was accused of official malfeasance and income tax evasion. The man was finally forced to flee into Mexico, running his affairs and the water company from Hermosillo. Finally, in 1970, he was cleared of all charges just before his death. At least his body came home with honor.

Among the Bonelli holdings was the old Baker-Hoot Gibson Rodeo Arena. In 1939 they started auto racing, the dirt track being tested by such notables as Troy Ruttman and Bill Vukovich. The stadium was closed during the war years, reopening to Circus Vargas, roundups, stock shows, and midget auto racing. During 1956 it was paved by manager Tony Coldeway for stock car racing and christened the Saugus Speedway. A Sunday swap meet was started by Coldeway in 1963, growing over the years to become one of the biggest in the state.

Out at the junction of Soledad and Mint canyons was a place called Solemint. A retired Los Angeles police officer threw up an 8-by-12 general store on the corner called variously Thompson's or Simmons'. Simmons sold out to Doc White, who resold to Alf Clark in 1945. Clark stocked his Solemint Store with everything from side saddles to fur-lined thunder mugs. Clark's advertising was unique and slightly erotic, roundly condemned by some and treasured by others. The store is gone but not forgotten by local old-timers.

The renowned ranch of Remi Nadeau, pioneer freighter of Los Angeles, which featured an extensive deer park, was sold to Helm Schmidt, who died in 1960. The 1,800 acres were acquired by the Jerry Snyder interests, who started development of the second tract in the valley, known as North Oaks, a year later. By 1963 the region was already being called Canyon Country, a name that became official five years later with the establishment of a Canyon Country Post Office.

Meanwhile, the Newhall Land and Farming Company, with its far-flung ranches, had experienced a series of ups and downs, slowly liquidating assets. On August 27, 1933, Atholl McBean was elected president and called in expert consultants and managers to galvanize the corporation into a producing, developing, and growing concern. McBean, by the way, was married to Margaret A. Newhall, a granddaughter of the company's founder. After serving nearly three decades as president, McBean became chairman of the board while, for the first time, a non-family member, George Bushnell, moved into the executive seat.

Between 1965 and 1967 a right-of-way for I-5 was sold to the State of California and California Land Co. was created to develop a new master-planned community on the eastern 4,000 acres of ranch property. The architectural and urban planning firm of Victor Gruen Associates was retained to create a whole town out of cattle pasture and onion fields. Like Athena of Greek myth, it would spring up fully grown. The town would have an industrial complex, a civic center, parks, and schools. This was to be Valencia.

The North Oaks subdivision, the valley's second housing tract, is pictured under construction in 1961. A couple of years later the area was being called Canyon Country. Courtesy, Santa Clarita Valley Historical Society

Don Cameron (car #25) and Walt Faulkner (car #7) test their racing skill in 1948 time trials at Bonelli Stadium (now the Saugus Speedway). Courtesy, Santa Clarita Valley Historical Society

Tract Homes and Shopping Centers

On Sunday, August 20, 1967, the new community of Valencia was born. Named for the Spanish town of ancient Moorish splendors, the town's inaugural day was highlighted by a ceremonial and symbolic passing of title from the King of Spain, through Franciscan missionaries, the Mexican government, Don Antonio del Valle, Henry Mayo Newhall, thence to the new owners.

Old-time residents were astounded when they found out that "flatlanders" from over the hill were willing to stand in line in order to lay out $25,000 for a house.

Valencians were not exactly settling down in "the sticks," although country living was a strong lure. Interstate 5 was nearing completion, making access easy to the San Fernando Valley and Los Angeles. Old Orchard Shopping Center was two years old, as was the championship golf course laid out by Robert Trent Jones. Development of an industrial park in Rye Canyon was at hand, while rumors of a major lake in the State Water Project at Castaic were turning to reality.

Meanwhile, at the other end of the valley, a conglomeration of tract homes and shopping centers was searching for a name. Long known as Solemint, after the junction of Soledad and Mint canyons, it was on its way to becoming the largest settlement in the region. In 1956 the Mint Canyon Chamber of Commerce was established. Among the early movers and shakers were Dr. Everett Phillips, a dentist who invested heavily in property, and Cliffie Stone, a well-known western entertainer. Phillips lured Ken and Ann Lynch out to sagebrush country, where they established a lumberyard in 1955.

Finally, there was Arthur W. Evans, who pursued a varied career, including Santa Barbara police officer, forest ranger, and rancher. Evans proved to be the catalyst who really got things moving in one direction. He was three times honorary mayor and twice president of the newly named Canyon Country Chamber of Commerce. In November 1963 these folks realized that the wide open spaces were rapidly being paved over and boxed in, so they started the first of a long series of Frontier Days celebrations.

By this time Canyon Country was widely used to designate the old Solemint district. There had been an attempt to make Solemint the official name; however, the post office thought it would be confused with Soledad up in Monterey County. Art Evans finally got postal officials to separate Canyon Country from the Saugus mail route, so that in 1968 the name became official.

Back in October 1963 Evans had established a small newspaper called the *Santa Clarita Sentinel*. It was an eight-page affair with typed news notes, a column by Cliffie Stone called "Rolling Stone," and lots of advertising.

At about the same time, Scott Newhall had acquired the *Signal*. Newhall, a great-grandson of the town's founder, had edited the *San Francisco Chronicle* for many years, building it into the second-largest paper in the state. While *Chronicle* editor, Newhall heard that the weekly *Newhall Signal* was for sale. Wanting a newspaper of his own, he bought it for $90,000, ultimately increasing circulation from 2,500 to 32,600.

A glorious newspaper war broke out (harking back to the days of Hearst and Pulitzer), between the *Sentinel* and *The Signal*, culminating in Scott Newhall challenging Art Evans to a duel under the Valley Federal Clock Tower at high noon. Though the town turned out to watch the duel, Evans failed to appear, and the challenge was followed shortly by the demise of the *Sentinel*. Newhall left San Francisco and moved to Piru, and for a quarter century the *Signal* was published and edited by Newhall, his wife, and sons.

Halls of Ivy

While most of Los Angeles County once regarded the upper reaches of the Santa Clara River valley as the domain of cowboys and sodbusters and now as suburbia, it is not without its institutions of higher learning, one of which is world renowned.

College of the Canyons started out on a shoestring budget in the backroom of Hart High School, growing to an immense campus. Since 1967 it has graduated many thousands of scholars who have gone on to universities across the country.

Out of the wilds of Placerita Canyon, construction started on modern stone-and-glass buildings

This aerial view of College of the Canyons was shot in 1978, about a decade after the school held its first graduation. This fully accredited, two-year community college covers a 158-acre campus in Valencia. Courtesy, Santa Clarita Valley Historical Society

during 1960. Los Angeles Baptist College opened on 28 acres with a faculty of 12 teachers. Actually incorporated on May 8, 1927, under the name Los Angeles Baptist Theological Seminary, it changed in 1957 as there were more college than seminary students. While still offering major Bible studies, the institution, now known as The Masters College, does have a wide spectrum of classes, preferring to be called a Christian liberal arts college.

The school's first prospectus listed Newhall as having:

a population of over 4,000 . . . It has a more Western flavor than many which are Spanish in character . . . It is either warmer or cooler (than Los Angeles), but not as humid, and is blessedly devoid of smog.

Classes for working people are conducted in the evenings at Golden Oak Adult School. Courses are given at various junior and senior high schools, providing solid practical education at convenient locations. The school also grants high school diplomas.

Perhaps at the other end of the scholarly spectrum are those starkly modernistic structures crowning a 60-acre hilltop in Valencia. This is the unique California Institute of the Arts.

Walt Disney incorporated CalArts in 1961 as the first fully accredited, degree-granting school devoted to visual and performing arts. It was a merger, actually, of the Los Angeles Conservatory of Music, which started back in 1883, and the renowned Chouinard Art Institute, founded in 1921. In November 1971 it relocated to the Santa Clarita site, opening its doors to students of music, film, theater, dance, art, and design.

Continually reaching out to the community, CalArts provides ongoing programs (either free or at nominal charge) that feature both the performing and visual arts.

When The Masters College first opened its Placerita Canyon campus, the school was still called Los Angeles Baptist College. Today this Christian-oriented, four-year liberal arts college sits amid 43 acres. Courtesy, Santa Clarita Valley Historical Society

A Great Place to Play

The most renowned local landmark in the Santa Clarita Valley consists of 200 acres of gardens, waterfalls, and some of the wildest rides in the world. It is a place called Magic Mountain.

Walt Disney proved that theme amusement parks could be impressive money makers, a fact not lost on the directors of Newhall Land and Farming Company. These creative businessmen followed in the footsteps of Atholl McBean, charging the company's president, James F. Dickason, to consult and then form a partnership with Sea World, Inc., engaging Randall Duell & Associates as architects.

Magic Mountain opened its gates on May 29, 1971, featuring a series of rides called "white knucklers." Frankly catering to the younger set, the Mountain hurled thrill seekers down a water-filled flume, flung riders into a full 360-degree loop on the *Revolution*, or dared them to challenge the mighty *Colossus*, billed as the world's fastest roller coaster. The Sky Tower stood 285 feet above a knoll, providing an impressive vista of the Santa Clarita.

More than 7,000 trees were set out, along with 30,000 shrubs and flowers and miles of gracefully curving walkways, plus bridges over streams adding beauty to the place. There were scaled-down rides in a one-acre children's park, a petting zoo, and craft area known as Spillikin's Corner.

The economic impact on the community was tremendous. Magic Mountain patronized local business, brought in millions of tourists, and became the largest employer in the valley, especially of teenagers looking for summer work.

In 1979 Newhall Land sold the park to Six Flags Corporation for $53.3 million. The Texas-based firm added new rides, diversifying into some less hectic activities that mom and dad might enjoy without getting their teeth jarred loose.

During May 1985 the Mountain got some new symbols. Swept away were the trolls, to be replaced with characters nearly as famous as M. Mouse and D. Duck. "Magic Mountain is going Bugs," read the advertisements, for here were Bugs Bunny, Daffy Duck, Yosemite Sam, a coyote, and a roadrunner.

After 20 years, Magic Mountain has become an institution in the valley.

Val Verde is the scene of physical fitness displays of men and women with enough muscle to probably cart off a Cadillac if one of them had a mind to do so. Also there is the boisterous Cinco de Mayo extravaganza complete with mariachi bands and the best-tasting Mexican food this side of Vera Cruz.

Various clubs, such as Kiwanis, Moose, Elk, and VFW stage barbecues, pancake breakfasts, and other events. The Historical Society has become famous for its "Old Fashioned Ice Cream Socials" held at the Saugus Station (which is now in Newhall) and Old Towne Days. Canyon Country Frontier Days features top-notch Western entertainment and championship rodeos. However, the granddaddy of them all is Newhall's gala Fourth of July parade.

The first procession of coaches, carts, and cars wound its way up San Fernando Road in 1932, getting bigger and longer as time went by.

The Western Walk of Stars was the brainchild of Milt Diamond and the Downtown Newhall Merchants Association. Memorialized in bronze plaques are the names of many stars who made movies in the area. Included in the sidewalks of Newhall are the names of Roy Rogers, Gene Autry, Tom Mix, William S. Hart, Tex Ritter, and Andy Jauregui.

Sagebrush Reservoirs

The Santa Clarita Valley, with its high-desert ecology and streams that run only a couple of months out of the year, would seem an unlikely place to find four fairly large lakes. Of course, they are all man-made, generally supplying the needs of residents well out of the local area.

The oldest of these existing dams is Bouquet, completed in 1933 by the City of Los Angeles' Department of Water and Power. Twenty-four years later the United Water District impounded Piru Creek just across the county line. Bouquet is part of the Los Angeles or Owens Valley Aqueduct supplying DWP customers in the city. Piru Dam keeps orchards green in Ventura County by recharging groundwater tables so that growers' pumps don't go dry.

The most renowned and largest water delivery system in the world is the massive California

Aqueduct, the only local landmark listed in the *Guiness Book of World Records*. It is said that Space Shuttle astronauts can see only two of the works of man back on earth—The Great Wall of China and the California Aqueduct.

Castaic and Pyramid lakes are part of what has been variously called The Feather River Project or State Water Project, owned and operated by California's Department of Water Resources (DWR) and stretching 684 miles from Oroville to Perris.

Although many people were involved in the planning and construction, two men were generally regarded as the prime movers. A burly state engineer named Arthur D. Edmonston pretty much laid out the route and proved that water could be moved 2,000 feet up the Tehachapis in a single lift. Governor Edmond G. "Pat" Brown campaigned vigorously for it, staking his political career on the outcome.

In 1960 voters approved a bond act that provided funds for construction. In fact, it was the largest measure ever passed by a single state, amounting to about $3 billion. Principal and interest were repaid by those who bought water and power, along with operating and maintenance costs. (DWR does not levy a tax and from time to time even shows a profit, which is rare for a state agency.)

Construction of Castaic Dam started in 1967 at the junctions of Castaic and Elizabeth creeks. Removed were such venerable institutions as Kasababian's Pig Farm, Castaic Brick Yard, and the Lyon, Daries, Cook, and Cordova ranches. Some moved to higher ground, while others left for good.

The dam was the earth-fill type with six zones and a clay core designed to withstand an earthquake registering 8.2 on the Richter scale.

On February 9, 1971, the dam was subjected to a test when a 6.6 temblor knocked over a hospital in Sylmar, collapsed freeway bridges, ruptured a boiler at Thatcher Glass, shook down chimneys around Valencia, and caused general disruption of day-to-day activities. Although still being built, Castaic was not affected in any way.

When completed during June of 1972, the embankment stood 425 feet high, was 45 feet across the top, and 2,000 feet at the bottom. Sliced in half, it would look like an earthen pyramid. A pond in front, called the Lagoon, covered 198 acres with 3 miles of

ABOVE: *California's Department of Water Resources was given the green light to begin construction on its 684-mile State Water Project in 1960, when voters approved a $3-billion bond act. Here, rebar pipe frame awaits further work as construction continues on the project. Courtesy, California Department of Water Resources*

LEFT: *Roy Rogers is among the cowboy stars immortalized in Newhall's Western Walk of Stars. From the Windsor Archives*

shoreline. Actually a catch-basin for the main lake, it quickly became popular for swimming, sailing, fishing, and picnicking. Castaic Lake itself swelled to a 29-mile shoreline, covering 2,235 acres, with about 105.5 billion gallons of water sloshing around. Although Castaic is primarily a drinking water supply for Los Angeles and Ventura counties, more than a million people a year flock to it for waterskiing, windsurfing, and other aquatic sports.

Seven miles north looms the 400-foot-high Pyramid Dam, impounding 171,196 acre feet of water and flooding 1,297 acres. Also built by DWR, since 1974 it has been open for recreation and includes a 93-unit campground.

THE GREAT REBELLION

The population of the Santa Clarita Valley literally exploded during the decade of the 1960s, jumping a dramatic 250 percent. During the next 10 years this increase had slowed down to only 42 percent, with the 1980 census recording 81,816 residents. This represented 1.1 percent of the total dwellers in Los Angeles County—a small portion, yet an increasingly vocal one.

Like their pioneering predecessors, newcomers and old-timers alike were becoming frustrated with a distant bureaucracy that seemed indifferent to their needs. It was taxation without representation!

There was tremendous pride in the area's churches, schools, and public buildings. Valencia was one of the best-planned communities in the country. Bermite was building sophisticated weaponry, and Hydraulic Research helped put men on the moon and launch space shuttles. Visitors came from all over the world to study the water project at Castaic and Pyramid lakes. In spite of this cosmopolitan development, the county's rulers in downtown Los Angeles always pictured the valley as some sort of rural backwash.

In order to get some kind of "home rule," studies were made to incorporate Newhall, Saugus, and Valencia. Spearheading these efforts were Carl Boyer III, a slender, sandy-haired educator, and a burly businessman, H. Gil Callowhill. Voters, who generally feared another layer of government and taxes, rejected these notions.

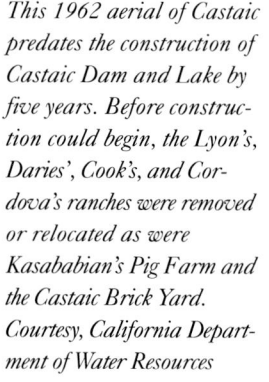

This 1962 aerial of Castaic predates the construction of Castaic Dam and Lake by five years. Before construction could begin, the Lyon's, Daries', Cook's, and Cordova's ranches were removed or relocated as were Kasababian's Pig Farm and the Castaic Brick Yard. Courtesy, California Department of Water Resources

Castaic Lake covers 2,235 acres of the valley and contains more than 105 billion gallons of water, while the "Lagoon" or lower lake (foreground) covers 198 acres. Courtesy, California Department of Water Resources

During December 1974 a group of rebels got together and formed a committee to study the complete secession of Acton, Agua Dulce, Gorman, Castaic, Val Verde, Canyon Country, Saugus, Valencia, and Newhall from Los Angeles County. This new entity was to be called Canyon County.

The chairman of the group was an attorney by the name of Daniel Hon. Connie Worden was a well-informed Valencia resident who involved herself in many community activities. Lee and Frank Turner, owners of Lyons Bowl, headed up publicity. Bill Light gathered petitions, while Art Evans rounded up financial backing.

These and many other people gathered enough valid signatures and submitted the proper paperwork to Governor Edmund G. (Jerry) Brown, Jr., for a commission to be appointed to study the feasibility of a new county. After nine months the five-member panel finally met on April 26, 1976, in (where else) downtown Los Angeles. At last, in August, they concluded that Canyon County could get along very well on its own so the measure was placed on the November ballot as Proposition F. County employees, spearheaded by the firefighters, fought the proposal with a huge war chest.

On the night of November 2 hundreds gathered at the Mint Canyon Elks Lodge. The group included Jo Anne Darcy, George Wells, Bonnie Mills, Janice Heidt, Alice Kline, Ken and Ann Lynch, and many others who had worked long and hard. The festive atmosphere deteriorated along about midnight when it became apparent that, while Canyon County was approved locally by a 55 to 45 percent vote, it had gone down to defeat in the rest of the county by a margin of 68 to 32 percent.

Out of the rubble of despair pluckily rose a second attempt, joined by other regions trying to secede, and even a proposal to carve Los Angeles into five separate counties. Faced with fragmentation and loss of power and positions, county supervisors pushed a bill through the state legislature that any new county would have to have a minimum population of 350,000. Just 15 days before the law went into effect (January 1, 1978) Canyon County petitions were delivered to the registrar's office, wrapped up like a Christmas present. The great rebellion was off and running again. This time it was Proposition K on the ballot of November 7, 1978, and was, as before, voted down by the county at large while approved locally (Yes—59 percent; No 41—percent).

The wheel of history turned its full circle. For as soon as the dust settled, there were Gilbert Callowhill, Carl Boyer, Carmen Sarro, and others getting together to incorporate, not only Newhall, Saugus, and Valencia, but also, the whole region that might have been Canyon County, into one gigantic city.

The Birth of a City

As early as 1920 there had been attempts to incorporate some of the communities of the Santa Clara. Four years later a chamber of commerce was formed in Newhall with one of its goals being to form a city. Each of these early attempts met with general apathy.

After the defeat of Canyon County, the "home rule" movement gained strength, but seemed to be mired down for the next decade. If any one group could be credited with spurring the cityhood movement back to life, it was the developers. Almost overnight it seemed that hills were leveled, historic structures were bulldozed, and ancient groves of oak trees ripped out by their roots. Thousands of tract homes sprung up like weeds, most with single-road access. Traffic became a nightmare, with such major thoroughfares as Interstate 14, San Fernando Road, and Sierra Highway becoming virtual parking lots between 4 p.m. and 6 p.m.

In 1985 the Chamber of Commerce, now called the Santa Clarita Valley Chamber, again pursued its goal of cityhood, and, in a move spearheaded by Chamber president Lou Garasi, implemented a feasibility study making sure revenues were sufficient to form the new city. Positive findings indicated an excess of $3 million, and the committee proceeded to fund the official cityhood application.

A city formation committee listened to residents, gathered petitions, and generally proposed to incorporate the whole valley into the City of Santa Clarita. These plans had to be approved by a Los Angeles County-appointed Local Agency Formation Commission, or LAFCO. The commission acceded to every developer request to be excluded, paring down the city to about half its original size.

On Tuesday, November 3, 1987, a record turnout of voters within the proposed boundaries of the new city approved cityhood (Proposition U) by 67.15 percent. From a field of 26 candidates, 5 were elected to the first city council. These were Jan Heidt, JoAnne Darcy, Carl Boyer, Dennis Koontz, and Buck McKeon. Howard "Buck" McKeon, with the most votes (7,219) became the first mayor of Santa Clarita, while Jan Heidt, with 6,091 ballots, was installed as assistant mayor. One of their first acts was to stop the cutting of heritage oaks.

City boundaries were set at 39 square miles instead of the original 95, including Newhall, Saugus, Valencia, and parts of Canyon Country. Cut off were Castaic, Agua Dulce, everything west of Interstate 5, including Magic Mountain, the land south of the Antelope Valley Freeway, and parts of Saugus. (These areas may vote to join the city at a later date.)

Less than a year after the City of Santa Clarita was incorporated, community residents and West Coast journalists were astounded to learn that the Newhall family (Scott, Ruth, and Tony) had suddenly resigned from the *Newhall Signal and Saugus Enterprise* after presiding over the paper for a quarter of a century. The Newhalls had sold most of their stock in *The Signal* to the Morris Newspaper Corporation and then walked out after a dispute concerning a buy-back arrangement. A month later, in September 1988, the Newhall family began publishing the *Santa Clarita Valley Citizen*, which put out its last issue only eight months later, thus ending an era of flamboyant journalism in the valley.

While the community's print media were undergoing dramatic changes, plans were developing for the valley's own radio station. Lawrence B. Bloomfield, an engineer with 30 years of experience, began setting up radio station 1220 AM, KBET. Bloomfield designed the state-of-the-art station and installed Mike Levine as program director. They envisioned broadcasting plays from Cal Arts, local history minutes, interviews with prominent individuals, and blanket coverage of regional events. Unfortunately for Bloomfield, he ran short of cash even before he could take to the airwaves, so he sold his stock to eastern investors. When they became exasperated at the length of time it was taking to get revenue to pour in, the new owners assumed operation of the station, and, at last, KBET made it to the air with "oldies but goodies" tunes, local news and weather, and traffic reports, a format that has proven successful.

Among the locals to make the most recent news were the members of the Santa Clarita City Council. While the city council held generally high marks with the citizens who elected them, some city residents felt that the council was not doing enough to slow or stop area development, and they criticized the council members for not taking a strong stand against turning Elsmere and Towsley canyons into landfills. Two council members, Carl Boyer and JoAnne Darcy, were targeted for recalls, but the movement failed to gain any momentum.

In 1990 Jill Klijac, who had been active in civic improvement and canyon preservation efforts, won election to the council, unseating Dennis Koontz. Though Koontz was generally regarded as a slow-growth advocate, Klijac was certainly a far more vocal individual.

Santa Clarita Valley residents were opposed to the City of Los Angeles' plans to pour millions of tons of offal into the oak-studded historic canyons of Elsmere and Towsley. Aside from their natural scenic beauty, both canyons have artesian wells that feed streams flowing into the groundwater table, the supply sources for most Santa Claritans.

Then, like the cavalry in a Western, the Santa Monica Mountains Conservancy swept in and saved the day. It purchased most of the mouth of the canyon to create a state park that features a lodge, hiking trails, and a visitor center named for Sonia Thompson, a deputy director and project analyst for the Conservancy.

When the 1990 U.S. Census reported that there were 110,642 residents in the City of Santa Clarita, the city council immediately challenged the figure, claiming that many minority residents had been overlooked and that the actual figure was closer to 145,000 citizens. (An accurate population count is very important since the City receives rebates from state and federal taxes based on its population.)

Though most of the local citizens had reacted quite indifferently to military actions in Korea, Vietnam, Grenada, and Panama, the seven-week Persian Gulf War of 1991 saw valley residents whip themselves into a patriotic frenzy. American flags flew from light poles, businesses, and private homes, and yellow ribbons were everywhere. Meager antiwar demonstrations were overwhelmed by flag-waving youths standing shoulder to shoulder with older veterans on street corners and in shopping centers, shouting "Support our troops." Motorists honked their horns in approval, often displaying American flags and yellow ribbons on their antennas. More than 180 locals served in the brief conflict, and they were honored by a special display of banners at city hall, in the Newhall Fourth of July Parade, and at the Fourth of July Carnival in Newhall Park.

In 1991, the fifth year of a statewide drought, Santa Claritans were attempting to conserve water. Like their predecessors, these resourceful residents would do their best to triumph over the forces of nature. Yet, even as there were calls for no new water hookups and for a moratorium on building, the State Water Resources announced plans for a massive visitor center complex at Pyramid Lake, and Newhall Land and Farming had graded and staked out land for a regional shopping mall. This optimism and forward thinking, part of Santa Clarita's heritage, is a legacy to be cherished and preserved in the "Valley of the Golden Dream."

Valley of the Golden Dream*

In the shade of Magic Mountain,
between I-5 and the 14,
I make my home in Santa Clarita,
valley of the golden dream.

We've got cowboys and horses,
trains and trucks and cars,
movie makers and stock car racers,
and the Western Walk of Stars.

Santa Clarita,
you're much more than you seem.
Santa Clarita,
valley of the golden dream.

We've got hills full of oil
and canyons rich with gold,
the River Santa Clara,
and oak trees so old.

Santa Clarita,
you're much more than you seem.
Santa Clarita,
valley of the golden dream.

● ● ●

The colorful heritage of the Santa Clarita Valley lives on in a myriad of ways—from its streets named after early movers and shakers to the restored houses surrounding the Saugus Station to its landscape dotted with ancient oaks. To weekend visitors, Santa Clarita immediately brings to mind a rush of images: Sunday swap meets and Saturday-night races at the Saugus Speedway; white-knuckler thrill rides at Magic Mountain; swimming, boating, and windsurfing at Castaic Lake; and the William S. Hart estate, an ever-present echo of the valley's Hollywood connection. To residents, the Santa Clarita Valley is all that and more. It is a suburban oasis for families, offering a sense of security, good schools, abundant recreational opportunities, and an affordable piece of the American Dream.

The following pages capture, in full color, the essence of the valley as it stands ready for the twenty-first century.

*Song lyrics from "Valley of the Golden Dream"
© copyright 1991 Teri Davis Greenberg
All rights reserved.

Six Flags Magic Mountain features Viper—the world's largest, looping roller coaster. An 18-story drop, a double barrel boomerang, a classic corkscrew, and three 360-degree loops make for a positively thrilling ride. Photo by Larry Molmud

RIGHT: *The Santa Clarita Valley has experienced a housing boom in recent years in response to the rapid population growth of the Los Angeles area. Photo by Patty Salkeld*

FACING PAGE: *Picturesque San Fransiquito Canyon is located between Saugus and Castaic in the northern part of the Santa Clarita Valley. Photo by Jerry Reynolds*

La Loma de los Vientos (Hill of the Winds) was the home of famous actor and director William S. Hart from the late 1920s until his death in 1946. It is now a public museum on the grounds of William S. Hart County Park. Photo by Teri Davis Greenberg

The ever-popular Saugus Swap Meet is held every Sunday at the Saugus Speedway. Photo by Justine Hill

Antique cars join the festivities of Newhall's Fourth of July parade. Photo by Jeff Greenberg

FACING PAGE: Built on the site of the old Newhall Depot, the Saugus Train Station opened on September 1, 1887. After nearly a century of service to the community the station was closed and later donated to the Santa Clarita Valley Historical Society by Southern Pacific. It now serves as the society's headquarters at its location in William S. Hart County Park. Photo by Patty Salkeld

ABOVE: *Castaic Lake is a great place to beat the summer heat. Photo by Justine Hill*

RIGHT: *Students of the California Institute of the Arts perform a production of Scapino— just one of many theatrical events produced by the school each year. Photo by Stephen A. Gunther/California Institute of the Arts*

LEFT: Colorful sails skim the waters of Castaic Lagoon. Photo by Jerry Reynolds

FOLLOWING PAGE: Located on the grounds of William S. Hart County Park, The Village is dedicated to the preservation of historic Santa Clarita Valley structures. The Ramona Chapel pictured here is one of a fine assortment of buildings restored by the Santa Clarita Valley Historical Society. Photo by Patty Salkeld

BELOW: The Saugus Speedway was originally constructed as a rodeo stadium in 1924 and it wasn't until 1947 that its first automobile race was held. Courtesy, Saugus Speedway

Santa Clarita Valley Milestones
A Chronology of Historic Highlights: A.D. 450-1991

A.D. 450 ✯ Tataviam Indians (Shoshone Serranos) arrive in the valley

1769 ✯ Don Gaspar de Portolá Party crosses mountains at Newhall Pass and camps at Rancheria del Corral (Castaic Junction) • Father Crespí names Santa Clara River for Saint Clare

1797 ✯ Mission San Fernando Rey de España formally dedicated

1804 ✯ Asistencia de San Francisco founded at Castaic Junction

1821 ✯ California becomes territory of Mexico

1839 ✯ Rancho San Francisco granted to Don Antonio del Valle

1841 ✯ Antonio del Valle dies

1842 ✯ Ignacio del Valle claims western section of Rancho San Francisco • Francisco Lopez, Manuel Cota, and Domingo Bermudez discover gold in Placerita Canyon

1843 ✯ Rancho Temescal granted to Francisco Lopez

1845 ✯ Rancho del Buque granted to Francisco Chari in what is now known as Bouquet Canyon

1846 ✯ Mexican War starts • California declared a U.S. possession

1847 ✯ John C. Frémont camps at Rancho San Francisco (Castaic Junction) • General Andrés Pico surrenders to Frémont in the Capitulation of Cahuenga

1848 ✯ With the Treaty of Guadalupe-Hidalgo, California lands become part of U.S. • John W. Audubon camps at Castaic Junction • Placerita gold rush ends as mines give out

1850 ✯ California admitted to the U.S. as 31st state

1854 ✯ Fort Tejon established • 1st elementary school in Newhall founded • Phineas T. Banning drives his first stage through Fremont Pass

1855 ✯ Sanford and Cyrus Lyon buy stage stop (site of present Eternal Valley cemetery) • General Edward Fitzgerald Beale purchases the first of several valley ranchos

1856 ✯ Severe drought hits L.A. County, resulting in the death of at least 10,000 head of cattle

1857 ✯ Major earthquake rattles Ft. Tejon

1858 ✯ Butterfield-Overland Stage Route is started through Fremont Pass and San Francisquito Canyon

1860 ✯ Colonel Thomas F. Mitchell arrives in Soledad Canyon

1862 ✯ Three-year drought begins, eventually resulting in a 71 percent reduction in the number of L.A. County's cattle

1863 ✯ Construction begins on Beale's Cut through Fremont Pass

1865 ✯ Rancho San Francisco sold to Thomas R. Bard and Thomas Scott

1866 ✯ General Beale buys Rancho Castac and changes the name to Castaic

1868 ✯ Soledad Post Office established • Soledad City renamed Ravenna

1869 ✯ Sanford Lyon, Henry Wiley, and William Jenkins spring pole first oil well in Pico Canyon

1871 ✯ John Lang kills a record 2,350-pound grizzly bear in Soledad Canyon • Elizabeth Lake School District established

1872 ✯ Sulphur Springs School founded

1873 ✯ Governor Newton Booth offers $8,000 reward for capture of outlaw Tiburcio Vásquez

1874 ★ Outlaw Tiburcio Vásquez sets up hideout in Soledad Canyon • Vásquez captured

1875 ★ Henry Mayo Newhall buys Rancho San Francisco • Tiburcio Vásquez hanged in San Jose • Soledad Judicial District set up with John H. Powell as first judge • Charles "Alex" Mentry begins drilling for oil in Pico Canyon

1876 ★ Placerita white oil displayed at Philadelphia Exposition • 6,940-foot San Fernando Railroad Tunnel "holed through" • California's first commercially successful oil refinery located at Lyon Station • 1st train through San Fernando Tunnel • Gold spike driven at Lang Station completes California's north-

south railroad • Pico No. 4 becomes California's first commercial oil well • Newhall founded at site of present-day Saugus

1878 ★ Pioneer Oil Refinery, moved from Lyon Station, starts production in Newhall

1883 ★ Newhall Land and Farming formed by the widow and five sons of Henry Mayo Newhall

1887 ★ Southern Pacific establishes Saugus and Castaic railroad stations • Town of Saugus founded

1888 ★ Acton Post Office established • Acton Community Church founded by the Reverend F.W. Pattee • Southern Hotel in Newhall burns to the ground

1889 ★ Castaic School founded

1891 ★ President Benjamin Harrison at Saugus Station • Valley's 1st Presbyterian Church formed by the Reverend F.D. Seward in Newhall • R.E. Nickel founds *Acton Rooster*, valley's first newspaper • Surrey Post Office established at Saugus

1893 ★ Pico Canyon-Newhall Earthquake

1898 ★ Brothers Dick and Martin Wood take over Saugus Station eatery and rename it the Saugus Cafe

1903 ★ Theodore Roosevelt at Saugus Station and Acton Hotel

1906 ★ Bercaw General Store opens in Surrey

1908 ★ Sterling Borax Works begins production

1915 ★ Valley's first Catholic parish mission church dedicated • Construction begins on Ridge Route • Town of Castaic founded

1916 ★ Last Tataviam Indian, Juan José Fustero, passes away

1917 ★ Castaic Post Office set up in Sam Parson's General Store

1919 ★ Edward H. Brown founds *Newhall Signal* newspaper • William S. Hart is one of Hollywood's top three stars

1921 ★ William S. Hart buys Horseshoe Ranch from Babcock Smith

1924 ★ Reginaldo del Valle sells Camulos

1925 ★ Angeles National Forest created

1926 ★ Dr. Peters opens offices that eventually become Newhall Community Hospital

1928 ★ St. Francis Dam breaks in San Francisquito Canyon—Southern California's worst disaster • William S. Hart moves into his Newhall home— La Loma de los Vientos

1929 ★ Great Saugus Train Robbery by "Buffalo" Tom Vernon

1930 ☆ Newhall Refinery reborn as "The Pioneer" Refinery

1932 ☆ First Newhall 4th of July parade • Highway 99 through Weldon Canyon completed, bypassing part of the old Ridge Route

1933 ☆ Bouquet Dam completed by the Los Angeles Department of Water and Power

1938 ☆ Highway cut through Newhall Pass eliminates car tunnel

1940 ☆ Santa Clarita Valley population is 4,000 • First movie theater in the valley is built by William S. Hart

1946 ☆ First high school in William S. Hart District dedicated • William S. Hart dies, leaving his Newhall estate to L.A. County

1947 ☆ Valley's first tract of homes—Rancho Santa Clarita—built in Seco Canyon

1952 ☆ Gene Autry buys Ernie Hickson's "Western" town, renames it Melody Ranch, and uses it as set for his TV show • Two oil wells on the Jenkins Ranch come in on the same day—a million-to-one longshot that makes national headlines

1956 ☆ Baker-Hoot Gibson Rodeo Arena paved and renamed Saugus Speedway

1957 ☆ Piru Dam and Lake completed

1962 ☆ Melody Ranch destroyed by fire

1963 ☆ Canyon Country founded • First Canyon Country Frontier Days celebration • Sunday swap meet begins at Saugus Speedway

1965 ☆ Santa Clarita National Bank opens

1967 ☆ Community of Valencia dedicated • Tract homes in Valencia sell for $25,000

1969 ☆ College of the Canyons established

1971 ☆ Magnitude 6.5 earthquake rocks Southern California • Magic Mountain opens • Southern Pacific demolishes Lang Station • California Institute of the Arts, incorporated by Walt Disney, relocates to Valencia

1972 ☆ Term "Santa Clarita" becomes official • Castaic Dam and Lake completed

1975 ☆ Henry Mayo Newhall Memorial Hospital founded • Santa Clarita Valley Historical Society founded

1979 ☆ Newhall Land sells Magic Mountain to Six Flags Corporation

1980 ☆ Santa Clarita Valley population is 81,816

1985 ☆ Chamber of Commerce (now Santa Clarita Valley Chamber of Commerce) implements study on economic feasibility of cityhood

1987 ☆ Voters approve City of Santa Clarita • Santa Clarita becomes incorporated city

1989 ☆ Santa Clarita Post Office dedicated

1990 ☆ Paul Veluzat family purchases Melody Ranch and soon begins restoration and construction of new sets • U.S. Census reports 110,642 residents in City of Santa Clarita

1991 ☆ More than 180 local residents serve in the Persian Gulf War • Ground is broken for the valley's first regional shopping mall

SPONSORS

AES Placerita • ATC Cablevision • Elisha Adajanian Family • American Beauty Homes • Andy Gump Inc. • Aquafine Corporation • Baxter Pharmaseal • C.A. Rasmussen, Inc. • California Institute of the Arts • Canyon Country Chamber of Commerce • Castaic Lake Water Agency • Castaic Union School District • Center for Women's Health • Chevron USA, Inc. • City of Santa Clarita • Clanton Block, Inc. • Country Oaks Escrow • First Care • Galpin Motors, Inc. • Gruber Systems, Inc. • Hale & Associates • Henry Mayo Newhall Memorial Hospital • KMGX MAGIC-FM • KGIL-AM • M.W. Sausse & Co., Inc. • The Master's College • Dr. M.D. Mullenax • The Newhall Land and Farming Company • Newhall School District • Patterson & Neavitt • Dr. Edward A. Pechter • Polycarbon Inc. • Fred W. Rio, M.D., F.A.C.S. • Santa Clarita Disposal • Santa Clarita Valley Association of Realtors • Santa Clarita Valley Chamber of Commerce • Saugus Union School District • The Signal • Sikand Engineering • Six Flags Magic Mountain • Stevenson Ranch • Sulphur Springs School District • Tan Medical Group/Newhall Community Hospital and Clinic • George J. Thomas III, M.D. • The Travel Bug • Valencia Country Club • Valencia National Bank • William S. Hart Union School District • Williams Instruments Company, Inc.

BENEFACTORS

Santa Clarita Valley Historical Society • A-1 Blueprint (Thanking you for 10 years of continued support) Angeles National Forest • Arnold Talking Yellow Pages • Bank of America, Newhall Branch • Joseph M. Caruso, D.D.S., M.S. • Ann Darcy (Compliments of) Facey Medical Group • Guyer Accountancy Corporation • Gerald H. Heidt Family • Henry Mayo Newhall Memorial Foundation • Raymond Kutylo • Joseph M. & Dorothy A. Morelli • Tom & Dody Rogers • Tips Valencia, Inc. • Valencia Mazda • Hondo Oil & Gas Company • Envicom Corporation

Courtesy, Santa Clarita Valley Historical Society (Security Pacific National Bank Photograph Collection/L.A. Public Library)

Santa Clarita Valley Chamber of Commerce

The Santa Clarita Valley Chamber of Commerce has served a variety of roles since its inception more than 60 years ago. It has been an organizer of community events such as the Miss Santa Clarita Valley Pageant and the July 4th parade. The chamber has brought business to the area, brought government leaders to the valley to discuss issues, helped resolve community needs and issues, and been a source of information about people and places in the Santa Clarita Valley.

The chamber's role in recent years has shifted away from social functions as the community has grown large enough that other groups have shouldered responsibility for those events. Now the chamber is increasingly an advocate for business. It has seven specific goals: promote a favorable climate for business; keep enterprise free from unnecessary regulations; work closely with the City of Santa Clarita; provide information about the valley to potential businesses and people considering moving to the area; inform both the public and government of the need for a strong business and industrial climate; influence government decisions affecting the environment, economy, transportation, and energy supplies; and always maintaining the unique atmosphere of the beautiful valley.

To meet its goals, the chamber has organized a continuing support system. Committees review legislation, act as a clearing house for information about economic development, assist firms to work with local schools; help solve transportation problems; review city government actions; establish business networking; deal with international trade; and promote film development in the valley.

The historic Pardee Home on the corner of Walnut and Newhall Avenues was home to the chamber from 1977 to 1988. Formerly the Newhall-Saugus-Valencia Chamber of Commerce (photo B), it became the Santa Clarita Valley Chamber of Commerce in 1980 (photo C) © 1991, Creative Image Photography

With 1,200 members it is the largest business organization in the Santa Clarita Valley. Its functions include monthly business mixers, an annual installation banquet, a tribute to teachers in the spring, a business exposition in October, the Cliff Sales Oak Tree Fall Classic golf tournament, and numerous grand openings.

Among the materials made available by the chamber is a videotape titled "Santa Clarita Valley: The Valley of Choice" and an accompanying brochure. The chamber also has a comprehensive map of the valley, as well as an annual business directory and community guide. It publishes an economic profile and a roster of industries.

The chamber was originally chartered in 1923 for the community of Newhall with a subsequent addition for the communities of Saugus and Valencia. In 1980 it became the Santa Clarita Valley Chamber of Commerce reflecting its desire to serve the entire area, thus living up to its name.

Prior to cityhood (1987), the chamber acted in an unofficial, quasi-governmental capacity. In 1985 it undertook the initial study for incorporation and gave key financial support to application for cityhood. Throughout the years it has been a key resource for all issues facing the area.

LEFT and ABOVE: In the early 1900s Newhall's Main Street was a bustling center of activity. Courtesy, Santa Clarita Valley Historical Society

Santa Clarita Disposal

When Steve Arklin and his brothers Phillip and Levon became involved in a landscaping job with their father, Florindo, in 1970, none of them had any idea how instrumental the job would be in their lives.

The landscaping job was for a successful San Fernando Valley disposal company owner, and the pay was a 1959 Diamond Reao garbage truck. From there, a business was born.

As Florindo remained in the landscaping business, a profession in which he had made a modest living, his sons slowly built a disposal business that started with the one truck in 1970 to more than 60 trucks and several 100 acres of family-owned landfill property by the year 1990.

But the business was not an instant success. "It was back-breaking work," Steve says. In the beginning Steve, Levon, and Phillip built a client base in the Santa Clarita Valley near their Sand Canyon residence, driving the truck themselves and then parking it outside the family home at night. "Mother did the billing from the kitchen table," Steve remembers.

In 1971 the Arklins purchased their second truck and soon after started buying up smaller garbage companies in the Santa Clarita and Antelope valleys. In 1975 the Arklins purchased a yard on Sierra Highway.

Today Santa Clarita Disposal continues to operate out of the 2.5-acre parcel of land in Canyon Country, utilizing more than 15 trucks and 40 employees to cover all areas of the valley.

However, as Santa Clarita Disposal continues to grow with the city, the Antelope Valley enterprise has evolved from a few trucks into a sprawling 400-acre base of operations with more than 45 trucks and 100 employees. "The Antelope Valley has turned out to be quite a pleasant surprise," he says.

The early 1980s had its ups and downs with the Arklins. Their father passed away after suffering a heart attack—a setback that was taken very hard by the family.

The brothers also expanded their business, opening Cal Coast Recycling in Canyon Country, an operation that Levon operates with his mother. The recycling firm has been incorporated into the waste-disposal business, with the Arklins holding high hopes for eventually being able to successfully recycle almost all waste materials.

"We plan on having an extensive curbside recycling project by the end of 1991," Steve says. In the meantime the Arklin brothers split profits and titles among the three enterprises, with each serving as president of one and secretary and treasurer of the others.

"One of the key things is being able to work with my brothers," Steve says. "That's the way our dad raised us." The Arklins attribute their success to treating customers right and offering good service at fair prices. And if the customers are not happy, their business cards carry a firm reminder that they mean business. They read, "Satisfaction guaranteed or double your rubbish back."

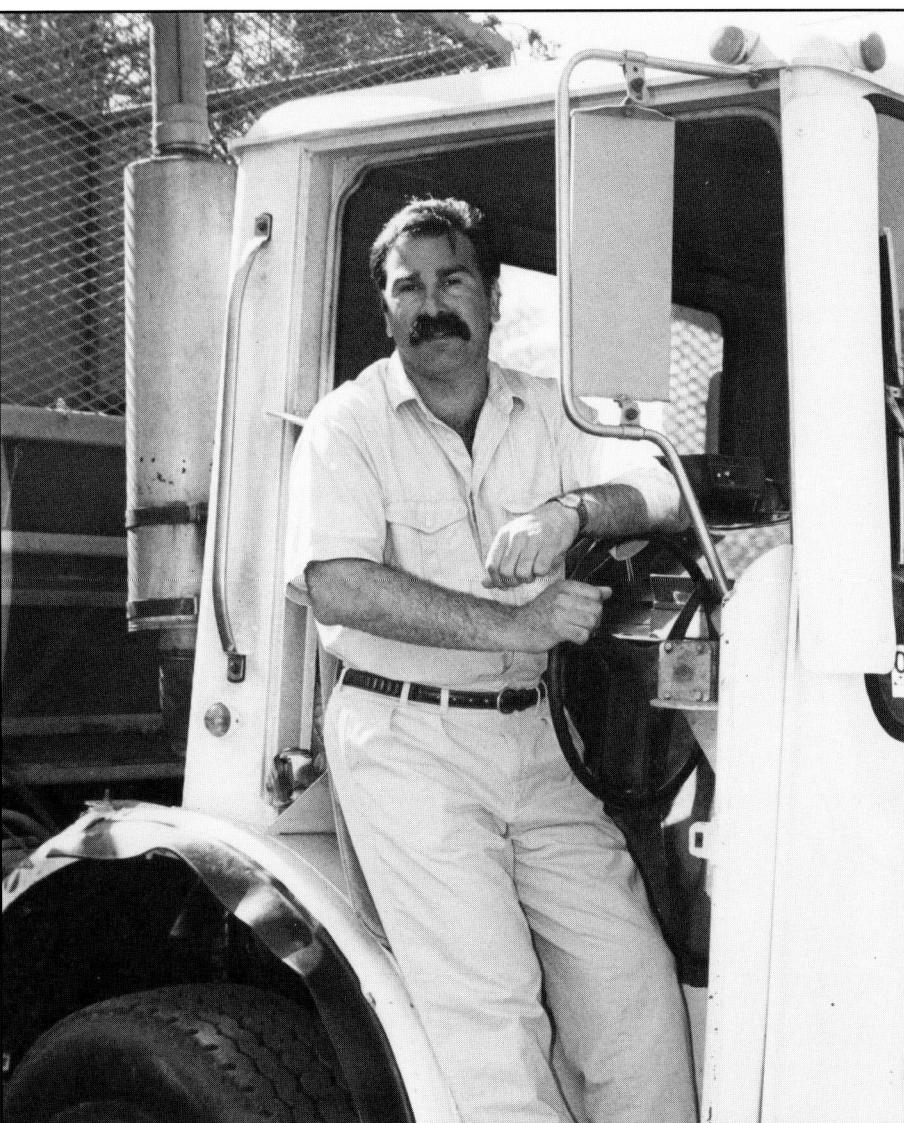

Steve Arklin, one of the founders of Santa Clarita Diposal. Photo by Douglas Ferber

Clanton Block, Inc.

When Hollis Clanton, Sr., asked his family to pitch in and help him make a go of the family masonry block and supply business in 1971, his wife, Alyne, sons Hollis Jr. and Steven, and daughter, Julianne, all came to his aide.

Today, through the hard work and dedication of the Clanton family, the business is flourishing in both the Santa Clarita and Antelope valleys.

With Steven serving as corporate president, Hollis Sr. as chief financial officer, and Alyne as secretary/treasurer, the Clantons are as much a part of the Santa Clarita Valley as the block walls that stand within it.

In the beginning Hollis Sr. began a block-making business with his father and brother in the mid-1940s. They developed a method to manufacture masonry blocks that eventually would revolutionize the industry.

In 1955 they purchased 25 acres of real estate zoned for heavy manufacturing in Saugus with the intention of moving the business from the San Fernando Valley. However it would be several years before the family would utilize the property off San Fernando Road.

In the meantime the Clanton Block remained in the San Fernando Valley until Kaiser Steel bought it out in 1960. Just prior to the sale, Hollis Sr. had set up a block-making facility for Kaiser in Hawaii.

Along with his brother Ray, Hollis Sr. continued manufacturing block-making machinery, working within the Saugus location until deciding to go back to school in the mid-1960s.

He emerged from San Fernando Valley State College (now California State University Northridge) with a degree in finance at the end of the decade and decided to give the business another chance.

Following the February 1971 Sylmar earthquake, Hollis Sr. took over the business from his brother and enlisted the help of his family.

Steven was working to save money for a planned trip to Europe. After two years Steven had saved enough and went on his way. But he did not get beyond Yosemite before deciding that Europe did not necessarily have the answers he was looking for.

"I came to the conclusion that if I were going to learn about life, I could do it anywhere," Steven says. So it was back to the block business, where Steven has remained ever since.

In the meantime Clanton Block went from a tiny trailer-based operation in the early 1970s to a company that employed 23 workers in 1990.

Due to extreme competition brought on by bigger companies, the Clantons dropped their block-making enterprise and focused on selling masonry supplies. The move has paid off. Now boasting a second location in the Antelope Valley, there is no question that the success of Clanton Block, Inc., is all in the family.

LEFT: The Clantons (left to right), Alyne, Hollis, and Steve, started out manufacturing masonry block, and now the company is a masonry and general building supply operation. Photo by Douglas Ferber

BELOW: Steve Clanton has helped build a business with his parents, Hollis and Alyne Clanton. Photo by Douglas Ferber

Dr. Edward A. Pechter

While working on his residency in plastic surgery at UCLA, Dr. Edward A. Pechter's introduction to the Santa Clarita Valley was treating the victim of a motorcycle accident whose arm was severed off.

The victim was sent from Henry Mayo Newhall Memorial Hospital to the Veterans Administration Hospital in Sepulveda, where Pechter was working a rotation. Pechter treated the patient, closing the wound left by the severed arm and grafting skin to complete the job.

As he became acquainted with the patient, Pechter found out there was a shortage of plastic surgeons in the Santa Clarita Valley. "The patient told me about Valencia—it sounded like a nice place," Pechter says.

That was in 1980. In the fall of the following year he decided to take a closer look at the valley, where he discovered it was just the place he was looking for to set up his practice.

His reasoning was that the Santa Clarita Valley was still close enough for him to remain within driving distance of UCLA, where he maintains a position as an assistant clinical professor. "There were no full-time plastic surgeons in the Santa Clarita Valley area," he says.

Pechter, who began his medical career in his hometown of Chicago, moved to Los Angeles in 1980 to complete his plastic surgery residency. Upon completion, Pechter became a board-certified plastic surgeon and opened his practice on Tournament Road in Valencia.

Pechter considers his profession both challenging and fulfilling. "I like taking care of the problems that plastic surgeons face," he says.

Besides his sometimes complex duties of reconstructing intricate facial and body irregularities caused by accidents and birth defects, Pechter has also established a reputation as one of the finest cosmetic surgeons in the city.

He says that increasing a patient's self-esteem and self-image is his reward. "Taking something bad and turning it into something positive is what it's all about," he says.

Pechter, who lives in Newhall with his wife, Sondra, and two daughters, Jacqueline and Greta, is very active within the community. Among his long list of involvements, Pechter is a Henry Mayo Newhall Memorial Hospital board member and has written a medical column for the *Newhall Signal*. Pechter has served as chairman of the HMNMH Health Foundation Founders' Circle since its inception in 1987. The Founders' Circle raised more than $500,000 for the construction and operation of the hospital Adult Day Health Care Center.

"I really love this community," Dr. Pechter says. "I enjoy being involved in it."

Edward A. Pechter is the only full-time board-certified plastic surgeon in the Santa Clarita Valley.

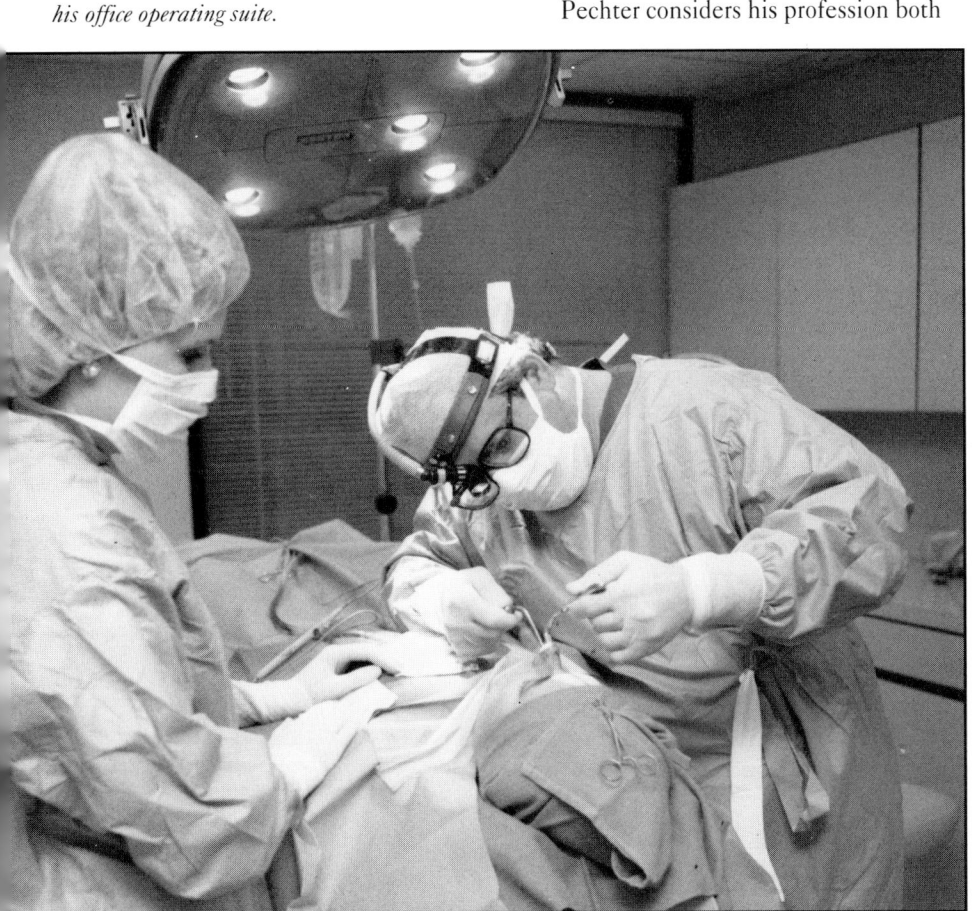

Edward Pechter performs plastic surgery in his office operating suite.

Applied Energy Services-Placerita

Applied Energy Services (AES) is a company that strives to be neither heard nor seen. But the products AES supplies to the Santa Clarita Valley and beyond are not easy to come by.

Contracting with Southern California Edison, AES supplies the Santa Clarita Valley with 110 megawatts of electricity, allowing residents to confidently flick a light switch and bask in illumination.

Bob Muir, former assistant plant manager of AES-Placerita, says AES' move into Southern California came with a built-in assurance of work. In the early 1980s Southern California Edison had been slowly losing its electricity reserves and suffering brownouts, which are considered dangerously low drops in voltage output.

"It had made them extra nervous," Muir says, adding that Edison soon put out a standard offer: a contract for an independent company that could supply them with electricity. AES was one such company.

As if the electric company's offer was not reason enough to set up shop in Southern California, there was also an oil company seeking a firm to provide it with steam for oil extraction purposes.

Steam is a natural by-product of cogenerated electricity. Cogeneration, says Clem Palevich, business manager at AES-Placerita, a subsidary of Virgina based AES Corporation, produces both electricity and steam from the same fuel source, saving valuable natural resources and improving air quality. Muir says the opportunity to sell both electricity and steam was too good to pass up.

Before long, TOSCO, an oil conglomerate operating off of Placerita Canyon, contracted for steam with AES, who built a cogeneration plant by the end of 1988. By using the steam produced by AES, TOSCO was able to save the resources that would have otherwise been spent to power portable steam generators. The old way, using fuel to produce steam, was also producing nitrogen oxides, known to create smog.

AES sought financing from several banks for the construction of the cogeneration plant. These banks insisted AES purchase the oil fields from TOSCO, who was seeking to sell its oil operation. AES quickly agreed.

After spending several months acquiring the necessary permits, AES-Placerita

ABOVE: Dan Hunter, Maintenance, in front of POCI (Placerita Oil Company, a subsidaiary of AES Placerita) Oil Well.

BELOW: Tim Martin, Plant Technician, doing some testing in the Water Treatment Lab.

took its place among Santa Clarita Valley industry.

While the oil business has its ups and downs, AES intends to continue its operation for at least the length of its contracts for the electricity production. As of 1992 the plant was pumping out approximately 25,000 barrels of crude oil a month from beneath the 60 acres of land the company occupies off Placerita Canyon. In addition to 105 megawatts of electricity.

Despite the fact that oil has been pumped from that land for more than 50 years, the venture still frequently comes under fire. Because of that, he says AES-Placerita is continually trying to improve the oil fields.

"We're trying to make the oil field as unobtrusive to the community as possible," Palevich says. In addition, when the electrical cogeneration power plant was being built in the mid-1980s, AES invested $4 million in noise insulation.

Nestled neatly on the eastern portion of Placerita Canyon and Sierra Highway, AES maintains an elaborate landscape around the perimeter of the plant as a way to blend in with neighboring residential areas.

Davis says that from an environmental standpoint, AES-Placerita is in the forefront of the industry. "We are among the safest, cleanest utility-size power plants in the country," he says, adding AES installed selective catalytic reduction equipment to reduce nitrogen oxide emissions to well below permitted levels.

But Davis says there is always room for new ways to cut down on emissions. "The truth is, we know we need to continue to improve, and that is where a bulk of our work is geared toward," he says.

AES Corporation, founded in Arlington, Virginia, in 1981, by a group of people studying low-cost environmentally concious energy strategies, found cogeneration as the key to their study.

Davis says the company is not as financially motivated as it is value based, adding that it is run with four basic values in mind: fun, fairness, integrity, and social responsibility.

For each new cogeneration plant the company builds across the country, AES sponsors major reforestation efforts. Davis says one such effort has led to the planting of 52 million trees in Guatemala. "The idea is that the trees that we plant will offset the carbon dioxide emitted," he says.

In the years ahead Applied Energy Services-Placerita will continue to supply much needed energy to Santa Clarita residents while working harder to improve its operations, keeping AES environmentally safe and sound, and maintaining AES' good neighbor status within the Santa Clarita Valley.

ABOVE: Mark Green, Plant Technician, checking gauge on the Steam Turbine

BELOW: Overall view of AES Placerita.

City of Santa Clarita

A promise is generally defined as the reason to expect something—usually success, improvement, or excellence. The residents of the newly incorporated City of Santa Clarita have made a promise to themselves and it is one that they intend to keep.

On December 15, 1987, the people of the Santa Clarita Valley voted by a two-to-one margin to take absolute control of their own destiny by agreeing to articles of incorporation, thus succeeding from the umbrella of Los Angeles County governance and becoming the largest city incorporation in the state of California. In effect, the people were voting for local control, self-determination, and easy access to government so that local services would be improved. Additionally, they hoped that their perspectives would finally be listened to and given an opportunity to mesh with ideas of their elected leaders.

Prior to incorporation, residents would often attempt to influence and lobby officials of the County or the City of Los Angeles. More often than not, those attempts at interactive government resulted in failure. Tired of being ignored, the people organized under the auspices of the Santa Clarita Valley Chamber of Commerce, then operating as a kind of quasi-government, and formed a city of some 43 square miles in a valley of more than 200 square miles. After several meetings with the Local Agency Formation Commission, a state agency charged with determining the boundaries of new cities and determining if they are economically viable, officials placed an initiative on the ballot along with a slate of candidates for city council. The resulting mandate was overwhelming with a large turnout at the polls voting in favor of the formation of a city, the right of self-determination, and the promise of a new tomorrow.

The promise of the good life has surrounded the valley throughout its colorful history. It was in the Santa Clarita Valley that the state's first gold strike was unearthed. The discovery, made six years prior to the more publicized occurrence at Sutter's Mill, began the transformation of an area where the once-ancient Alliklik Indians, wild horses, Spanish explorers, and European colonists roamed the gently

ABOVE: Thanks to the City of Santa Clarita, more than 2,300 trees have been planted in the City since incorporation. The City hosts an annual Arbor Day event every year to provide residents with tree information and to plant even more trees!

BELOW: The City of Santa Clarita celebrates Cinco De Mayo every year at Newhall Park with a pinata, folklorico dancers and ethnic treats.

rolling hills.

Henry Mayo Newhall was one of the earliest settlers in the valley in 1870, and he started the area on the road to modernization through his auctioneering and railroad interests. After purchasing Rancho San Francisco (later known as Newhall Ranch) in 1875, Newhall sold a right-of-way to the Southern Pacific Railroad for one dollar and a town site known as Newhall for another dollar. Not only did it become a rail center, but the first commercially-producing oil well began operation in nearby Pico Canyon in 1875, closely followed by the state's first oil refinery in Railroad Canyon.

In the early 1900s Hollywood chose the valley, where its rugged canyons provided appropriate backdrops for the western silent movies of the day. Still, the actual population in the valley remained relatively low.

But then, during the boom years of the 1970s and early 1980s, the valley saw unprecedented growth. Resulting partly from the outward migration from Los Angeles combined with the unique life-style and rural amenities of the area, the valley experienced a doubling of its population. Present population figures reveal approximately 150,000 permanent residents in the valley. That figure is expected to grow to nearly 300,000 by the year 2010.

The Santa Clarita Valley forms an inverted triangle with the San Gabriel and Santa Susana mountain ranges separating it from the San Fernando Valley and the Los Angeles basin to the south, and the San Joaquin Valley, Mojave desert, and Angeles Forest to the north. The Santa Clara River and its tributaries drain over 490,000 acres of mountains and canyons that form the valley.

Resting in the heart of this idyllic setting is the incorporated area of the City of Santa Clarita. It is comprised of four major communities: Newhall, Valencia, Saugus, and Canyon Country.

Newhall Land and Farming Company selected the area known as Valencia for the development of its premier master-planned community. The Spanish-style paseo system of lighted walkways with easy access between homes, schools, and shopping is an example of a perfectly planned community.

Valencia houses City Hall, the Santa Clarita Valley Chamber of Commerce and the Civic Center, which includes the Valencia library, sheriff's station, courthouse, and county services. It is also the home of Six Flags Magic Mountain amusement

ABOVE: In just two years, the City of Santa Clarita completed a 17 acre park in Canyon Country, on time and on budget!

BELOW: The City of Santa Clarita celebrates its third birthday with a 3 Mile Run, beginning at City Hall in which more than 300 people participated.

park, which brings thousands of visitors to the area. Valencia is also home to numerous students who attend the College of the Canyons and California Institute of the Arts. The Valencia Industrial Center is comprised of more than 300 firms employing 10,000 workers while providing additional jobs and business opportunities for the future.

The community of Newhall still maintains its rustic beauty in the midst of rapidly expanding developments. The oldest community in the area (established in 1876), Newhall, is the home of the Williams S. Hart Park and Museum, the beautiful Placerita Canyon Nature Center, and Heritage Park, a refuge for Santa Clarita's most historic buildings. Also located in the area are The Master's College, a four-year liberal arts Christian college, while the Newhall Hospital/Tan Medical Clinic continues to provide excellent health care.

Saugus began as a railroad stop with the Southern Pacific Railroad bisecting the area. It has continued to grow as a popular residential area on its gentle rolling hills and in its canyons. As the population of the area has grown, businesses have flourished. Examples of this growth include Santa Clarita Place, a newly refurbished shopping center, and Bouquet Canyon Center. Saugus is also home to the famous Saugus Speedway where exciting car races and the Sunday swap meet are held.

Canyon Country is the site of diverse residential developments offering a variety of price ranges. The rural atmosphere is heightened by the number of equestrian estates scattered throughout the canyons. Sand Canyon, bordering Highway 14, is an ideal residential area with excellent shopping nearby, including a Price Club.

Soledad Canyon Road, which runs directly through Canyon Country, is the main shopping artery of Santa Clarita. In addition, the recent opening of the 17 acre Canyon Country Park, the largest park in Santa Clarita, and the five acre Begonias Lane Park provide a wide variety of recreational activities for children and adults alike.

Surrounding the incorporated City of Santa Clarita are the communities of Castaic, Val Verde, and Agua Dulce, which remain part of Los Angeles County.

Castaic, known as the gateway to the Santa Clarita Valley, is a major recreational center. Castaic Lake provides swimming, fishing, boating, and waterskiing. Val

ABOVE: Santa Clarita youth enjoy seasonal events at local parks, including an Easter Egg Hunt and related festivities.

BELOW: The City of Santa Clarita began a new transit service, providing 11 bus routes, 13 local transit buses, 10 Dial-a-Ride vans and 9 commuter buses for transportation to Los Angeles and Century City.

Verde, a small, active community, still maintains its rural charm with the residents striving to maintain the natural beauty of their surroundings. And finally there is Agua Dulce (meaning "sweet water"), where the famed Vasquez Rocks continue to draw numerous visitors and film crews, while providing a beautiful backdrop to the horse ranches and country-style homes in the area.

Interstate 5 is the major artery for north/south traffic through the valley, linking it with Los Angeles and San Diego to the south, and Bakersfield and San Francisco to the north. Highway 14, the so-called Antelope Freeway, emanates from the northern San Fernando Valley and is utilized by traffic going to the Palmdale/Lancaster area and Las Vegas. In the planning stages is a realignment of Highway 126, which eventually will become an expressway crossing the northern portion of the valley and linking I-5 with Highway 14.

The entire valley is blessed with Southern California's much-heralded Mediterranean climate: Summers are warm, dry, and sunny, with highs in the 90s and lows in the 60s. Winters are temperate and semi-moist, with highs in the 60s and lows in the 40s. Moderate rain of about 15 to 18 inches falls between November and March. The skies are mostly sunny the remainder of the year.

Businesses moving to Santa Clarita can choose from many locations, either leasing existing space or building to suit their needs. Companies that build or buy facilities will realize a generous return on their investment due to the continued escalation of the area's real estate values.

At present, the Valencia Industrial Center is the fourth-largest industrial park in Los Angeles County and the valley's leading source of employment. The center's 1,500-acre site has seven million square feet for light industry and a potential for 11 million square feet.

Other industrial and commercial parks throughout the valley offer facilities for small and medium-size businesses, including room for expansion, and parks under development will substantially increase the number of square feet available for industrial and commercial use. The City of Santa Clarita's "Pro Business" policies continue to encourage an influx of new businesses.

The film and television industry does an extensive amount of production work in the valley. A new $10-million, six-stage film studio has been constructed that will further

ABOVE: The City recognizes the importance of its youth and sponsors an annual "Youth in Government" program for junior and senior high school students.

BELOW: Hundreds of Santa Clarita residents enjoyed free concerts and theater in the parks during the summer at various city parks.

expand the area's production capabilities.

Santa Clarita's strong continued consumer demand, generated by its rapid population growth, has already drawn more than 5,000 retail businesses to the area that has resulted in a considerable upward curve in retail sales. The valley's many fine shopping centers come in a variety of shapes and sizes and can be found throughout the area. The newest and largest of these centers, now under construction, will be a $180-million regional shopping center. When completed, it will have 1.5 million square feet of retail space in a two-level enclosed mall, six major department store anchors, and 160 shops. The new mall will occupy an 80-acre site in the heart of Valencia. Its first phase is expected to open in late 1992, with three major department stores and 700,000 square feet of retail space.

The valley's 50 child-care facilities provide a full range of programs: preschool, cooperative, school age, year round, infant, parent/toddler, kindergarten, and special education. For primary and secondary education, the area has six public school districts that include 21 elementary schools, three junior high schools, five senior high schools, and an adult education program.

Overall, valley students consistently score high on statewide academic tests, putting area schools among the top 20 percent in the state. And more than 70 percent of those who graduate high school go on to four-year or community colleges. The valley itself has three institutions of higher learning: California Institute of the Arts, the nation's first fully accredited, four-year visual and performing arts college; The Master's College, a Christian-oriented four-year liberal arts college; and the College of the Canyons, a fully accredited two-year community college.

The major medical centers serving the valley rank with the best of any large city. Using the latest medical techniques and technologies, these centers provide the full spectrum of diagnostic, acute-care, and trauma services.

In addition, the valley offers more than 60 places of worship encompassing most religious beliefs. And, throughout the valley, there are nearly 200 clubs and organizations for people of all ages.

Today the City of Santa Clarita has a city council/city manager structure of government, common among California cities. The council is a part-time legislative and policy-making body with five members,

ABOVE: More than 250 Santa Clarita Valley residents served in Operation Desert Storm. The City erected a flag at City Hall for each of the soldiers, with their names on them, which remained at City Hall until the end of the war. Each soldier received their flag at a 4th of July celebration..

elected at large on a nonpartisan basis, which enact ordinances and resolutions essential to the city. The meetings are open to the public. The city manager, the city's chief executive officer, oversees all city operations.

The newly incorporated city only recently adopted its general plan. The plan functions as the city's master plan for guiding and improving economic development and quality of life. Included in the published plan are long-term standards for land use, transportation, housing, noise, safety, air quality, and much more.

The Santa Clarita Valley represents the perfect location for companies that want to capitalize on the region within a 40 mile radius of downtown Los Angeles. The Santa Clarita Valley's high concentration of capital, labor, transportation, energy, and other vital assets make it a strong, economically viable community.

Among the wealth of resources in L.A. County is its population of more than 13 million people, of which Santa Clarita is a part of, giving it the second-largest labor market in the United States. In addition, L.A. County is a major trade center for nations worldwide and for Pacific Rim countries in particular; its ports of Los Angeles and Long Beach handle the highest tonnage in the nation; and Los Angeles International Airport has the third-largest U.S. passenger volume.

For companies seeking easy, profitable access to the circle's solid-gold economy, relocation to the Santa Clarita Valley is the strategy of choice.

Says city manager George Caravalho, "The citizenry of the Santa Clarita Valley represents the quality of people that can create the finest twenty-first century city in the State of California. This is especially true in terms of providing a solid economic foundation for the future. We at city hall, feel very good about the positive gains made so far in the development of our community. We promise to do even more in the future."

The promise of a new future is unfolding before the people of the Santa Clarita Valley. They took a calculated gamble a few short years ago and promised themselves something better. They promised themselves a successful city, bursting with innovation and excellence in all phases of community life. Judging from its track record and its supporters' obvious pride, the City of Santa Clarita represents the promise of a new and better tomorrow, a promise that should last forever.

Castaic Lake Water Agency

With their sights set on the future, Santa Clarita Valley's visionary leaders of the early 1960s laid plans to assure residents and those looking to relocate to the northwestern area of Los Angeles County and within the Santa Clara River watershed that an adequate water supply would be available. To that end, the Upper Santa Clara Water Agency was formed in 1962, changing its name to the Castaic Lake Water Agency (CLWA) in 1970. The agency was founded through the combined efforts of the Bouquet Canyon Water Co. (now known as the Santa Clarita Water Co.), The Newhall Land and Farming Co., and other water users in the Santa Clarita Valley.

However, it was the first members of the agency's board of directors and the agency's founders that paved the way to ensuring that the valley would be adequately supplied with the precious resource of water. Members serving on that first board were William G. Bonelli, Jr., Robert L. Essick, Ray Fisher, O.L. Martin, Roger C. Morey, Everett W. Nichols, and Earl Schmidt. Max Bookman of Bookman and Edmonston Engineering, Inc., and Stanley C. Lagerlof of Burris & Lagerlof were retained as the agency's engineer and attorney, respectively.

"Creating the agency was very important for this valley because of the limited groundwater that was available," explains Betty L. Castleberry, former Secretary of the Castaic Lake Water Agency. Castleberry, who retired after 26 years with the agency in 1992, believes the foresight of the agency has paid off handsomely. "The growth of business and housing in this valley has made it an ideal location for people to settle," she says. Through the years the water agency has kept pace with the increased water demands of the community, says Robert C. Sagehorn, general manager of the agency since 1980.

In 1963 the agency contracted with the State of California for 26,500 acre feet of water supply. Three years later the contract was increased to 41,500 acre feet.

Early agency leaders had to overcome adversity from those who shunned the need for more water in the valley. After failing in its initial effort, the CLWA in 1976 obtained voter approval of an $18.6-million bond issue to finance construction of a 12.5-million-gallon-per-day water-treatment plant and the necessary transmission pipelines that were as large as 54 inches in diameter.

The Earl Schmidt Filtration Plant, located in Castaic and named after one of the early members of the agency's board of directors, began operation in 1980. The facility was expanded in 1986 to a capacity of 25 million gallons per day.

Toward the mid-1980s the CLWA, led by Sagehorn, studied development plans being approved for the valley and began a search for additional sources to increase the water supply. In 1987 an opening arose that would afford the agency that opportunity. A corporation, which owned and farmed in Kings and Kern counties, found that its cotton crop had become pro-

ABOVE: 25 Million gallon per day Earl Schmidt Water Treatment Plant at Castaic Lake. Photo by Air Views

ABOVE, RIGHT: Angelina Gleason, CLWA Chemist, examines tubes and Jonie Wyatt, laboratory assistant, take notes during water quality check at the Earl Schmidt Water Treatmnet Plant. Photo by Creative Image Photography

hibitively expensive to irrigate with state water served by the Devil's Den Water District.

"They agreed to sell their land to the Castaic Lake Water Agency," Sagehorn recalls. In October 1988 Devil's Den Ranch and its 8,454 acres became the property of the CLWA. A contract amendment with the Department of Water Resources in 1991 transferred 12,700 acre feet of the State Water Project entitlement of the Devil's Den Water District to the Castaic Lake Water Agency and increased the agency entitlement to 54,000 acre feet.

Financial planning for the extensive local treatment and transmission facilities needed beyond the year 1990 led the agency to seek increased authority to charge facility capacity fees to new development and to implement a stand-by charge. Secured by the expanded financial authority of the agency, a $132-million issue of Certificates of Participation was sold during 1990. The major improvements to the agency water system planned for construction with the financing include a second water-filtration plant and the initial phase at a reclaimed water distribution project. The second plant, named the Rio Vista Water Treatment Plant, is being built on the site of the former City of Los Angeles' Saugus Rehabilitation Center. Bids for construction were called for during the fall of 1991 with completion of construction slated for early 1994. The project will include agency administrative facilities and will feature a garden that focuses on low-water use plants and trees. Tours of the garden and instruction on plants, planting material, and irrigation will offer the public an opportunity to learn methods of beautifying home and business by maximizing the use of a minimal amount of water.

"We see reclaimed water as an important element in the future water supply picture," says Sagehorn. "We are planning for our reclaimed water project to treat water from the Los Angeles County Sanitation District facilities for use in irrigating golf courses, freeway landscaping, and other non-potable needs."

CLWA's growth is clearly dictated by the demands placed upon it by development approved by city and county. "We continually analyze the future demand estimates of developments in the approval process and advise the planners of the limits of the available water supply," states Sagehorn. "We plan and construct additional water supply projects to maintain a comfortable lead on the service needed." In the future CLWA will continue to look for additional sources of water and will maintain a focus on methods to conserve and reclaim. If history is any indicator, CLWA will continue to be in the right place at the right time, allowing the Southern California residents of the Santa Clarita Valley to rely on an ample supply of high-quality water.

C.A. Rasmussen Inc.

C.A. Rasmussen Inc. is one of the dominant firms of the Santa Clarita Valley, helping develop the city's business community.

The heavy-equipment company was already seven years old in 1971 when it came to the aid of the developers of Magic Mountain. The theme park was just months from opening and the developers recognized they would need an alternate route into the park—one that would have to be built quickly in time for the grand opening.

Rasmussen put all the equipment it had on the project, undertaking unfamiliar specialty work, such as a large storm drain. The firm not only finished the job on time, but it won praise for the quality of its work. The Magic Mountain contract marked a new beginning for C.A. Rasmussen, showcasing its ability to handle difficult projects on a tight schedule.

Since then, C.A. Rasmussen's clients have included builders who have been active in the Santa Clarita Valley, such as American Beauty Homes, Kaufman and Broad of Southern California Inc., Larwin

ABOVE: C.A. Rasmussen, Inc., purchased the first Caterpillar D10 tractor in Southern California in 1979. Its debut marked a milestone in local construction history. Vicki Rasmussen, Dean's wife, inaugurates the new Cat D10.

LEFT: Rasmussen takes pride in its position as an industry innovator. All equipment and methods used by the company are state of the art.

Construction, Saunders Development, Southern California Gas Company, The Newhall Land and Farming Company, Warmington Homes, and Watt America. Other clients range from the County of Los Angeles to Jet Propulsion Laboratory to Security Pacific National Bank.

C.A. Rasmussen Inc. was founded in 1964 at a time when the Simi Valley was beginning to develop. Its founder, Carl Rasmussen, left M.L. Wilson Company of Simi Valley to start C.A. Rasmussen.

Carl Rasmussen soon brought his sons, Dean, Larry, and Charlie, into the business. In 1978 Carl rewarded their efforts by selling the company to them.

The company's highlights include an equipment demonstration in the late 1970s. The event, held at the intersection of Sand Canyon and Soledad Canyon roads, celebrated delivery of the first Cat D10 to Southern California.

The firm Carl Rasmussen started has become the largest of its kind in Southern California, operating more than 250 pieces of heavy equipment, including seven Cat D10 tractors and 19 D9Ls. The equipment is capable of moving from 25,000 to 50,000 yards daily. The payroll includes more than 500 union workers, more than 300 of which are operating engineers. C.A. Rasmussen Inc. endeavors to keep its employees to eight-hour days. In addition to realizing that employees work better when they have time to go home and get a full-night's rest, C.A. Rasmussen Inc. also wants its employees to have full lives outside of work.

C.A. Rasmussen Inc. is headquartered in Simi Valley. Its market area includes all of Southern California, especially the western San Fernando Valley and the Santa Clarita and Antelope valleys.

RIGHT: Company founder Carl A. Rasmussen, seen here in 1972, envisioned a promising future through innovation.

BELOW: C.A. Rasumussen's corporate office, located at 2360 Shasta Way in Simi Valley.

Newhall School District

The Newhall School District has its roots in the nineteenth century, but it is moving into the twenty-first century as a modern elementary school district, ranking among the top 10 percent of California districts in academic achievement.

As it enters the 1992-93 school year, the district is expecting an enrollment of almost 5,000 students in grades kindergarten through sixth, a full-time faculty of almost 200 teachers, and a support staff of about 250 people.

It is a far cry from the size of the district when it first opened. In 1879-1880 there were only 53 school-age children living in Newhall, and an average of only seven attended school each day. The most students to show up at one time was 13. Today the district boasts an outstanding attendance rate of more than 95 percent— close to 99 percent counting excused absences.

The first school in Newhall actually opened in 1878, but it was one student short of the necessary seven to be officially recognized. The first teacher was Kate A. Kaystile, and the school was held in the Sanford Lynn home on U.S. Highway 99.

In 1879 a school building was constructed on the northeast corner of Ninth and Walnut. That building was destroyed by fire in 1890. A residence at 719 Spruce Street was used until another building could be built at Ninth and Walnut.

In 1892 the school was enlarged to two rooms for an enrollment of 60 students. The school taught through the ninth grade until 1899.

Since the site was too small to accommodate expansion, a new two-story, three-room building was built on the corner of Newhall Avenue and what is now Lyons Avenue (then called Pico Road).

Newhall School moved to is present site on Walnut Street in 1928, although the original building, except for a few rooms in the north wing, was destroyed by fire on Valentine's Day in 1939. Gradually the school was rebuilt on the same site, starting in 1939 with additions in 1946, 1950, 1954, and 1958.

As the student population expanded, other schools were added to the district. Peachland Avenue Elementary was built in the 1950s, Wiley Canyon in 1966, Old Orchard in 1971, Meadows in 1976, and Valencia Valley in 1988. The average class size was 29 students as of mid-1992.

A rapidly growing district, Newhall currently has almost 1000 students in portable classrooms and is introducing multi-track year-round education in an effort to house its growing student population until financing can be found for new schools.

District superintendent is J.M. McGrath, Ed.D., who has held the position since 1972. He was previously a teacher, assistant principal, and principal in the district, and his mother taught kindergarten in the district for 12 years.

RIGHT: The first Newhall Elementary School was long on Victorian architecture but short on modern facilities. This three-room building was located on the corner of Newhall Avenue and what is now Lyons Avenue (then called Pico Road). It boasted 42 pupils when this class photo was taken. Photo courtesy Santa Clarita Valley Historical Society

BELOW: Valencia Valley School is the district's newest campus, which opened in 1988. The school has more than 800 students this year, in grades kindergarten through sixth.

Patterson & Neavitt

"I believe you can assess the quality of a law firm by what its attorneys contribute to the community in which they work," says Richard A. Patterson, co-founder and partner in the law firm of Patterson & Neavitt.

Calvin Coolidge once said, *"No successful enterprise can exist for itself alone, it ministers to some great need. It must perform some great need. It must provide some great service, not for itself but for others or failing therein, it ceases to be profitable and ceases to exist."*

Judging by the quantity of community service donated by the lawyers of Santa Clarita's oldest and largest law office, this is one successful legal firm indeed.

Vitally active in nearly all aspects of our community's life since 1973, Patterson and Neavitt are two of those rare individuals who fashion a plan and then stick to it until success is achieved. Patterson attributes his pattern of setting high goals to his wife Ann. "She has always been generous with her confidence in me and as a result I have been able to achieve goals, which, I myself, would not have thought possible."

When asked about his reputation for being an aggressive negotiator and his involvement in facilitating many of the major business transactions in the Santa Clarita Valley, his response was, "Our clients understand the importance of obtaining sound legal advice in any legal transaction, whether it involves the sale of a corporation or negotiating with a tight-fisted insurance adjuster over an injury claim. Clients expect value for the fees they pay." Then with a smile he asked, "Who wants a wishy-washy attorney when your life or future is on the line? We don't mind letting the opposition get up to bat and take a few swings, but we insist on winning the game.

"We find it easy to be committed to winning because our representation is limited to clients and cases we believe in."

His partner, James T. Neavitt, is equally successful. He enjoys the elite designation of being a Certified Specialist in Family Law, a distinction achieved by less than one percent of all practicing attorneys in California. Neavitt enjoys a state-wide reputation among his peers as an accomplished litigator specializing in major divorce, child custody and spousal support cases. Most of his waking hours are spent in trial.

In addition to directing the affairs of Patterson and Neavitt, Patterson is also a successful businessman. He and a couple of close friends founded the Valencia National Bank in 1987, now the only community owned bank in Santa Clarita. It became profitable in just its second year and today has some $60 million in assets which are used to support local businesses and consumers.

Together, Patterson & Neavitt have assembled a high quality staff of attorneys, paralegals, legal secretaries and clerks. Their primary areas of practice encompass Personal Injury, Family Law, Business and Real Estate, Probate and Estate Planning.

But it is these individuals' care and concern for the community that elevates them to even higher levels. As a group, the firm touches nearly every aspect of community life in the Santa Clarita Valley. Activities include involvement with Food Pantry, the

> *"We find it easy to be committed to winning because our representation is limited to clients and cases we believe in."*

STANDING: James T. Neavitt
SEATED: Richard A. Patterson

Rotary Club, the College of the Canyons, Boy Scouts and the Parks and Recreation Department. They are also active in the hospital's "I Can Cope" program, which provides legal advice to patients with serious or terminal illness. In addition, Patterson serves as Bishop in the Church of Jesus Christ of Latter Day Saints.

When asked about his thoughts concerning the firm's rise to the top of the legal firms in Santa Clarita, the unassuming Patterson simply says, "I see the Santa Clarita Valley as a land of opportunity for anyone who is willing to work hard and strives to give something back to the community. I've seen many people move here and do just that. Invariably, they are successful."

Valencia Country Club

The world's most renowned golf course architect, Robert Trent Jones, Sr., has not forgotten the diamond he created in Valencia.

Every hole he designs is intended to be a difficult par and an easy bogey. He has said no course better typifies that philosophy than the Valencia Country Club.

Talking to club officials in 1991, Jones spoke of the course as if it were a fine wine. "It is particularly gratifying to see how well it has maintained its golfing challenge over the years," he said. "Indeed, the challenge seems to have been enhanced by a natural maturing process that was begun 27 years ago. For example, the par-three third, one of my all-time favorites, is still one of the great short holes anywhere."

Jones has designed hundreds of golf courses, criss-crossing both the nation and world to do it, so he was choosing from a large and illustrious number of holes.

And Jones was as complimentary of the entire course as he was of a single hole. "Valencia Country Club is considered to be one of the great golf courses in this country today," he said.

Through the years a chorus of voices has joined Jones in praising the course. Notable are the things that were said when the course opened in 1965, offering 105 sand traps, eight holes with water hazards, long tees, 12 dog-leg fairways, and large greens.

"You may need an illegal ball to stay out of the lakes," wrote *Los Angeles Times* staffer Bill Shirley.

"I was proud of Valencia when I designed it," said Jones, during an in-person return visit to Valencia in 1991, 26 years after it opened as a then-public golf course, "and I'm proud of it today. It has character, even more so now with the trees and foliage that have grown. This course is an excellent test of golf. Each green has good shot value. I'm really pleased with it," he added.

Thompson promised that the course would gain favor as one of the most challenging and attractive in Los Angeles County.

Art Rosenbaum of the *San Francisco Chronicle* called the Valencia course "gorgeous but treacherous."

An editorial in *The Signal* suggested that even non-golfers might want to visit the golf course to note its beauty. The editorial urged visitors to find out just how captivating the course is, describing it as an "enchanted garden" and a "fragrant oasis."

In 1984 the course was named one of the 75 best public courses in America. It has been the site for PGA qualifying rounds, and it was one of four Southern California courses named as a qualifying site for the 1992 U.S. Open and will host

A 45,500-square-foot country club is one of the many new features at Valencia Country Club.

ABOVE: Even non-golfers visit the course to enjoy its beauty.

RIGHT: Large bunkers and rolling greens at the Valencia Country Club are trademarks of courses designed by Robert Trent Jones, Sr.

Sectional Qualifying for the 1993 U.S. Open, one of just 13 clubs in the nation to be so selected.

Today, a mature golf sanctuary of sculpted terrain, crystalline lakes, lush green foliage and towering shades trees, the Valenica Country Club is a more stunning test to a golfer than ever.

With the coming of more hotel rooms in the area, the course is being touted as a possible site for a PGA tour tournament.

It is one of the few courses anywhere with a three-stroke differential between Blue (championship) and White (regular) tees, offering a course rating of 73.7 and 70.8 respectively.

Total yardage ranges from 7,105 for the the Gold to 5,733 for the Red, virtually making the course four courses in one, allowing for comfortable adjustment to a golfer's ability without forsaking its demand for strategy and accuracy.

The third hole (which was the 12th hole before the course was recently restructured) remains one of the toughest par threes in golf, demanding a long, true drive to a deceptive green sloping toward a lake on the right.

The 16th hole (previously the seventh) also continues to draw attention. Surrounded by four cavernous bunkers, it can only be reached by an all-carry straight drive over a tee-to-green lake.

The back nine's fitting finale is the prodigious 18th hole, a 567-yard, par-5 hole that requires a solid fairway distance and a delicate approach and putting.

Uniden Corporation, which purchased the golf course in 1985 and converted it to a private course two years later, has been mindful not only of preserving the quality of the course itself, but also of providing amenities equal to it. A two-tiered clubhouse on 45,500 square feet has been completed, offering a pro shop, locker rooms, snack bar, and an elegant dining room. The Inagiku Restaurant provides a top-notch Japanese-style dining experience. Uniden's care for the Valencia Country Club stems from the company's commitment to excellence. Established in 1966 as a small manufacturer of citizens band radios, Uniden has established its reputation as one of the world's top specialists in radio communications. Uniden's business now ranges from electronic components to cosmetics to travel services.

Its Valencia office, charged with caring for the Valencia Country Club, employs about 120 people. Their responsibility is to maintain a Robert Trent Jones, Sr., golf course that made history from the moment it opened. At that time it was the first public course Jones had designed in Southern California. And now it is gaining stature as a private course.

Santa Clarita Valley Association of Realtors ®

By becoming a member of the Santa Clarita Valley Association of Realtors (SCVR), more than 1,000 professional real estate agents and brokers have made a strong statement to the community in which they reside and do business.

According to the Santa Clarita Valley Association of Realtors®, the association is made up of members of the community. Usuallly, when people conjure up the image of Realtors they think of a bunch of people who only sell homes and make money. What they don't realize is that 95 percent of the association membership lives and works in the Santa Clarita Valley. Our members share the same concerns about our schools, overcrowding, roads, and unchecked growth. While the association is an advocate of a growing community, it seeks growth that is organized and environmentally compatible with the community.

And, in order to assist the community in organized, quality growth, members of the SCVAR give unselfishly of their time and resources.

One of our most popular volunteer programs is the "Sing No to Drugs" program. Begun in 1990 in the Saugus, Sulphur Springs, and Newhall school districts, the program involved more than 4,000 first, second, and third-grade youngsters. The Santa Clarita Valley Association of Realtors contributed kits that included coloring books with songs accompanying the pictures, peel-off stickers, and audiocassettes with 10 anti-drug messages. In addition, each school received a videotape as a teaching tool. Using the videotape in the classroom provided a background for open discussion about the dangers of drug use. Association leaders agree that the popularity of the program will lead to an expansion of this positive campaign.

Another top priority of the SCVAR is rasing monies for the College of the Canyons Foundation and the SCV Scholarship Foundation. In order to raise the funds, the association holds an Annual Las Vegas Night. In addition to the money raised during the evening's festivities, the association also pledges up to $5,000 in matching funds. Each year the association releases thousands of dollars for scholarships for eligible students from William S. Hart High

Photos Above and opposite page by Creative Image Photography

School District and the College of the Canyons.

Many members of the SCVAR also participate in an annual golf tournament. Although designed to be exciting and encourage competition, the tournament also accomplishes the more important goal of charity to the community. Each year the proceeds from the event are equally divided between the American Red Cross and the Santa Clarita Senior Citizens Center.

Issues of even bigger importance are also of concern to the organization. One good example of this concern is the SCVAR's commitment in helping to solve the problem of hunger across the state and throughout the nation. To this end, members continue to actively support the annual Christmas Cantree canned food drive program. Members not only donated thousands of canned good items but also gave money and resources to the cause. Working in tandem with other area community groups, the effort effectively symbolizes the aggressive volunteerism spirit present in the residents of the Santa Clarita Valley.

As an association, the SCVAR's primary goal is to promote and maintain high standards of conduct in the real estate profession by conducting real estate transactions with competence and integrity as expressed by the code of ethics of the National Association of Realtors (NAR), the association's parent body. In addition, the association is the only organized protector of private property rights in the country. Association committees monitor and lobby local, state, and national legislatures about pending bills affecting private property.

Established in 1965, the SCVAR also provides its members with continuing education, research services, and experience. Governed by 18 realtor members elected by the respective membership, the SCVAR sets policy within the framework of its bylaws, the professional standards rules, and nonprofit corporation laws. Its parent body, the NAR, is comprised of more than 800,000 members nationwide and represents the largest trade organization in the nation.

Members of this multi-level organization are also provided with a multiple listing publication, produced annually, which contains a comprehensive list of homes and property on the market; hundreds of forms standardized to meet the ever-complex field of transferring property; and an ongoing educational process to keep realtors in touch with changes in the industry. Additionally, members can access a legal hotline to help them understand the nuances in the area of real estate law.

The association, similar to the valley itself, has experienced unparalled growth during the past few years, growing from approximately 500 members to more than 1,000 today. In order to meet the demands of its increasing membership, the association's directors, with the approval of the membership, have begun construction on a new facility to house the SCVAR. Scheduled to be completed in 1993, the 15,000-square-foot facility will be located on a two-acre parcel of land on Redview Drive off of Golden Triangle Road. In addition to office space, the new building will also feature banquet rooms and training facilities.

With an eye to the future, the Santa Clarita Valley Association of Realtors continues to meet the needs and demands of its members as well as the community that it so proudly serves.

WILLIAMS INSTRUMENT COMPANY, INC.

James F. Williams, founder and president of Williams Instrument Company, Inc., has reason to be proud.

"More than half of the pneumatic chemical injectors made are based on our designs and concepts," he told his employees in a company publication in 1985. "Now that is flattery."

Williams Instrument Company has continued its influential role. The firm has now passed its 25th anniversary and is entrenched as one of the giants of the industry.

James Williams was working for Pacific Lighting Gas & Supply Company when the seeds for Williams Instrument were planted. Williams became aware of the need for several products not on the market, so he roughed out sketches on everything from drafting paper to napkins, then began building prototypes on the kitchen table and garage workbench.

Some of the items Williams designed used electric current in corrosion. He also designed control panels, battery backup devices, and natural-gas odorization devices.

Pacific Lighting Gas & Supply Company, realizing the need for the products, backed Williams' efforts and became one of his first customers. Many of Williams' co-workers helped him out during those early years—assistance for which Williams remains grateful.

In 1965 Jim and his wife, Dorothy, mortgaged their personal property to finance the founding of Williams Instrument Company Inc. They had been working part time on the business, but they had realized it would take a full-time effort if the project was to succeed.

Part of a building in Pacoima served as the company's first permanent home in 1965. The budget was tight in those early years, but the introduction of the oscillamatic controller and pump in 1967 sparked a sales upswing, helping the company as it began to put its lean years behind. By 1972 sales had increased so much that the company was able to buy the rest of the building.

The odorant and chemical pump lines expanded, eventually including custom-engineered systems and accessories. Filters and valves were also developed.

When the firm grew out of the Pacoima facility in 1979, it moved into a 12,000-square-foot building in Valencia. As sales continued to grow, the company purchased its own machining company in 1982 in order to maintain better control over the

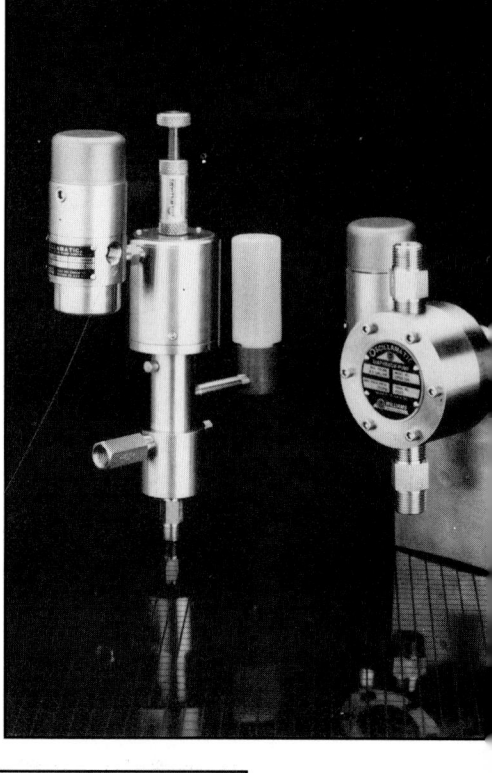

One of the original designs of the Williams pneumatic metering pumps (BELOW) and "present-day" designs of the Williams pneumatic metering pumps (RIGHT). This is what the customer would purchase in the 1990's as contrasted to the other photo, which shows one of the original designs in the late 1960s.

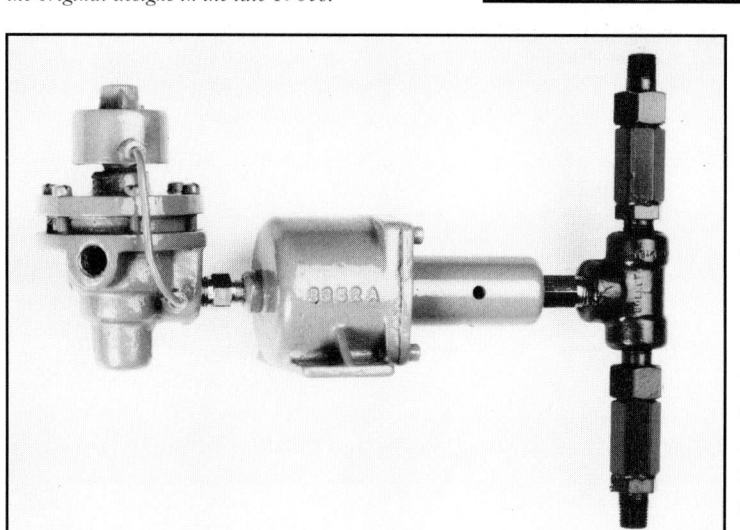

quality of its products. The first overseas office opened in Aberdeen, Scotland, in 1980. Four years later, an office was opened in Edmonton, Canada. An office in Singapore started up in 1986. As the international business continued to grow, the company also opened sales offices throughout the United States. Williams offices service the authorized distributor network that has been expanded worldwide.

Williams Instrument Company's pneumatic metering pumps and chemical injection systems are used in many different ways. For example, some applications are the metering of chemicals used in refining oil; measuring solutions to control Ph levels in water treatment; the metering of biocides, liquid caustics, defoamers, corrosive control chemicals, and solvents in the pulp and paper industry; monitoring chemicals used to treat boiler feed water for corrosion and scale control at power generation plants; the metering of chemicals used in food processing and the pharmaceutical industry; and the metering of chemicals in such industries as fertilizer, plastics, paint, foundries, textiles, electronics, shipping, rubber, printing, and cement.

James F. Williams, the son of textile mill workers, grew up in the Carolinas. He joined the U.S. Navy in 1942 when he was 17. He served with distinction on two ships, seeing combat in both the northern and southern Atlantic, the Mediterranean Sea and the Pacific.

Returning to California in 1950, Williams went to Bakersfield, where he met and married Dorothy Jeffrey.

Williams' early jobs ranged from farm worker to insurance salesman to appliance salesman to operator of a government surplus store. After he was promoted to manager of the government supply store, he was given a chance to buy a store in Taft, California. Unfortunately, the outbreak of the Korean War eliminated the supply of government surplus items. At Pacific Lighting & Gas Supply Company, Williams began as a construction worker, then progressed to instrument foreman.

Williams Instrument Company, Inc., has built its reputation on a commitment to quality design and quality manufacturing. The firm is firmly committed to expanding its product lines, improving the products it has, and promoting its operations worldwide.

At the time of the company's 25th anniversary, James F. Williams says the company will continue to manufacture all of its products in Valencia, as well as conduct its research and development at the Valencia office.

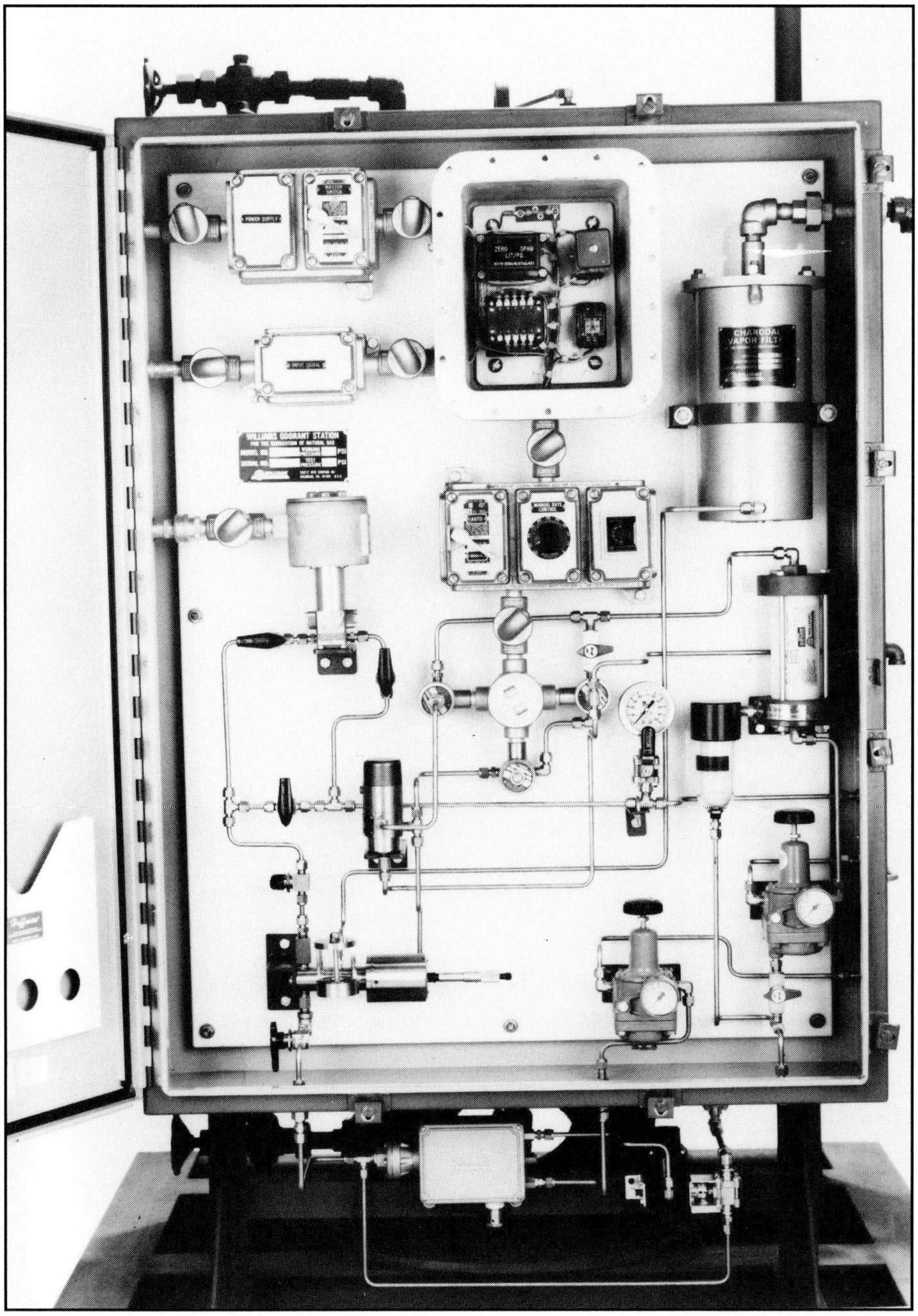

ABOVE: This is a photo of a B-100 odorizing pump being tested in a Baytown, Texas, plant in 1967. This pump was the result of William's background at Pacific Gas & Supply Company, and his knowledge for the need of a way to accurately inject odorant into a gas pipeline.

LEFT: This is a photo of a "present day" design of a Williams odorizing system that features a Williams pump (lower left corner). This is in contrast to the system (ABOVE) that shows one of the first odorizing pumps that did not include the sophistication of the current odorant systems.

SIKAND ENGINEERING

Since 1959 Sikand has been committed to a tradition of excellence, innovation, and technological improvement. Backed by the extensive professional experience gained through more than three decades of service, Sikand continues to provide the highest quality of civil engineering, surveying, and land planning and environmental services to private developers, public agencies, and municipalities. To date, Sikand has provided services for improvements valued in excess of one billion dollars. To find a high-quality civil engineering firm that has successfully shaped much of Los Angeles County and its environs, a Southern California developer or home-builder need look no farther than Sikand Engineering of Van Nuys, California.

Besides being one of the largest construction surveyors in the Los Angeles area, Sikand is adept in all phases of residential, commercial, and industrial development. The firm is noted for its expertise in hillside design, but its capabilities range from computer-aided design of tract maps to creating whole new infrastructures for communities responding to the fast-paced growth of the area.

This enterprising and dynamic firm had its auspicious beginnings in India, where its founder and president, Gunjit Sikand, earned a bachelor's degree from the University of East Punjab. From there Sikand ventured to the United States, where in 1950 he earned a bachelor of civil engineering degree from Auburn and a master's degree in civil engineering from the University of Colorado in 1953. Five years later he settled in Los Angeles, and it was there that the foundations for Sikand Engineering Associates were laid.

Sikand began teaching at California State University, Los Angeles, and a year later, with a partner, formed his own consulting firm. In 1964 Sikand bought out his partner and changed the name of the company to Sikand Engineering Associates. Nine years later Sikand's home office settled at 15230 Burbank Boulevard in Van Nuys, the company's current address. Satellite offices are located in Orange County, the Antelope Valley, and the Inland Empire.

Gunjit Sikand's professional affiliations are impressive. A member of the Urban Land Institute, he also serves on the board of the California Council of Civil Engineers and Land Surveyors (CCCE&LS) and is past president of its Los Angeles chapter. He stays connected to the education community as Professor Emeritus at California State University, Los Angeles, as a member of the advisory board of its School of Engineering, and as a member of the board of counselors of the School of Urban and Regional Planning at the University of Southern California. The central theme of these organizations is a commitment to design excellence and professionalism within the engineering community, a theme that is readily apparent at Sikand.

Sikand's junior partner, executive vice president, and head of planning, Ronald R. Horn is equally well qualified. Also a registered civil engineer, he earned a bachelor's degree in civil engineering in 1962. Horn serves as state chairman of Community

Gunjit Sikand, founder and president of Sikand, brings more than 30 years of experience to every project with his personal touch.

Planning & Enviormental Affairs for CCCE&LS (1990-92) and is past president of the L.A. County Chapter. He will serve as its 1992-93 Chairman of the Board of Directors for the recently merged Consulting Engineers and Land Surveyors of California (CELSOC) comprised of CCCE&LS and CEAC. In the Santa Clarita Valley, Horn serves on the board of directors for both the Henry Mayo Newhall Memorial Hospital Foundation and the Boys and Girls Club, and on various committees and task forces for such things as the City of Santa Clarita Hillside Ordinance, and transportation planning of the Route 126 Corridor. Horn has also served as a part-time faculty member at California State University (L.A.) and as a speaker at local governmental planning seminars.

Other key members of Sikand's talented staff include Kurt Rheinfurth, a licensed architect and director of planning, and vice presidents Gerald R. Price and Mark R. Sikand, both of whom had extensive experience with Los Angeles County's Flood Control District before joining the firm.

Sikand's award-winning and ongoing projects give best testimony to the company's talents and capabilities as a whole. Working hand-in-hand with the Santa Clarita Valley's largest and most respected

Ron Horn, executive vice president at Sikand, has been a key player in the development of Valencia.

developer, The Newhall Land and Farming Company, Sikand has garnered esteem while assisting the home builder in developing an entire valley.

The relationship between the two companies began with the design of a network of major highways that opened the 44,000-acre Newhall Ranch and resulted in, among many other ongoing ventures, two residential communities that received 1989 "Project of the Year" awards from the CCCE&LS. Valencia Northbridge, the winner in the engineering/surveying category, posed the challenge of designing a community of 1,800 hillside homes while preserving the privacy and views for homes already adjacent to the project. Other problems were achieving compatibility with existing MWD and CLWA water lines and relocating electrical transmission lines during construction.

Valencia Westridge was acclaimed in the planning category for its recreation-oriented community of 1,900 homes designed around a championship golf course. Preservation of the oak trees in the area was the major challenge and required an innovative cluster design of the homes. In addition, a water reclamation system was incorporated for purposes of irrigation to help solve drought-related problems in the Santa Clarita Valley.

The Valencia Commerce Center, a 1,400-acre light industrial development, is another hallmark of Sikand design excellence and presented the firm's planners and engineers with one their most unique environmental challenges. Conceived to provide needed employment in a housing-rich area, the project involved approximately 20 million cubic yards of grading while preserving specific habitats for endangered species. Sikand's innovative design for the environmentally sensitive site addressed the concerns of government agencies, local residents, and client needs, resulting in a center that accommodates a broad range of businesses and offers such recreational amenities as jogging and equestrian trails.

The expansion of the Valencia Industrial Center is another project, the primary objective of which is to provide a high school site with a capacity of 2,000 students in an

ABOVE: The Newhall Ranch as it appeared in the mid-1960s when Valencia Boulevard (S-curved road in the center of photo) was being graded for construction. Old Route 99 (now Magic Mountain Parkway) is in the foreground. A recently constructed Interstate 5 cuts in front of the Santa Susana mountains.

RIGHT: Newhall Ranch as it is today, with the City of Santa Clarita Civic Center buildings along Valencia Boulevard. The large graded area will soon be a regional shopping mall. In the distance are (left to right) California Institute of the Arts, College of the Canyons, and Six Flags Magic Mountain.

area that in the 1980s saw overcrowded schools develop into one of its chief concerns. As part of the Valencia master-planned community, the Industrial Center expansion also includes retail commercial and light industrial space and is designed to serve the growing business and educational needs of the surrounding communities. Sikand has provided services for the development of various recreational and public use facilities such as Magic Mountain amusement park, the Henry Mayo Newhall Memorial Hospital, and College of the Canyons. Residential developments, such as East Copperhill in San Francisquito Canyon and numerous developments comprising the Mountain View communities, integrate thousands of homes with acres of commercial development, schools, parks, and open space in projects that continue to reflect the master planning excellence to which Sikand commits itself.

Sikand Engineering in the 1990s will continue to grow as the firm plays a major role in reshaping the area's long-neglected infrastructure. "We want to have an active part in the reconstruction process," says Gunjit Sikand, "and help close the gap." With his firm's penchant for tackling and solving major problems, Southern California will soon see few gaps in need of closing.

M.W. Saussé & Co., Inc.

In the time-honored way of all successful entrepreneurs, Michael William "Bill" Saussé introduced his vibration control systems in 1949 because he knew he would be tapping into a potentially large market that was being served in the eastern United States, but not yet in the West.

The young engineer had worked for a vibrations control systems manufacturer following graduation from New York University, and he correctly anticipated the need for vibration isolation products for the growing air conditioning equipment industry. Thus Bill Saussé and his wife, Sheila, bravely began to manufacture and sell their own vibration control systems, which they trade registered under the name Vibrex, out of their garage in West Hollywood.

Bill Saussé knew that the real key to success lay less in the product itself than in the special engineering knowledge and skills required for the custom design for each type of installation. "That unique expertise is a rare commodity outside of our industry even now," says Mark J. Xitco, the firm's president.

Before long, the fledgling company was flourishing and could expand into better quarters in West Hollywood. In 1962 the firm moved to a larger facility in Van Nuys, and by 1964, the year Mark Xitco joined Bill Saussé, there were 11 employees and the business was continuing its dynamic growth. The company moved to its present location in a modern manufacturing plant in the Valencia Industrial Center in 1968.

Saussé's growth took its most dramatic upturn following the 1971 Sylmar earthquake, which resulted in the enactment of more stringent building codes, especially those affecting schools and hospitals.

Sheila M. Xitco, the company's general manager and daughter of the late Bill Saussé, says, "The earthquake brought with it a new, urgent awareness of the need for seismic restraints for all mechanical equipment, which from then on became an integral part of our product line."

Secretary/Treasurer Barbara A. Saussé, daughter of the founder, adds, "Our company was already widely respected both for the quality of our products and the dependability of our service, so we were in an ideal position to meet the increased demand of our services."

Today M.W. Saussé & Co., Inc., has 50 employees, serves customers in seven western states, and has sales offices in San Diego and San Francisco. It has custom designed and manufactured Vibrex systems for California Institute of the Arts and for some of the largest buildings in California, including the Moscone Convention Center in San Francisco and the Security Pacific Bank building and the First Interstate World Center in the heart of downtown Los Angeles.

Bill Saussé, who died in 1980, lived to see his dream come true, and today his widow Sheila continues to actively participate in the business they founded together. Barbara, speaking of her parents, says simply: "It is their knowledge and skills and above all, their integrity, that have been and always will be the driving force behind the company's success."

Micheal William Sausseé and his wife, Sheila M. Saussé.

Center for Women's Health

It is not by chance that the Center for Women's Health has become the most active and largest private practice at the Henry Mayo Newhall Memorial Hospital in terms of admissions, and births. Everything about this medical practice is by design.

The Center for Women's Health, established in the Santa Clarita Valley in 1978, was created to satisfy the total health requirements of women of all ages. It is designed and equipped to provide a comprehensive range of medical and health-related services in a congenial and comforting environment.

The center encourages each patient to select one of the five practicing physicians as her own personal physician. All physicians are specialists in obstetrics and gynecology, and each has a subspecialty interest and expertise. Whenever the need arises, physicians call upon the collective multidisciplinary skills and knowledge of other Center physicians in support of their efforts. With the utilization of shared expertise and multiplicity of skills, Center doctors assure patients of the most prompt, efficient, expert, and caring medical attention available.

The Center specializes in several areas of health care. Center physicians have pioneered prepared childbirth techniques and procedures and are acknowledged experts in the field of obstetrical care. Over the years new diagnostic and treatment methods have been developed, enabling physicians to more accurately prevent the loss of early pregnancies. Physicians at the Center for Women's Health utilize these newly developed concepts and technologies offering intense evaluation and attentive monitoring during the early states of pregnancy.

In addition, Center physicians provide extensive and comprehensive evaluation and treatment of infertility. Applying state-of-the-art diagnostic techniques, this intensive evaluation process encompasses male, female, and combined factors. The Center also provides the essential health care services relating to the diagnosis and treatment of both minor and major gynecological conditions. Finally, Center physicians use the latest proven technologies in hormonal therapy and preventive medicine, specifically created to satisfy the needs of older women.

Says Dr. Gary D. London, M.D., "The woman of today wants to know that her physician is up to date with all the latest medical developments. She also wants the medical facility that she visits to be big enough to handle all of her health needs, yet small enough to provide for her own personal health care." The Center for Women's Health fits those requirements and is an innovative concept in health care that has grown with the community and has succeeded admirably well.

ABOVE: Standing from left to right: James L. Creighton, Leslie I. Novikoff, Kelly T. Harkey Sitting from left to right: Charles Gassner, Garry D. London

BELOW: Center For Womens Health Staff

THE NEWHALL LAND AND FARMING COMPANY

Among the thousands who hurried west after gold was discovered at Sutter's Mill in 1848 was a young Massachusetts native named Henry Mayo Newhall. At age 24, he was already a successful auctioneer—experience that proved very useful when his prospecting efforts failed. He soon became head of San Francisco's largest auction house and, a decade later, invested some of his earnings in that city's first railroad company.

When Southern Pacific bought the railroad, Newhall received more than one million dollars and decided to buy California land, which was selling at distressed prices. During the 1870s he purchased six ranches totaling 143,000 acres at an average price of two dollars per acre. The most promising was the 48,000-acre Rancho San Francisco, now known as the Newhall Ranch, located 30 miles north of Los Angeles, on which he raised cattle, fruit, and wheat.

Newhall also sold a right-of-way to the Southern Pacific to build the tracks that would connect Los Angeles and San Francisco. He donated ranch land along the tracks, which became the site of the town of Newhall.

When Henry Newhall died in 1882, his property was inherited by his wife and five sons, who all had been urged by Henry not to sell the land. Following his advice, they incorporated their inheritance in 1883 as The Newhall Land and Farming Company.

A variety of problems plagued the company during the first half-century of its existence. Its cattle operations lost money and, with debts mounting, some of the more remote ranches were sold. In 1928 a dam burst just north of the Newhall Ranch, killing 420 people and causing widespread destruction. Another calamity, the 1929 stock market crash, wiped out the livelihood of some Newhall family members and threatened the company with bankruptcy.

At that point William Mayo, Henry Newhall's sole surviving son, made a move that was to stem the tide of misfortune. He called in his son-in-law, Atholl McBean, to take over the operation. A successful businessman, McBean instituted strict controls and soon had the company on solid footing. By 1934 the company was profitable and, in 1935, was able to resume dividend payments, which have continued without interruption to this day. Late in 1937, oil was discovered under the Newhall Ranch. The field yielded 44 producing wells, adding substantially to the company's earnings and financial stability.

With a population explosion taking place in the West after World War II, the company began to de-emphasize its cattle operations and to buy additional land to expand its farming activities around the state. When, in 1964, the state acquired a strip of land through the ranch for construction of the Golden State Freeway, the Newhall area was soon to be within a half-hour drive of downtown Los Angeles. The time for urban development had arrived.

In 1965 the company embarked on its most ambitious project to date, the development of the planned community of Valencia, located adjacent to the town of Newhall on the Newhall Ranch. The ranch was large, more than twice the size of New York City's Manhattan, and the land was contiguous, presenting planning opportunities found in few other metropolitan areas.

The Old Orchard Shopping Center, Newhall Land's first major commercial development, and the Valencia Golf Course were among the first projects opened, along with the formation of Valencia Water

Henry Mayo Newhall, founder of the company.

A rendering of Valencia Town Center, Valencia's regional shopping center which is scheduled to open in 1992.

Company. In 1967 the first residents moved in, a second golf course opened, and development of Valencia Industrial Center began.

The company went public in 1969, and its stock was listed on the New York Stock Exchange in 1970. In 1971 Six Flags Magic Mountain opened in Valencia, with the company as a partner with Sea World. In 1972 the company became sole owner and operator before selling the park to Six Flags, Inc., in 1979. By the end of the 1970s, Valencia's population exceeded 12,000, and the community had schools, parks, a hospital and a medical center, the county administration center for the area, several shopping centers and churches, and two colleges. Many of the important institutions in Valencia were brought to the community with financial help from Newhall Land.

The 1980s brought continued expansion, with about 4,000 of the ranch's 41,000 acres developed. By the end of the decade, Valencia Industrial Center had become the third-largest industrial park in Los Angeles County, with more than 8.5 million square feet of completed space, 500 companies, and more than 11,000 employees.

As the 1990s began, the community's newest business/industrial park, Valencia Commerce Center, was opened. The new decade also saw the beginning of a major regional shopping mall, Valencia Town Center, the first in the Santa Clarita Valley. Numerous community celebrations in 1990 marked the 25th anniversary of the Valencia Master Plan.

New arrivals to the area can choose from a broad spectrum of single-family homes, condominiums, or rental apartments in well-maintained neighborhoods, surrounded by plenty of open space. Neighborhoods, shopping areas, recreation centers, and schools are linked by a network of landscaped walkways called "paseos," complete with tunnels and bridges, allowing pedestrians, joggers, and cyclists to travel throughout Valencia comfortably. There are eight spacious parks, several golf courses and tennis courts, lakes, and numerous other facilities, providing a wide variety of recreational, athletic, and leisure activities.

Valencia also provides excellent educational facilities. Elementary, junior high, and senior high school students are served by three respected school systems and several private schools. At higher levels there is the College of the Canyons community college and the world renowned California Institute of the Arts, a fully accredited visual and performing-arts college endowed by Walt Disney. Houses of worship, retail centers, and a wide variety of restaurants help make Valencia a community that has something to offer everyone.

Henry Newhall would be proud of what his descendants have done in their various

endeavors. Besides its primary activity of developing Valencia, The Newhall Land and Farming Company has become one of the 10 largest farming operations in California and is among the 100 largest in the nation. In 1985 the company converted from a corporation to a California limited partnership. Its partnership units are traded on the New York and Pacific Stock Exchanges.

Under the leadership of chairman Thomas L. Lee and president Gary M. Cusumano, the company has posted record levels in revenues and net income. The appraised value of its land holdings in Valencia has appreciated at an annual compound rate of nearly 20 percent and represents one of the premier real estate opportunities available in California to investors.

The people of The Newhall Land and Farming Company have every reason to be proud of what has been accomplished. Under their leadership, Valencia has become one of the finest master planned communities in the nation, creating an environment ideal for living, working, playing and enjoying the best that California has to offer.

LEFT: The paseo system, one of the master plan's trademarks, is the landscaped walkway system that extends through over 10 miles of the community.

BELOW: Valencia Summit, one of the community's premier neighborhoods.

First Care

First Care, the first walk-in medical facility in the Santa Clarita Valley, has grown to the point that more than 120 patients are seen each day between the two offices.

It was started by doctors Larry C. Barnhart and Ralph E. Farinella, who met while working at Golden State Hospital, which once stood on the corner of Lyons Avenue and what is now Wiley Canyon Road.

Barnhart and Farinella became friends and decided they would go into practice together once they finished medical school and their residencies. Years later, after their schooling and residencies were finished, Barnhart was working in an urgent-care facility in Orange County and Farinella in an urgent-care facility in Lancaster. They decided it was time to open their own practice.

Barnhart and Farinella selected the Santa Clarita Valley for their venture. Both valley residents, they knew it offered good schools and an enjoyable life-style. Also, the community was ripe for a walk-in medical facility, since there wasn't one in the area.

The Saugus office, at 22840 Soledad Canyon Road, opened in February 1985, and the Canyon Country office, at 16522 Soledad Canyon Road, opened in early 1986.

Those who go to First Care instead of to hospital emergency rooms are likely to find there is less waiting, less expense and more personalized service. No appointments are necessary. First Care is open until 10 p.m. every day of the year.

While walk-in medical centers have become a trend across the nation, many are failing, often because they are not as service-oriented as First Care. Sometimes they fail to have X-ray machines or a pharmacy on site. Such drawbacks decrease the value of the walk-in center. First Care provides X-ray services, pharmaceuticals, and has the personalized care that has allowed it to become a highly successful concern.

Another advantage of using First Care is that if a specialist is needed, First Care will refer the patient to the specialist directly, whereas often patients must wait until they are in the hospital before seeing a specialist.

First Care can provide medication during hours when pharmacies are closed. In addition, First Care strives to keep its pharmaceuticals priced as low those sold at pharmacies.

The company is innovative and patient oriented. It offers employment opportunities that most student nurses and young physicians just starting out find beneficial in helping them achieve their goals.

First Care's personalized care has made the company an important part of the medical community in the Santa Clarita Valley. The company witnessed the birth of the city of Santa Clarita and has been growing right along with the city.

Doctors Ralph E. Farinella and Larry C. Barnhart

Elisha Agajanian Family

Elisha "Aggie" Agajanian is the son of "Armenian" immigrants who fled to the United States from Armenia during the Turkish holocaust, which was in turn followed by the Russian Bolshevik Revolution. Aggie has two sisters; an older brother who pursued an illustrious career in automobile racing; and a younger brother who for many years held the field-goal kicking record in the National Football League.

Aggie, as he is affectionately known and referred to (even by his three sons), started as a pig farmer in Saugus after serving a tour in the Coast Guard in World War II. He also built up a successful waste disposal company that is now known as Blue Barrel Disposal.

The advent of garbage disposals soon eliminated the need for a garbage route. After more than 20 years in the trash business, he sold Blue Barrel Disposal and founded the First Community National Bank in the Santa Clarita Valley—known appropriately as Santa Clarita National Bank. After pursuing the banking business for another 25 years, he and the other directors voted to sell the bank to Security Pacific National Bank, which is now merged with Bank of America.

Danny, Roger, and Dennis Agajanian

ABOVE: *Elisha "Aggie" Agajanian.*
LEFT: *Maxine Agajanian*
Photos By Creative Image Photography

Maxine Agajanian, Aggie's wife of more than 50 years, moved with her four sisters, a brother, and parents from Oklahoma. It was a true *Grapes of Wrath* storyline complete with border checks at the California border for proof of income, employment, and lodging. As a result, the family moved to Oregon first, then settled in California. In addition to owning her own business with her friend, Jane Town, she also sold real estate. But she is best known for being a loving wife and wonderful mother to her three sons: Roger, a lawyer in Long Beach; Danny, a private investigator and professional entertainer in Fresno; and Dennis, a businessman and also a professional entertainer.

The entire family is musically talented. They often play at community functions, and the three brothers toured the Far East during the Viet Nam War. Dennis and Danny have toured almost every Third World country, fighting world hunger. This closely knit family, along with the eight grandchildren, spends every available moment together.

Aggie's involvement in civic organizations include the Lion's Club, Masons, and Shriners, of which he has been a member in excess of 40 years. He was instrumental in obtaining Santa Clarita's first junior college, College of the Canyons, where he petitioned the California State Senate for funding and approval. He serves on the local high school, hospital, and water district boards. He was the honorary mayor of Newhall, Castaic Lake commissioner, Santa Clarita Valley Chamber of Commerce Family of the Year, and Man of the Year for the City of Hope. In his spare time he participated in the Sister City Exchange Program with a city in Korea; performed with the local community players; and hosted exchange students from Japan and Australia.

He is a loving father and husband who personally shared with his three sons their accomplishments. He attends as many of Roger and Danny's trials as he can; and many of Danny's and Dennis' concerts. Dennis has recently returned home from a Third World Hunger Tour with the Billy Graham organization where the itinerary included Cambodia, Bangladesh, Lebanon, India, Ethopia, El Salvador, and Nicaragua.

Canyon Country Chamber of Commerce

The Canyon Country Chamber of Commerce has been working to promote the local economy and improve the quality of life in the area since 1957.

The chamber, with 530 members, is made up mostly of small businesses. "We are dedicated to bringing small business and the community together for the benefit of both," says Jack Watkins, chamber president.

He lists the Miss Santa Clarita Valley Pageant, Circus Vargas, Pride Week (started in 1986), graffiti removal, the Handyworker Program, and Frontier Days as some of the projects the chamber sponsors in order to reach its objective.

The Canyon Country Chamber of Commerce also holds business mixers, economic development committee meetings, business seminars, and an annual golf tournament and works with transportion and film development committees. The chamber says its mixers are a must for businesspeople wanting to network.

The chamber also provides monthly legislative analysis the assistance of business consultants, educators, and marketing people; a business directory; a clubs and organizations list; a monthly newsletter; an economic profile publication; and a general information service.

The chamber represents its businesses by voicing its concerns to federal, state, and local lawmakers. Chamber officials say they have developed a cooperative bond with officials of the City of Santa Clarita that is unequaled by other chambers in Los Angeles County. The chamber is represented at city council meetings, giving it the ability to assist its membership in reviewing city actions.

The founders of the chamber included Ken and Anne Lynch, Henry and Juanita Heinly, Gene Kronnick, Dr. Phillips, Ace Cain, Frank Collins, and Sam Hyman (who turned 100 years old in 1991). There were nearly 20 original members.

At the time of the chamber's founding, one of the big local issues was the widening of the Sierra Highway; the local community negotiated with government officials to get the funding for the construction.

The chamber was initially known as the Mint Canyon Chamber of Commerce, and it met in the Mint Canyon Community Building (which is now the Santa Clarita Elks Lodge). The name of the group was changed to the Canyon Country Chamber of Commerce in the 1960s.

The first Frontier Days kickoff barbecue was held in the 1950s at the Sand Canyon ranch of Art Evans to raise money for Frontier Days, which was held behind the Elks Lodge and included such events as burro races and chasing greased pigs.

ABOVE: Photo by Buzz Lawrence

LEFT: Photo by Buzz Lawrence
BELOW: The Chamber's working committee meets to discuss important and timely issues.

Saugus Union School District

Saugus Union School District was formed in 1908 from parts of the Castaic and Newhall school districts. After various boundary and name changes, the Clifton Union School District was established in 1938. Finally, on February 27, 1940, the formal name of Saugus Union School District was adopted. Minor boundary changes were made in 1944, 1951, 1981, and 1991.

Saugus Union School District, one of four elementary districts in the Santa Clarita Valley, serves more than 6,000 kindergarten through sixth grade students in 10 schools located in the communities of Valencia, Saugus, and Canyon Country.

Innovation, commitment, and excellence are hallmarks of the district. Phenomenal periods of growth have found the district conducting classes in newly constructed houses, an old Conservation Corps camp, and more recently, Seco Canyon School, which was constructed in six weeks of relocatable trailer classrooms. Additionally, the James Foster School, opened in 1989, was designed to be converted into a senior citizen residence when no longer needed as a school facility. Bouquet Canyon School, also opened in 1989, is totally composed of relocatable classrooms and was constructed, landscaped, and ready for students in less than nine weeks.

The district also offers two school calendars. One follows the traditional school year with classes beginning in September and concluding in June. The other, adopted in the mid-1970s, is a four-vacation plan that begins at the end of July and provides for three weeks of vacation time in October and January, two weeks in the spring, and six weeks in the summer. Enrichment classes for students on both calendars are offered during their scheduled vacation periods.

Technology and special needs have been addressed in exciting and creative ways. Computer labs were instituted in the early 1980s and have been expanded and updated through the years. Students are participating in video technology and multimedia presentations. Special education staffers personalize instruction both through in-class consultation and individual assistance.

Six schools have been recognized as California Distinguished Schools. The honor, based on state testing data, comprehensive self-studies, lengthy applications, and visitations, was bestowed on Highlands, Seco Canyon (now Charles Helmers School, Rio Vista, Rosedell, Santa Clarita, and Skyblue Mesa. These schools represent the commitment to quality and excellence demonstrated by all the Saugus schools.

Highlands School also received a National Distinguished School Award in 1990.

Saugus Union School District acknowledges the importance of parental involvement, excellent teaching, and community partnerships. Parents, teachers, and community members work diligently to provide educational experiences that challenge and motivate students toward higher levels of achievement and responsible decision-making. The district also offers extensive staff-development opportunities for teachers, paraprofessionals, and substitutes. The Los Angeles Sheriff's Department, the City of Santa Clarita, and Saugus Union School District established a partnership in 1988 to assist teachers in the delivery of drug, alcohol, and tobacco education curriculum. Newhall Land and Farm Foundation and the City provide support for after-school enrichment activities, including arts and crafts, language, computers, music, and drama.

The district anticipates increasing student enrollment, additional schools, and continued involvement in the educational process for students in the Santa Clarita Valley.

Students at Highlands School hold their National Distinguished School Commemorative Flag. Saugus Union School District has six California Distinguished Schools and one National Distinguished School.

Dr. M.D. Mullenax

"Treating the cause of a problem is as important—and often, more effective—than treating the symptom." This belief, and his profound caring for each patient as an individual, has built Dr. M.D. Mullenax's practice into one of the most successful and highly respected in the Santa Clarita Valley.

Recognizing that chiropractic treatment is an often-misunderstood procedure, Dr. Mullenax stresses that every function of the human body is controlled by the nervous system. When the spine is out of alignment in any number of ways, the body reacts to the impending imbalance, sometimes leading to chronic pain and disease. "We see patients who have tried everything else," explains Dr. Mullenax, "and in most cases that deal with chronic ailments, we can offer a solution. Through chiropractic treatment, the spine can be realigned and order can be restored."

"The real beauty of chiropractic care is that it is drug-free," adds Dr. Mullenax. He adheres to the theory that the human body is "the world's greatest drugstore" because of its ability to supply itself with necessary chemicals to sustain a healthy physiological balance. "The body working normally needs no help, if it has no interference. Our goal is to eliminate the interference."

While personal injury is a major portion of his practice, Dr. Mullenax also specializes in working with children. "Sadly, many children have spinal problems when they are born," Dr. Mullenax comments, "and it is estimated that 70% of all babies fall on their heads within their first year. Our goal is to help these children avoid serious and painful problems later in their young lives."

As part of Dr. Mullenax's work with children, especially toddlers and pre-teens, he thoroughly enjoys lecturing at schools about the spinal column and nervous system. In fact, sharing his experience and knowledge have always been a source of fulfillment for Dr. Mullenax. For 35 years, he has been dedicated to helping new doctors launch their careers based on the firm foundation of excellent professional treatment and sincere concern for the patient.

Opening the Mullenax Chiropractic Clinic in the Santa Clarita Valley in 1980 after 21 years in Tulsa, Oklahoma, Dr. Mullenax was raised and educated in Missouri, graduating from Chiropractic College in 1957. He also studied in the Orient, receiving his certificate in Acupuncture in 1973, and taught for two years with the Columbia Institute of Chiropractic.

Dr. M.D. Mullenax
Chiropracter

Fred W. Rio, M.D., F.A.C.S.

"Social architects attempt to divide society into segments of providers and consumers," says Fred W. Rio, M.D., F.A.C.S. "A sobering aspect of this is that sooner or later, everyone, including the 'providers,' becomes a consumer of health care. That's why I treat all of my patients exactly the way I'd like to be treated."

Dr. Rio continues, "There's no way around it; nobody enjoys being operated on. My job is to make my patients feel as good as they possibly can about the medical procedure and to make them as comfortable as possible." It is a sound doctor/patient philosophy that has been formed over years of medical practice and responsibility.

Upon graduating from the California College of Medicine in 1961, Dr. Rio served his internship at Los Angeles County Hospital. He began his own medical practice as a general practioner in Saugus in 1962 after visiting the area and sensing "fantastic opportunities" in the mostly rural community.

Dr. Rio became the first chief of staff of Santa Clarita Hospital, which became the Henry Mayo Newhall Memorial Hospital in 1964. He organized the medical staff and helped the hospital gain its first accreditation by the joint commission of hospital accreditation.

During his early years of practice in the Santa Clarita Valley, Dr. Rio served on the Saugus Unified School District board of directors—one year as president. He also, with the help of the Los Angeles County Health Department, established free immunization clinics at local schools, an effort that earned him an Outstanding Citizenship Award from the Junior Chamber of Commerce.

In 1967 Dr. Rio opted to leave his practice for four years for a surgical residency at Queen of Angels Hospital in Los Angeles. Rio says, "I did this because there were no medical specialists, and there was a real need for a local surgeon."

Upon his return to the Saugus area, Dr. Rio was named as the first chief of staff of the Henry Mayo Newhall Memorial Hospital. In the ensuing years he served as chief of surgery for 12 years, started the first trauma program in north Los Angeles County (years ahead of the Los Angeles County Trauma Program), and directed emergency and trauma services at the hospital for 14 years. In 1977 Dr. Rio was appointed regional liaison for the American College of Surgeons Committee on Cancer and obtained a grant that allowed him, along with Dr. Roscher and Dr. Hinkes, to establish the Cancer Program at Henry Mayo Newhall Memorial Hospital.

Dr. Rio presently practices surgery in the Valencia area in association with Max E. Rodriguez, M.D., F.A.C.S., and Darrell W. Carpenter, M.D.

Dr. Rio continues to bring new people, methods, and concepts to his practice in order to better serve the health care needs of the people of the Santa Clarita Valley. For example, his practice is actively involved in laparoscopic surgery (including removal of the gallbladder and other diseased organs through a laparoscope), laser surgery, and alternative treatments for breast cancer.

"Patients are what make my work interesting and exciting. It's helping them get well and watching them grow stronger—that makes my profession worthwhile," says Dr. Rio, on his way to still another surgery.

ABOVE: Fred W. Rio, M.D., FACS

BELOW: Dr. Fred Rio, Dr. Darrell W. Carpenter and Dr. Max E. Rodriguez prepare for a laparoscopic cholecystectomy. Photos by Gary Choppe, Creative Image Photography

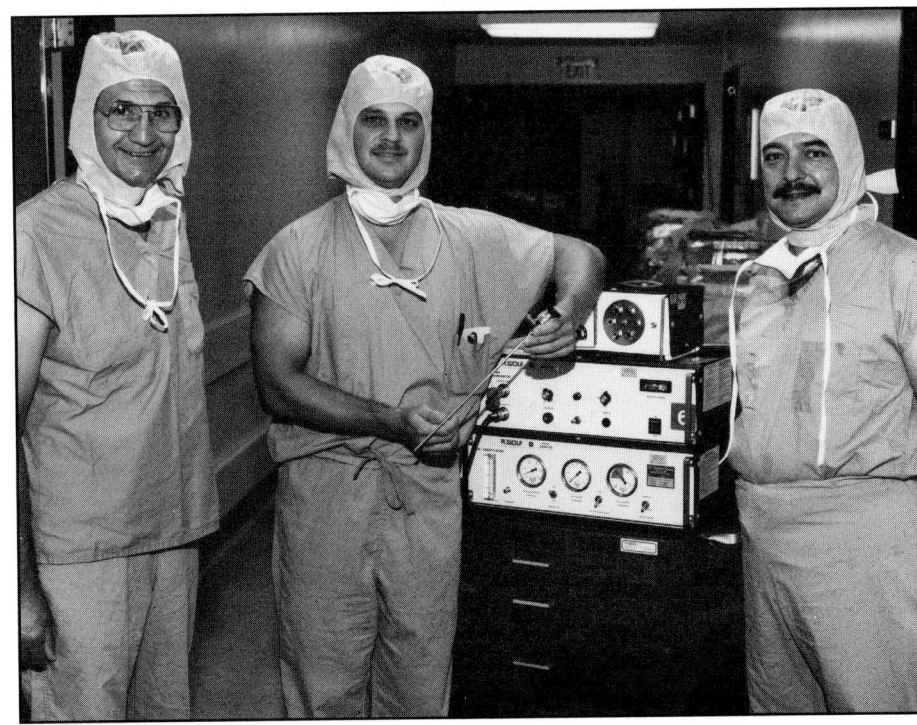

Galpin Motors

In 1965, the Santa Clarita Valley was just beginning to take shape, Saugus Speedway, formerly known as the Baker-Hoot Gibson Arena, was almost 10 years old and a young company president was about to achieve his dream of owning his own business by completing the buy out of Galpin Ford.

Those who have been associated with Bert Boeckmann over the years would call him a visionary. His achievements and innovations in the automobile industry have inspired the praise of many of the most prominent leaders in the business. Lee Iaccoa, former president of Ford Motor Company and Chrysler Corporation, called him, "The best in the business—bar none!" Phillip Caldwell, former chairman of the board of Ford Motor Company, wrote, "No one overlooks the remarkable record which your Galpin Ford has written over many years" and Harold "Red" Poling, current chairman of the board of Ford Motor Company, said, "The very best of the best! Bert has done a fantastic job for Ford Motor Company." His civic and community involvement has brought him endorsements and heartfelt appreciation from all walks of life. Former President Ronald Reagan has said, "When I think of what's right with America I will always think of men like Bert Boeckmann." President George Bush has said, "You exemplify many of our nation's most cherished traditions —duty, sacrifice, and a patriotism that finds its expression in taking part and pitching in."

It was with vision and dedication that Bert Boeckmann began what is now a 40-year involvement with the people in the Santa Clarita Valley. As expected, that involvement had its roots firmly planted in the automobile.

Galpin Ford-sponsored race cars had been racing up and down the coast of Southern California, including the Santa Clarita Valley, since the early '50s, but it was in 1965 that a young race car driver named Ron Hornaday, also Service Manager of Galpin Ford, was putting together back-to-back championships in Galpin-sponsored cars at Saugus Speedway by winning half of the 26 races he competed in that year. Ron would retire from racing in 1975 from a career that would see him and the Galpin-sponsored cars win numerous titles, awards and trips to the winner's circle. Today, his son, Ron Hornaday Jr., a past employee of Galpin who is now running his own business in the Santa Clarita Valley, is following in his father's footsteps. And in keeping with a tradition which began in the mid-'60s, Galpin Motors continues to provide the Saugus Speedway with the Official Pace Car.

Bert Boeckmann has a long-standing tradition of excellence and commitment. This basic foundation has helped him build one of the most successful car dealerships in the country. Under his leadership, Galpin Motors has been the proud recipient of more than one thousand awards and commendations for participation in national, civic and community affairs.

Demonstrating an example of a 40-year commitment that Galpin Ford has had in the Santa Clarita Valley, employees provide a courtesy car to William S. Hart High School in 1970.

Left to right: Ron Hornaday Sr., Bert Boeckmann and Ray Wilkings, Saugus Speedway Manager, at the Saugus Speedway. In the background is the Official Pace Car provided by Galpin Motors.

"Being a native of Southern California," Boeckmann says, "I am constantly amazed at the growth that has taken place here. Seeing that growth occurring in the Santa Clarita Valley makes me realize the potential of the area and the great things in store for the people living there. I'm proud that Galpin Motors has the opportunity to contribute to that growth and we hope to be a part of it for a very long time."

From those early beginnings when Galpin Ford had only 35 employees, its growth has been similar to that of the Santa Clarita Valley. Today Galpin Motors—adding to its Ford dealership a Hyundai dealership in 1986, a Lincoln Mercury dealership in 1988 and a Saturn dealership in 1990—now has more than 500 employees. With over 60 of these employees living in the Santa Clarita Valley, Galpin Motors is considered one of the area's leading employers. People like Shea Shaeffer, General Sales Manager for Galpin Ford and a 25 year employee, and Mel Summers Sr., a top mechanic for Galpin for 26 years, have been very active in youth athletics by coaching teams in the Canyon Country Little League and the William S. Hart Boys Baseball League for over 17 years. This type of community involvement helps to form the backbone of any community and is something that Bert Boeckmann has always encouraged.

And it doesn't stop there. From involvement and sponsorship of the Santa Clarita Warriors and Canyon Country Cowboy Football programs, to major contributions to Masters College, active support of Church of the Canyons and the Prison Satellite Ministries, Bert Boeckmann and Galpin Motors continue to reinvest in the area's future growth and development.

On the subject of the future, Galpin Motors will have even more impact as an employer in the Santa Clarita Valley by opening their second Saturn Dealership, the area's first Saturn of the Valley.

From the early beginnings to the present day location.

The Galpin Ford-sponsored car with Ron Hornaday driving at the Saugus Speedway in 1965.

Bert and Jane Boeckmann (second and third from the left) with (second from right) Dennis McCroskey, General Manager of Saturn of the Valley, a fourth-generation employee and a resident of Santa Clarita, with executives of the Saturn Corporation at the opening of the first Saturn of the Valley.

George Jefferson Thomas III, M.D.

George J. Thomas III, M.D., arrived in the Santa Clarita Valley in 1973, during the time of Hillside Community Hospital when there were still the fairly rustic three communities not yet named Santa Clarita: Newhall, Saugus, and Valencia. He saw the need for more orthopaedic surgeons since the valley's only local orthopaedic surgeon, Dr. William. C. Allen of Stanford, was moving for health reasons. After covering Allen's practice during Allen's vacation, Thomas decided to add his expertise to the service of the community. He became the first orthopaedic surgeon in the area to perform arthroscopic surgery, the first to use orthopaedic laser surgery, and among the first to perform total joint arthroplastics of the hips, knees, and shoulders, in addition to all of the customary practices of general orthopaedics.

Thomas' training had afforded him access to excellent teachers at Howard University Medical School in the District of Columbia, including Howard Epps, M.D., and LaSalle D. Lefalle, M.D. After med school, Thomas began internship training as the first African-American male intern at Washington Hospital Center in the District of Columbia, and then undertook general surgery training with James Yee, M.D., and James Smith, M.D., at Veteran's Hospital in Martinez, California, in 1969. Thomas' orthopaedic teachers at the San Francisco Orthopaedic Residency Training Program included doctors Lloyd Taylor, Gar Wynne, Ralph Soto-Hall, Richard Welch, and Gerald Strange, all world-renowned orthopaedic surgeons. Thomas put his education to good use from 1973-1975 while serving his country in the Navy, including one year as chief of orthopaedic surgery, USNR Port Hueneme, California Naval Hospital.

Thomas knew early in life that he wanted to pursue a career in medicine. His grandfather, the Reverend George J. Thomas, Sr., of Winston-Salem, North Carolina, was already proud of Thomas' dad, George J. Thomas, Jr., M.D., a urologist of some fame in New Orleans, Louisiana, who often took his son on rounds with him and allowed him to spend much of his youth exploring and working in hospitals. In college at the University of New Orleans (then known as Louisiana State University in New Orleans), the younger Thomas also volunteered to do laboratory work with future Nobel Prize laureate Dr. Schaale, and did some of the actual work in amino acid gas chromatography in delineating the amino acid sequence of melanin. Further research on his own was accomplished in medical school with published works as a student of cardiac transplantation and alloxan-induced diabetes.

Thomas' interest in medicine and orthopaedic surgery still allowed time for him to marry Dianna Fields, whom he met while in college at the University of New Orleans. They are the proud parents of two sons and two daughters, all now grown.

"I feel I'm doing what I'm well suited for, where the need proved to be most," Thomas explains, adding that he still doesn't feel as if it's work.

George Jefferson Thomas III, M.D.

George Thomas III poses with his family: (clockwise, from left) his daughter Stephanie, his wife Dianna, his son George IV, his daughter Alicia, and his son Robert.

Hale & Associates

While working on the Owens Valley Aqueduct, the primary source of Southern California's water supply, Donald E. Hale recognized something different about the Santa Clarita Valley: It didn't lack the distinct seasonal changes that most of Southern California lacked.

"This valley had great potential," Hale recalls, adding that the change in seasons was an alluring feature. "It looked like a good area for investment, a great place to raise my family." Before long, Hale, his wife, Wanda, and the couple's two daughters, Deanna and Jerianne, moved to the Santa Clarita Valley.

In 1978 Hale, who had 14 years' experience with the Los Angeles City Department of Water and Power and a degree in civil engineering from Cal State Northridge, set out on his own, starting Hale & Associates. With the DWP, Hale worked on hydrology design for nuclear power plants, EPA studies including thermal and wastewater discharge alternatives, and various other projects in and around the northern Los Angeles area.

When Hale & Associates was formed, Hale focused his efforts on structural analysis and California energy standard design, which at about that time became a mandatory step in obtaining development permits. The following year Hale added architectural design to his company's repertoire.

Hale & Associates began to grow along with the Santa Clarita Valley, peaking at 31 employees in 1990. "I owe a great deal to the dedication of our staff," Hale says.

Today Hale & Associates, a full-service professional engineering consulting firm, is deeply involved in land planning and architectural, structural, and civil design in the Santa Clarita Valley.

Hale, who served as a member of the city's formation committee, believes cityhood has brought the government closer to the people of the valley. "It is better-able to serve the people," Hale explains. "The city should have been formed much earlier."

Before cityhood, Santa Clarita was often overlooked and not given the monies or attention it deserved from officials of Los Angeles County government. But the advent of cityhood has changed all that, according to Hale. "I see a more organized city now, giving the people what they want, not what the county of Los Angeles dictates."

Hale attributes the success of his business to the dedication and support of his wife, who sits on the company's board of directors. Wanda had spent several years working in the title insurance business before joining her husband's firm in the land-planning department.

Teamed with his wife and the new city, Hale feels confident that the chemistry will continue to bring good fortune.

BELOW: A home designed by Hale & Associates.

BOTTOM: In addition to single family residences, Hale & Associates has designed several neighborhood commercial centers.

BELOW: Single family residences designed by Hale & Associates in the Santa Clarita Valley and surrounding area.

THE SIGNAL

The Signal was the journalistic creation of publisher-editor-printer Edward H. Brown, who sought in 1919 to publish a newspaper "devoted to the Newhall-Saugus valleys."

The inaugural edition of *The Signal* hit the newsstands February 7, 1919, as Brown greeted readers with the words, "With this issue we unfurl the sails of *The Signal* upon the sea of journalism."

The Signal has published continuously ever since, and despite many changes over the years, *The Signal* remains deeply devoted to the communities in and around the Santa Clarita Valley.

That very first issue sported the motto, "Build up; don't tear down," and a subscription cost two dollars a year. Advertising rates were 25 cents per single-column inch per week and classified ads cost five cents per line.

Brown's career as publisher ended less than a year later with his death on February 3, 1920. His wife, Blanche, assumed control of the paper and quickly bought out the rival newspaper, *The Saugus Enterprise*.

In 1938 *The Signal* was sold to brothers Mark and Fred Trueblood for $1,500. The Arizona natives also acquired a building on San Fernando Road near Market Street, where the paper was produced. Fred Trueblood, Jr., who served as general manager, later succeeded his father as editor and publisher.

The Signal experienced tremendous growth in 1963 under the short-lived reign of owner Ray Brooks, who bought the paper, moved it to a location on Sixth Street in Newhall, and increased circulation from 3,000 to 7,000. He sold it six months later to Scott Newhall, a great-grandson of the town's founder, Henry Mayo Newhall.

Newhall, former editor of the *San Francisco Chronicle*, breathed new life into the

In 1939 The Signal *offices were located on San Fernando Road in Newhall under the ownership of Fred Trueblood, Sr.*

Scott Newhall, who bought The Signal *in 1963, breathed new life into the paper with his provocative and flamboyant editorial style.*

paper with his provocative and flamboyant editorial style, once calling the city of Los Angeles "the greatest aggregation of sneak thieves, rapists, child molesters, armed robbers, and phantom flashers ever gathered in one place in the long history of mankind."

Newhall's wife, Ruth, also took a leading role as managing editor and chief society columnist under the guise of "Mimi." Under Scott Newhall, the publication of the paper was increased from one to three editions a week.

The Signal joined the Morris Newspaper Corporation when it was purchased in 1978 by Charles Morris, president of the Savannah, Georgia-based corporation. While the Newhalls continued to operate the paper until 1988, the newspaper under Morris' ownership moved to its present building on Creekside Road in Valencia and increased publication to five and then six days a week.

In September 1988 the Newhall family left *The Signal* and Darell Phillips, publisher of five small Northern California newspapers, took over as publisher. Sammee Zeile, former marketing director at the Los Angeles metropolitan giant *Daily News*, assumed control of the newspaper's daily operations as general manager. Award-winning investigative journalist Chuck Cook became editor, was later replaced by Joseph Franco in July 1989, and John Green in March 1992.

Today *The Signal* publishes seven days a week and has increased its circulation to more than 46,000. Professing "vigilance forever," *The Signal* remains committed to serving the Santa Clarita Valley exclusively as it continues to sail "upon the sea of journalism."

KMGX, MAGIC FM

In 1958 an FM station was founded in the San Fernando Valley by a group called Pacific Western Broadcasting Corporation, a Cleveland firm. The company called it KVFM. Buckley Communications bought the station in 1976 and simulcast it with KGIL-AM. At that time, the FM station became KGIL-FM. However, in 1983, the two stations were separated by formats, and the FM station began playing adult contemporary music.

A new transmitter was installed on Oat Mountain, and the Santa Clarita Valley finally got a radio station of its own. Back then, KGIL-FM was "rockin' easy in the Valley." The station was very well received by the community and became an overnight success in Santa Clarita. Sales offices were opened in Valencia, and local businesses started getting great results on the air.

In the fall of 1989 KGIL-FM celebrated a new identity—KMGX, Magic FM. With the change in call letters came new personalities, new programs, new excitement, and the same great music that had made the radio station the most popular in Santa Clarita. Now, as Magic FM, the station continues to expand its audience as the Santa Clarita Valley experiences one of the highest population growth rates in California.

Special Magic FM marketing tools make the station a favorite of astute local businesspeople. Such tools as the familiar Magic FM remote van (Big Pink) continue to make valley customers aware of businesses that go the extra mile to ensure maximum impact from their marketing investment.

94.3, KMGX, Magic FM, is the only FM station designed to serve Santa Clarita Valley listeners with news, great adult contemporary music, weather, and community service, in addition to fun and entertainment.

ABOVE: *The widest variety of music!*

LEFT: *Magic FM's mobile studio, "Big Pink."*

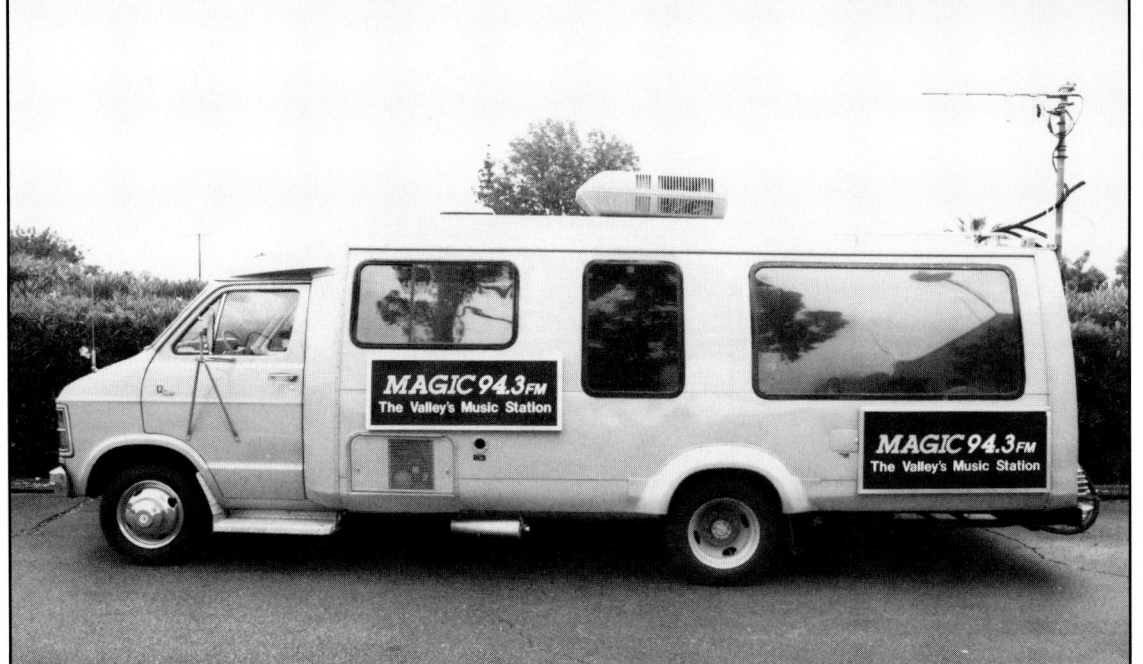

KGIL-AM

There were only some 350,000 residents in the San Fernando Valley when radio station KGIL first went on the air on October 19, 1947. The 1,000-watt station's programming included roughly 70 percent music and 20 percent news, with the remainder divided among several other features, including agricultural news. The Valley was still very much a farming area, and the orange and walnut growers would tune in to 1260 AM for the latest in weather forecasts that could affect their delicate crops.

The station was launched by the San Fernando Valley Broadcasting Company, which, shortly after its January 1946 founding, applied to the Federal Communications Commission for a license to operate a radio station licensed to the City of San Fernando. The station chose its call letters from the nickname of its first president and general manager, J. Gilbert "Gil" Paltridge, who was one of the founders of the company.

The early years were difficult ones. Between 1947 and 1960 there were several changes of ownership and management, although programming content remained much the same. One exception was the elimination of agricultural news, reflecting the changing character of the Valley from farmland to suburbs.

On July 28, 1960, KGIL was purchased by its present owner, Buckley Broadcasting Corporation, then called Buckley-Jaeger Corporation. At the time of acquisition, Buckley owned two other stations, both on the East Coast.

In November 1962 Richard "Rick" Buckley, Jr., became KGIL's program director and made sweeping changes in the traditional programming. He put together a modern music library, featuring contemporary selections aimed at the young adults who made up much of the listening audience.

The concept of KGIL as the "Valley station" was strongly promoted, emphasizing the long-standing ties between the station and the Valley, by then approaching the one million population mark.

News and traffic reports focused on local happenings. KGIL was only the second Los Angeles-area station to use an airplane to cover traffic, and it reported exclusively on conditions in or leading to and from the Valley. In 1963 KGIL built its own weather facility, again focusing on Valley conditions, which were often different from those in other parts of the Los Angeles basin.

That same year the FCC approved a full-time increase in power to 5,000 watts. In 1964 the offices and studios were moved to the transmitter site at 14800 Lassen Street in Mission Hills. It remains at that location, although growth has dictated considerable expansion.

In 1985 KGIL switched to an all-talk format, called "newstalk." It has proven to be a highly popular blend of news broadcasting and on-the-air talk with listeners.

The 1960 acquisition of KGIL by Buckley, now 16 stations strong, has worked well, enabling the station to grow and change with the burgeoning San Fernando Valley market, with which it has been so closely tied and which it has served so well for more than 40 years.

LEFT: Discussing the issues of the day.

BELOW: KGIL Radio

Stevenson Ranch

Stevenson Ranch is one of the largest master-planned communities of the Dale Poe Development Corporation of California, a company that has been in the land development business for more than 30 years.

The corporation has done developments and master-planned communities in the California cities of Valencia, Agoura Hills, Simi Valley, Long Beach, and Sacramento. In addition, the Dale Poe Development Corporation also has developments in Nevada, Oregon, and Texas. The diversified company also has cattle and farming operations in Ventura and Kern counties.

The large master-planned community of Stevenson Ranch is located west of the I-5 in Santa Clarita between Lyons Avenue and McBean Parkway. When completed, the carefully planned community will encompass approximately 4,000 acres and will include homes, schools, parks, shopping, and commercial centers.

GRUBER SYSTEMS, INC.

Beautiful coordinated bathrooms in cultured marble, onyx, granite, or solid color can be seen throughout the world as the result of the technology and designs created by Gruber Systems, Inc.

Louis Gruber, the company's founder, was one of the pioneers of the cast polyester industry. He experimented in the 1950s with the mixture of resins, fillers, and catalysts to develop a new material for the manufacture of bathroom products. His experiments produced a matrix created through the mixing of the resins and fillers, which was then poured into molds where it was allowed to cure. The products were then demolded, finished, and ready for installation. Products in the early days of the industry were limited to vanity tops or flat pieces. The technique of "veining" used by many manufacturers to create a "marble-looking" product led to the term "cultured marble," by which the manufactured product was commonly identified throughout the 1960s and 1970s.

As manufacturers of "cultured marble" cropped up not only in Southern California, but throughout the nation, Gruber saw the need for a source of molds for this rapidly growing industry. Gruber Systems, Inc., opened its doors in 1965 to fill that need and quickly became the recognized leader throughout the industry as a source for high-quality molds and manufacturing equipment.

In 1958 Louis Garasi joined the company begun by his father and became president in 1970 upon Louis Gruber's retirement. In 1978 Gruber Systems, Inc., relocated its operations from North Hollywood to the Valencia Industrial Center, becoming one of the park's first residents.

Over the years, cast polyester manufac-

RIGHT and BELOW: Gruber Systems, Inc., produces molds for cultured marble whirlpools, vanity tops, sinks, showers, and numerous other products.

turers throughout the world have been able to greatly expand their product lines with the help of mold designs from Gruber Systems: vanity tops, bowls, tubs, showers, waterclosets, bidets, fireplace surrounds, columns, kitchen sinks, countertops, and numerous other products. Gruber Systems also supplies the industry with state-of-the-art manufacturing equipment, mold care products, whirlpool systems, pumps and technical support. Manufacturing facilities are now located in Florida and Mexico, as well as in Valencia, with sales offices throughout the United States and distributors worldwide.

The corporate offices of Gruber Systems, Inc., are located at 26536 Avenue Stanford in the Valencia Industrial Center.

Valencia National Bank

When a satisfied customer mentioned to an officer at Valencia National Bank how important the staff made him feel each time he walked into the bank, it was typical of the many favorable comments the bank has received over the years.

Valencia National Bank, currently the only financial institution headquartered in the Santa Clarita Valley, was the brainchild of several local prominent businessmen, including Glen Rollins, Richard Patterson, Anthony Matthess, and Charles Albrecq.

In March 1986 Howard P. "Buck" McKeon was asked to join the group and serve as chairman of the bank organization effort. With McKeon accepting the offer, the five set out to form a board made up of a diverse cross-section of Santa Clarita Valley businesspeople who also shared a dream of establishing a true community-oriented bank.

The original board included Lou Garasi, Kathy Wiener, Eugene Burke, Richard Keysor, Orville E. Weaver, Kent Fortin, Peter V. Wiese, William Walsh, and the five named above. The group then selected a seasoned bank executive, Robert N. Manley, to fill the position of president and chief executive officer.

In addition to the board of directors, a "founders group" of 123 people were brought into the project, each offering $3,000 to help the bank with its organizational expenses.

As Manley stated in an interview shortly after the bank opened, "That group represents a real foundation for this bank. They are all local people who also saw a need for a new bank to be started."

Prior to opening, the group had to find a site, data processor, bank equipment, and support staff. The bank founders received preliminary approval to organize the bank from the comptroller of the currency in September 1986.

A citywide public offering of the bank's stock was made in the spring of 1987, with hopes of attracting local residents, Manley says. It was felt that local ownership would ensure the bank's local orientation as it grew in the ensuing years. The bank then issued 427,514 shares of stock at $10 per share. The bank was originally capitalized at more than $4 million—well above the minimum required to start a bank.

The excitement mounted as the vision of opening a bank that offered personalized service, local decisions, and a full range of banking services became a reality.

Ironically, the bank opened its doors for business on October 15, 1987, now referred to as "Black Monday" due to the near collapse of the stock market. Nonetheless, the bank managed to take in approximately one million dollars in deposits for the day, Manley says.

The concept of a locally owned community bank, oriented to the needs of local businesses and individuals,

Valencia National Bank's opening day ribbon-cutting ceremony on October 15, 1987: (from left to right) James Perkins, Glen Rolins, Paul Rohl, Howard P. (Buck) McKeon, Kathy Wiener, Robert Manley, Terry Martin, and D.M. (Mike) LaTurner.

continues to be the formula for Valencia National Bank's success, says Gail Pinsker, spokesperson for the bank. Customers like the fact that they are treated like friends, greeted by name, and that their deposits are kept in the Santa Clarita Valley to be loaned out as needed to local consumers and commercial customers.

The future looks bright for Valencia National Bank, with more than 35 employees and 14 officers and assets exceeding 60 million, Pinsker says. The bank was seeking to expand in 1992, with branches planned for Canyon Country and Newhall.

The board of directors, bank management, and staff hold the bank's original mission statement as its continued philosophy. It reads, "To provide our shareholders an equitable return on their investment by becoming the finest Santa Clarita Valley financial institution, offering our community professional, competitively priced banking services with an emphasis on personalized quality service."

Valencia National Bank headquarters on West Valencia Boulevard.

The Travel Bug

The writing was literally on the wall for Geri Jacobs, founder and owner of The Travel Bug, a Valencia-based travel agency. While growing up in West Los Angeles, Jacobs and her family moved into a house that had a world map painted on the wall of one of the rooms. It became Jacobs' bedroom.

When her mother offered to give the wall a fresh coat of paint, Jacobs declined the offer and instead familiarized herself with the world, via the map. And her fancy for maps has propelled her and her business into the limelight of Santa Clarita business travelers and tourists alike. In a drawer beside her desk are maps, and lots of them.

Jacobs, who began her career in the travel business in 1967 as a reservation clerk with United Airlines, immediately took to the business, although she was an admitted "white knuckle flyer." "But it never stopped me from traveling," she says.

It also did not stop her from opening her own travel agency. In 1978, after coming to the conclusion that Valencia was in dire need of a corporate travel agency, she opened The Travel Bug in The Newhall Land and Farming Co. building in Valencia.

"Finding a professional location was important to me," Jacobs says. "Getting that lease is what started the ball rolling—it put me in that corporate environment."

In the early years the business was not computerized. She made reservations by phone, typed travel itineraries, and delivered tickets in person. Through her persistence, Jacobs went from a staff of two people to seven employees, prompting her to move into a larger office. Jacobs moved down the street to the Valencia National Bank building in 1987, which is where the company remains today.

By 1990 The Travel Bug had expanded to 11 employees with clients all over the world including a client that called Jacobs for assistance during the May 1989 student demonstrations in China, where violence marred the streets of Beijing.

Jacobs was asked to arrange transportation out of the country. "We were already closed, but I phoned and got him out of the country," she remembers.

Jacobs attributes the success of The Travel Bug to getting the job done under any circumstances. "The most rewarding time is when you help people who rely on your expertise to get them where they want to go," she says.

Jacobs explains that the corporate traveler, who she has built her business on, provides her with some of her most demanding work.

"It is fast-paced, energetic, and demanding, but it is the most exciting aspect of the business," she says. Jacobs believes the real service she can offer clients is information and options.

In her spare time Jacobs keeps involved in the community, having served on the board of directors of the Henry Mayo Newhall Memorial Hospital and the Santa Clarita Boys and Girls Clubs. She says she has benefitted from the community's patronage of her business, and she enjoys returning the favor.

Geri Jacobs attributes the success of The Travel Bug to getting the job done under any circumstances.

Baxter Pharmaseal

Baxter Travenol Laboratories, Inc., and American Hospital Supply Corporation merged in November 1985. The merger was a natural; both companies had maintained a working relationship for many years prior to 1985. Each had attained some degree of leadership in their respective industries.

Baxter Laboratories began with Dr. Donald E. Baxter, who founded Don Baxter, Inc., a Glendale-based company that patented the first safe means of making commercial intravenous solutions. In 1931 Baxter licensed his patents to a small company in Chicago that adopted the name Baxter Laboratories, Inc.

Baxter Laboratories upheld Baxter's tradition of innovation, developing a host of pioneering medical products and systems. The company introduced the first sterile system to draw and administer blood. Other Baxter breakthroughs include the separation of plasma from red blood cells and the first kidney dialysis machine.

American Hospital Supply, founded by Foster G. McGaw in 1922, was also making its mark in the medical world as the premier distributor of hospital supplies. The company is credited with creating the first artificial heart valve, a range of disposable medical products, automated purchasing systems, and a variety of training programs for health care professionals.

Today, Baxter International offers some 120,000 products and the Baxter International's products play an integral role in almost every health care setting—a doctor's office, hospital, or dentist's chair. That's because Baxter is the world's largest supplier of products, services, and systems to health care professionals.

ability to meet more than 65 percent of a hospital's supply needs. The company, which is headquartered in Illinois, employs 60,000 people in more than 100 countries.

More than 400 of these employees can be found in Valencia, where Baxter's Pharmaseal Division is headquartered.

Originally part of Don Baxter, Inc., Pharmaseal was the trade name the company first used in the 1950s for its line of plastic disposable medical products. Since that time, Pharmaseal's product line has expanded tremendously, and today it features a broad range of surgical, medical, and respiratory care products. Specific products include procedure trays and needles, surgeons' gloves, sterilization wrap, thermal packs, wound cleansers and dressing, oxygen and aerosol therapy equipment, humidifiers, and nebulizers.

The Pharmaseal Division's headquarters are located at 27200 North Tourney Road in Valencia. While no manufacturing takes place in this four-level, 237,000-square-foot facility, a variety of other activities that are essential to Baxter's worldwide success do. In Valencia, Baxter Pharmaseal anchors the company's administrative services, customer service, engineering, finance, human resources, marketing, purchasing, quality assurance, regulatory affairs, research and development, and sales.

William S. Hart School District

When community leaders first established the William S. Hart School District back in 1945, their goal was to provide Santa Clarita Valley students with a quality education. Nearly 50 years later, that goal hasn't changed, and the Hart School District continues to stand for excellence and innovation in faculty, academic programs, and student services.

Originally known as Santa Clarita Union, the district's name was changed with the completion of the first five buildings of William S. Hart High School in 1947. Hart—then a junior and senior high school—was the first school in the new district.

The district's namesake was a Shakespearean actor turned cowboy star who made his home in the hilltops above Newhall. A well-known local figure, Hart gave generously to community causes and organizations, and eventually left his property and legacy to the valley's people.

One of seven high school districts in Los Angeles County, the Hart School District covers some 365 square miles between Davenport Road and the Ventura County line to the east and west, and between Templin Highway and the ridge of mountains between the Santa Clarita and San Fernando valleys to the north and south. The district comprises nine schools, including Hart, Canyon, and Saugus high schools; Placerita, Sierra Vista, and Arroyo Seco junior highs; Bowman Continuation; Learning Post; and Golden Oak Adult School. These schools serve more than 10,000 students attending grades seven through 12 and in excess of 2,700 adults each year.

The district's staff includes a full-time faculty of 520 certified teachers, counselors, librarians, psychologists, and administrators, as well as more than 300 classified employees. With an annual budget of $45 million, the Hart District is a major local employer, issuing more than 1,000 paychecks each month to its employees.

Teachers in the Hart District are excited about working with young people and actively participate in the district's team approach to education. Hart teachers work together on curriculum content and

ABOVE: High school students with councelor Edel Alondo.
LEFT: Junior high school students prepare to go on an archaeological dig.

student issues, striving to create a rich learning environment in which students feel connected to school.

Hart's team approach has certainly paid off. Students from the Hart District consistently rank among the top 25 percent in the California Assessment Program tests. Approximately 25 percent of Hart students continue their education in four-year colleges. And an overwhelming 80 percent continue on to some type of post secondary institution.

Equally important to the success of its students is the positive support the district receives from the local community. In the Hart District a real partnership exists between the schools and the parents; a partnership which has created an exceptional climate for academic excellence and student achievement.

And achieve they have! Students from

the Hart District perform well in academic competition. Hart High School, for example, recently claimed second place in the county's Academic Decathlon, and, for the second year in a row, fielded the highest scoring individual student. Saugus High School earned a perfect 1,000 score in mathematics in that competition.

Hart schools are frequently recognized for excellence and innovation. In 1988 Sierra Vista Junior High School was named a California Distinguished Middle School, an award given to less than 100 schools chosen by the state for their outstanding programs and academic records. For six years in a row Hart High School has been listed among Los Angeles County's top 100 high schools. And Arroyo Seco Junior High School was recently chosen as one of California's 100 Partnership Middle Schools.

But the district also strives to give students an opportunity to excel on the playing field as well as in the classroom, maintaining a healthy balance between academic programs and athletics. In addition to their academic achievements, Hart District high schools have earned championships in football, track, and basketball.

The district provides a number of special services, including special programs for vocational, college-bound, handi-

capped, learning disabled, gifted, and limited English proficient students. The district maintains a fleet of 72 buses, which travel over 700,000 miles a year from home to school, and an extra 72,000 miles a year for co-curricular activities. And the district's Food Services Program serves more than 4,000 meals each school day.

Over the past few years, the district has added computer labs to provide its students with everything from basic computer literacy to advanced business computer applications.

Through much of the late 1980s and early 1990s, the Santa Clarita Valley experienced one of the fastest rates of growth in the nation. The Hart District recognized the coming need for more area high schools and acquired land for a new high school and a new junior high. Both schools will be completed as soon as funds are available. A new campus for Continuation High School is scheduled to open early in 1992. This will double the size of the existing school from 200 to 400.

The district's students themselves are changing, too, reflecting the increasingly diverse makeup of the rest of the state and the nation. As of this writing, the Hart District student population is 15 percent Hispanic, 1.7 percent black, 1 percent Filipino, 2.5 percent Asian or Pacific Islander, .3 percent Native American, and 79.5 percent white.

The William S. Hart School District has grown and changed in many ways since it was first established, but the goals of yesterday and today remain the same. "Students deserve excellence in their schools," says district superintendent Hamilton C. "Clyde" Smyth. "So does the community. Here in the Hart District, we are committed to the pursuit of excellence in every area of educational endeavor."

ABOVE: A Junior high school activity day sponsored by the Associated Student Body.
LEFT: High school students with teacher David Crissman.

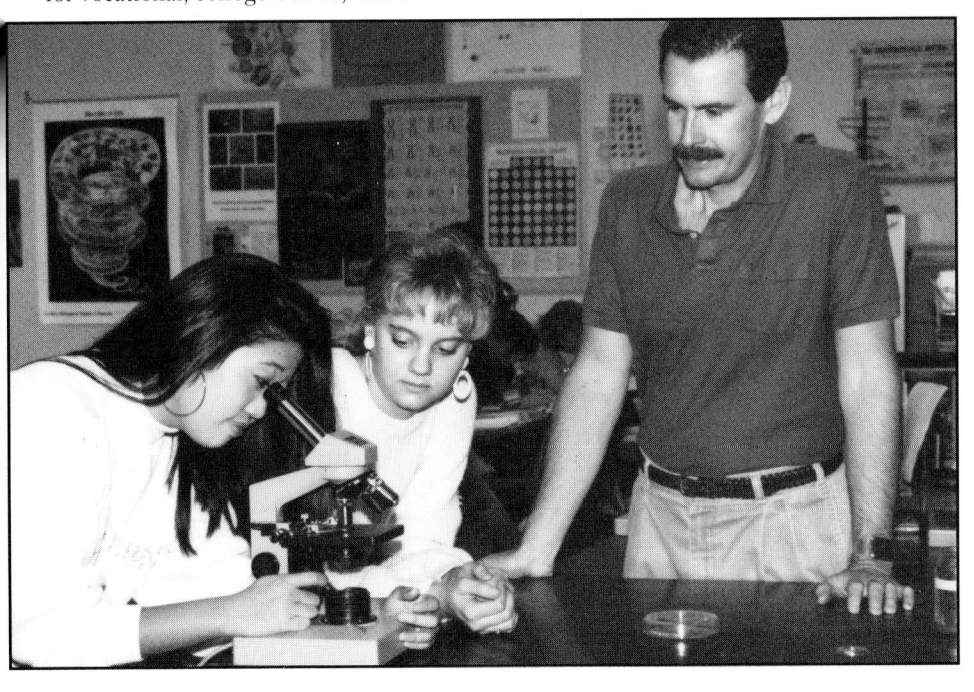

California Institute of the Arts

The reputation of California Institute of the Arts has grown steadily since the school incorporated three decades ago. In fact, many have suggested it is now the art world's dominant source of talent.

CalArt's incorporation in 1961 established it as the first degree-granting institution of higher learning specifically for students of both the visual and performing arts.

A year earlier, Walt Disney had initiated plans for the school. He dreamed of a school where the arts could be cross-cultivated as different disciplines were studied side by side, each artist drawing ideas from what he or she saw others doing.

Disney founded CalArts by merging Chouinard Art Institute and the Los Angeles Conservatory of Music. Lulu May Von Hagen, the chairman of the Los Angeles Conservatory of Music, played a leading role in the merger. Von Hagen was CalArt's first chairman of the Board of Trustees.

Although Disney died in 1966, his dream of a school of the arts was carried on by family members and benefactors. In 1968 Robert Corrigan became the first president of the school, which was initially housed in a building on Seventh Street in Los Angeles.

Ground was broken on the Valencia campus in 1969. Before it was completed, the school moved temporarily to what had been the Villa Cabrini High School in Burbank.

Finally, in the fall of 1971, 10 years after the school was incorporated, the Valencia campus opened with 659 students. The period from 1961 to 1971 has been referred to as an incubation period, the school not really hatching until it opened the Valenica campus.

William S. Lund was named chief administrative officer in 1972, serving until 1975, when Robert J. Fitzpatrick was named president. Fitzpatrick, whose fundraising skills put the school on a firm foundation, served until 1987. He resigned to become president of the new Euro Disney in Paris. Nicholas England was interim acting president until 1988 when the school's current president, Steven D. Lavine, was hired.

An article in the August 1989 *Vogue* magazine suggested CalArts is an art factory wilder than Warhol's. "The salient art academy of its time, the school has functioned for almost two decades as a free-floating cultural satellite, a communications link between the art scenes of New York and Los Angeles," wrote Ralph Rugoff. "In the process, it has changed the complexion of both. Its alumni, including David Salle, Eric Fischl, Mike Kelley, Ashley Bickerton, Randy Wicks (*The Signal*'s award-winning cartoonist), and Paul Reubens, better known as Pee Wee Herman, have helped establish a Who's Who for the art of the 80s."

Robert B. Woodward, writing for *The New York Times*, said students at CalArts are drilled to be suspicious of normal practices, to search out new ways to convey their work to their audiences. "Teachers such as the feminist critic Catherine Lord, the photographer Allan Sekula, and the conceptual

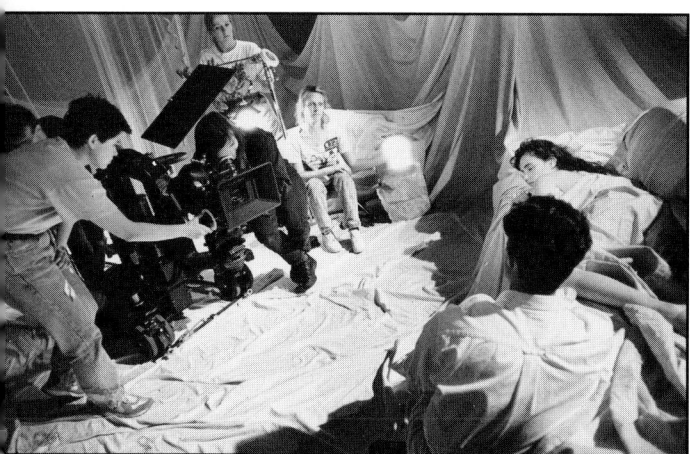

ABOVE; The set of The Blue Fiction, *a CalArts student film by Marco Puccioni. Photo by Steven A. Gunther.*

LEFT: *The front entrance of CalArts in Valencia. The Valencia campus opened in 1971, 10 years after the school was incorporated. Photo by Steven A. Gunther.*

LEFT: Faculty member Tina Yuan of the CalArts Dance Ensemble. Photo by Steven A. Gunther.

ABOVE: CalArts students Lily Barmor and Sandra Choi perform in a noon recital. Photo by Steven A. Gunther.

artist Michael Asher put students through rigorous classes that can go on for 10 hours at a stretch, the intent to begin to expose the premises and implications behind any given approach," Woodward wrote. He said that "whether CalArts graduates are more thoroughly schooled and self-conscious, or whether the art world has wanted to accept a CalArts degree as a badge of intelligence, its students have swarmed over both coasts like a pack of elite professional soldiers."

Tim Burton and Ed Harris are just two examples of those who have taken their lessons at CalArts. Burton's directorial and animation skills have combined to create the films *Beetlejuice* and *Batman*. Harris' acting credits include the Broadway production *Precious Sons* and the feature films *The Right Stuff, Under Fire, Sweet Dreams, Places in the Heart, Walker,* and *The Abyss*.

The CalArts faculty has included such luminaries as film and video experimentalist Ed Emshwiller, artists John Baldessari and Douglas Huebler, theorist Gene Youngblood, and photographer John Divola. The school also has such faculty members as dancer and choreographer Cristyne Lawson, composer Morton Subotnick, actor-director Robert Benedetti, and photographer Jo Ann Calli´s. Mel Powell, who won a Pulitzer prize for his composition "Duplicates," also teaches at CalArts.

Has Disney's dream been realized? The school clearly has become a training ground for some of the world's most creative minds. And it is a place where artists of different disciplines, all housed under one roof, benefit from each other's ideas.

And although it is not a place where a steady stream of tour groups watch students from balconies, the public is invited to view the artists' performances, exhibitions, and productions almost daily.

At many institutions, school officials herd students off the campus at a given hour each day to make room for evening classes, thus earning extra money at the expense of the full-time students. Not so at CalArts, a school where students have access to the campus 24 hours a day.

It is a school where students are taught not only what they should know, but also that they should question those same values. The faculty is encouraged to practice their art, not just teach it. Often the faculty and students work together on projects, allowing the students to learn by watching and sharing the creation of ideas as opposed to learning from lectures alone.

The institute, in realizing the founder's philosophy, now comprises five related schools and a program of general studies: schools of art, dance, film/video, music, and theater. CalArts offers both bachelor's and master's of fine arts degrees as well as certificate programs at the undergraduate and graduate levels.

The school draws students from around the world and interacts with art communities in various parts of the world, but the community in the best position to view the student and faculty works is Santa Clarita.

Andy Gump Inc.

Often portable versions of products—such as cellular phones and portable stereos—are more luxury than necessity of living.

But Andy Gump's portable product is one that comes close to being an essential item. Construction workers and others can thank Andy Gump for providing them with portable toilets.

Andy Gump's sons, Barry and Bill, helped him build his first portable toilets when they were in junior high school. Those toilets were so heavy by today's standards that it would be hard to call them portable.

It was the birth of Andy Gump, Inc., a firm now headed by Barry. The senior Gump, M.Z. "Andy" Gump, remains active in the company, but he turned the management over to Barry in 1979. Barry credits the company's success to hard work and the enthusiastic team spirit of nearly 50 "like family" employees.

The firm has built a client list that includes such firms as the Newhall Land and Farming Company, Kaufman & Broad, American Beauty, Dale Poe Development, Warmington Homes and Paragon Homes.

Their toilets, or "Andy Gumps," as they are known, have been at the 1984 Summer Olympics, The L.A. Marathon, the L.A. Open, Renaissance Pleasure Faire and many other prominent outdoor activities.

Andy Gump, Inc. has been recognized for not only supplying basic portable toilets, but also for introducing solar-powered portable toilets with fresh running water, flushing toilets, sinks, interior lighting and mirrors.

The company has become one of the largest and most respected suppliers of portable toilets. Barry Gump's reputation in the industry led to his election as president of the Portable Sanitation Association International in 1989.

Barry's reputation in the business world led to his being named as the Small Business Administration's 1990 Small Business Person of the Year.

It was his involvement with community and charitable causes that gave him the edge against the other candidates in being named the Small Business Person of the Year. He has been involved with the Cystic Fibrosis Foundation since his daughter died of the disease more than 20 years ago. He served as president of the Los Angeles chapter of the foundation. Gump is co-founder of the L.A. Dodgers "Sixty Five Roses" Club which has raised hundreds of thousands of dollars to help fight cystic fibrosis. Gump is also a member of the California Building Industry Association and belongs to local chambers of commerce.

Andy Gump, Inc. is a firm that does more than it gets credit for. Not just a provider of portable toilets, Andy Gump supplies temporary power to construction sites along with temporary fencing, field offices, hole drilling and services residential septic systems.

Barry Gump not only carries on the tradition of his father, but credits his father for providing him with the work ethic that has allowed him to build the business. Barry's wife, Pati, is director of personnel and their daughter, Nancy, joined the firm in 1989 and represents the third generation of Gumps serving the Santa Clarita community.

BELOW: Barry, Nancy, and Andy Gump.

RIGHT: The Andy Gump VIP, "Very Impressive-Portable," a solar-powered, flushing portable toilet with fresh water, sink, light, and mirror.

COUNTRY OAKS ESCROW

Harold and Kathy Wiener represent the truest meaning of commitment and dedication. They have combined a loving and caring family and a very successful escrow business. They have conquered a major health problem. Maybe that is why Harold and Kathy take such great pride in their company slogan, "Commitment to excellence."

The Wieners are blessed not only with the success of their business, but truly fortunate that they have their health, especially where Harold is concerned.

Harold, the recipient of a heart transplant in January 1989, has overcome his ailment to combine his more than two decades of bank management experience with his wife's real estate escrow savvy to form Country Oaks Escrow.

It was Harold's 14-year bout with a congenital heart condition that led the Wieners into the escrow business. In the late 1970s Kathy came to the realization that her husband's sometimes vulnerable condition could at any time worsen, leaving her with the responsibility of raising their son Jeffrey, 16, and daughter Becky, 14. Thus, Kathy opened a small escrow office in Newhall in March 1981 with the hope of doing well enough to support the family.

Kathy, with the help of her husband, has attained her goal and more. In 1991 Country Oaks Escrow celebrated its 10th anniversary. It has more than 100 employees and four offices: Valencia, which is the corporate office, Arcadia, Lancaster, and Palmdale. Country Oaks has come a long way since its first day, March 1, 1981, when it had one secretary and a telephone not yet connected.

Dedication and commitment have made Country Oaks Escrow one of the largest escrow companies in California and have given it a reputation for excellent service.

During the lean years, the Wieners have remained optimists and never let the 1990 real estate slowdown affect their ideals or goals.

The Wieners, who met while working together in the banking industry in the late 1960s, married within weeks of their meeting.

Harold and Kathy Wiener with their children, Jeffrey and Becky.

Harold and Kathy Wiener

Their marriage has endured not only financial and business setbacks but also the difficult years while Harold fought for his life.

Through it all, Country Oaks Escrow has prospered with the expertise of Harold's banking experience and Kathy's perseverance to be able to support her family. Country Oaks Escrow can quite literally be called the escrow company with a "heart."

The Wieners are very active in the local community on a personal as well as a business level. Their activities include hosting seminars for the real estate industry on a bimonthly basis, teaching classes on the escrow process, serving as chairpersons of the Boys and Girls Club 1992 auction, serving on the Henry Mayo Newhall Hospital Corporate Partners Program, and founders of the Valencia National Bank. Harold and Kathy Wiener also serve in many capacities in the banking and escrow industry statewide.

Polycarbon Inc.

With 220 employees, Polycarbon rates as a midsize company in the Santa Clarita Valley. But it is a firm with a reputation that stretches far beyond the valley, thanks to the quality of its workers and products.

Polycarbon Inc. was founded by Pat Sterry in 1967 in North Hollywood. Sterry had reached the point in his career where he was not only eager to start his own firm, but he had the experience and know-how to do so.

Sterry worked for Boeing in Seattle, Washington, from 1957 to 1960, getting solid work experience. He was then offered and accepted a job as vice president for research and development of Hitco, a Southern California maker of composites used in the aerospace industry.

Not long after leaving Hitco, Sterry had his own firm, Polycarbon Inc., up and running. It was the start of a success story. The company has grown rapidly, going from two to 220 employees and from $500,000 to $35 million in annual sales as of 1990.

In each of the eight years preceding 1990, Polycarbon Inc. has boasted a 20 percent increase in sales. "Our markets grew much more than I expected and we were able to capture a larger share of these specialty material markets," Sterry says.

Most of Polycarbon Inc.'s customers are in the Midwest, but the firm has customers scattered around the globe in about 20 countries. Twenty percent of the sales come from customers overseas.

One of Polycarbon's most high-profile products is the insulation used in the throat and exit cones of the space shuttle solid rocket boosters. Polycarbon makes the insulation for ICI Fiberite, which in turn sells a product to Thiokol, the maker of the solid rocket boosters. This account provides Polycarbon with about 20 percent of its sales. Polycarbon Inc. has been working with the space shuttle program since 1973.

Other Polycarbon products are likely to be underneath the hood of a car. The company makes graphite sheets used in the making of automotive gaskets.

In 1980 Polycarbon Inc's achievements had attracted the attention of the respected Sigri Group of companies. Sigri purchased Polycarbon Inc., giving the Valencia firm added stability.

In 1983 Polycarbon Inc. moved into the Valencia Industrial Center, becoming one of the better-known firms in the large industrial park. The firm's offices are at 28176 North Avenue Stanford. The area was ideal, with reasonable land prices and near to the freeway and accessible to the airport.

The Valencia location has also benefitted Polycarbon Inc. by attracting quality workers. "The recruitment of employees has been relatively easy because people enjoy the Southern California environ-

In 1983 Polycarbon Inc. moved into the Valencia Industrial Center at 28176 North Avenue Stanford.

Polycarbon Inc. produces high-quality fabric, felt, rigid felt, yarn, foil, and composites.

ment," Sterry says.

Through all the moves and changes, Sterry has remained a head of Polycarbon Inc., giving it the direction that has enabled it to achieve success.

The firm has five product lines. In the yarn industry, Polycarbon leads the field in carbon/graphite yarns. This leadership is largely a result of the company's unique manufacturing processes. The graphite yarn is used in pump and valve stem packing worldwide.

As a maker of carbon and graphite composites, Polycarbon's rigid quality-control standards have helped the firm establish an enviable "no-rejects" record.

In the carbon fabric industry, Polycarbon has spent years developing a fabric with the graceful suppleness of a fine textile without sacrificing heat resistance or stability properties.

As a maker of carbon and graphite felt, Polycarbon engineers are constantly developing new ways of using felts in heat treating. For years, vacuum furnaces have used molybdenum shields and carbon graphite felt for insulation. The soft felts are excellent insulation materials and are used in conjunction with other materials.

In the graphite foil field, Polycarbon's Calcarbon Division has developed numerous pure forms and introduced unique homogeneous materials. Polycarbon has the world's largest foil line. The firm's laminates ensure leak-proof performance while effectively affording an environmentally safe alternative to asbestos.

The company's success has been attributed not only to its continuous efforts to develop new technology, but to its rigid standards, sound management, and its responsiveness to its customers.

Whether the product is fabric, felt, rigid felt, yarn, foil, or composites made by the firm, it must meet the high standards of Polycarbon Inc.

The Master's College

For an aspiring student who wants to honor Christ while preparing for a lifetime of service to Him in both the workplace and church, there's no better place to start than The Master's College.

Although officially known as The Master's College only since 1985, the 110-acre campus that is now nestled in the rolling hills of Santa Clarita was actually founded in 1927.

From 1927 until 1959, the college was primarily a theological school located in central Los Angeles. During the late 1940s, a liberal-arts program was started and the term "college" was added to the name. In 1959 Dr. John R. Dunkin became the president of Los Angeles Baptist College and Seminary. The school relocated to its present site in 1961; in 1974 it separated from the seminary, which moved to Washington State.

After 25 years of service, Dr. Dunkin retired in 1984, yet he still serves in an honorary capacity as president emeritus. A new, two-story student center that overlooks beautiful Placerita Canyon has been named after him as a reminder of his faithful dedication to the school.

In May 1985, Dr. John F. MacArthur, Jr., renowned Bible expositor on "Grace to You" radio and pastor of Grace Community Church in Sun Valley, was appointed president of the college. With the frequent exposure through the "Grace to You" radio ministry, the school suddenly became one of the fastest-growing Christian colleges in America. Present enrollment numbers nearly 900 students in the college and 175 students in the seminary. These students represent 37 states and 20 foreign countries.

Today The Master's College has 32 fields of study. In addition to baccalaureate degrees, teaching credentials and the one-year Master's Institute Bible diploma are also offered. The college provides a distinctive program offering personalized scholarship and discipleship to every student. Sound academic preparation in the liberal arts and sciences is combined with a biblical Christian foundation. The college is also a member of the National Association of Intercollegiate Athletics as well as the National Christian College Athletic Association.

Graduate programs in ministry are now available for students of The Master's College. Under Dr. MacArthur's leadership, The Master's Seminary was started in 1986 with the goal of producing pastors and church leaders skilled in Bible exposition. Strategically located on the campus of Grace Community Church, the seminary offers two degree programs: the Master of Divinity and the Bachelor of Theology.

Both the college and the seminary are accredited by the Accrediting Commission for Senior Colleges and Universities of the Western Association of Schools and Colleges.

Friendships flourish in the personal atmosphere on campus, in the dorms, and in the classrooms.

Personalized scholarship allows the students to interact with faculty inside and outside the classroom.

Six Flags Magic Mountain

As the city of Santa Clarita continues to evolve, so does one of its most notable residents, Six Flags Magic Mountain, a Time-Warner affiliated company.

Since opening its doors in May of 1971, the family-oriented Magic Mountain has induced a strong geographic presence for the Santa Clarita Valley. Magic Mountain has employed more than 60,000 people and entertained 50 million guests since it opened. The park's world-renowned roller coasters have given nearly 500 million rides, which exceeds the populations of the U.S., Japan, and Canada combined.

Over the years Magic Mountain's growth has paralleled the fast-growing Santa Clarita Valley. In 1990 the park had grown to feature more than 100 rides and attractions, with each year bringing forth a new adventure.

In the bicentennial year of 1976, the park introduced the world's first 360-degree looping roller coaster, the Great American Revolution (now called the Revolution). Two years later Colossus, the world's largest roller coaster, was introduced. Colossus, built on 10 acres at a cost of $6 million, sports nearly two miles of wooden track and features drops of 115 and 105 feet.

In 1979 Magic Mountain joined a national chain of seven theme parks after being purchased by the Texas-based Six Flags Corp.

The new owners quickly spent $6.5 million on the park, adding the Aqua Theatre, home to the Dolphin and Sea Lion show and the high diving stunt show. In addition, the Magic Moments Theatre was opened, a landscaped picnic pavilion was added, and a gas station and expanded parking areas were developed for the convenience of park visitors.

In following years the park introduced Roaring Rapids, a white-water rafting ride on a quarter-mile long river. The park also added Mystic Lake (1983), where a water skiing spectacular was staged. The following year, in commemoration of the Olympics being held in Los Angeles, Magic Mountain introduced the Sarajevo Bobsled ride.

In 1985 Magic Mountain attained a licensing agreement with Warner Bros. to bring Bugs Bunny and all his Looney Tunes friends to the park. In conjunction with the new association, Magic Mountain opened Bugs Bunny World, a six-acre children's wonderland with scaled-down rides and adventures.

Joseph R. Schillaci, who became president of the park in 1986, vowed to offer a "new and compelling" attraction each year. And over the next four years, Magic Mountain added Ninja, the West Coast's first suspended roller coaster, and Tidal Wave, called one of the wettest rides ever conceived.

Also during the latter part of the decade, Magic Mountain added weekend entertainment for teens, After Hours (an outdoor dance club), Back Street, and Z-Force, a looping starship ride. In 1990 the park introduced Viper, a twisting, turning suspended roller coaster that has been touted as the most frightening coaster on earth.

By 1990 Magic Mountain had grown from 50 acres to more than 260 acres, being recognized as one of the 10 largest theme parks in the country. The park also employs annually more than 3,000 seasonal workers, and more than 300 year-round employees.

In 1992, the park introduced Flashback, a $4 million steel coaster which features six steeply banked vertical 180-degree hairpin drops and a gravity-defying 540-degree horizontal corkscrew.

"Six Flags Magic Mountain is proud to have attracted the attention of Southern California, the nation, and the world to the Santa Clarita Valley," Schillaci says. "We are proud to be an active part of the valley's business environment and an integral part of our community's identification."

LEFT: With its thrilling rides, live shows, and spectacular attractions, Six Flags Magic Mountain has been one of Southern California's most popular family fun spots for more than 20 years.

BELOW: The Colossus is one of the world's longest, fastest, and highest dual-track wooden roller coasters. It covers 10 acres, is 1,608 feet from end to end, and is 125 feet from ground level to its highest point.

Castaic Union School District

The board members of the Castaic Union School District are becoming well acquainted with governing the district in a time of growth. John W. Johnson, a former board member, had been with the district 24 years, since there were about 200 students in grades kindergarten through sixth grade.

Irene L. Massey has been with the district 11 years, watching it grow from one to three school sites. And Jane Wakeham-Lopez, a former board member, with the district for about four years, notes it has more than doubled in size during the past five years.

The booming expansion of the district has also been witnessed by the other school board members, Gloria E. Mercado and Jane S. Pederson.

Gloria Mercado was the first Hispanic woman elected to a school board in the Santa Clarita Valley. Growing up in Castaic, she has seen the area grow "from a rural community to a more suburban commuity."

RIGHT:: Castaic's original schoolhouse, 1922.

BELOW: Castaic School, 1933.

Dr. Scott Brown was named superintendent of the Castaic Union School District in October 1988. "The enrollment as advertised in the job announcement was 991 students," he remembers. "Since that time the enrollment has grown to 1,539. In January 1989, Live Oak Elementary was completed and opened. The staff has grown in proportion to the enrollment increases and programs such as music, home arts, computer labs, and other electives have been added to the curriculum."

In addition to Live Oak Elementary, the district has Castaic Elementary and Castaic Middle School. The school district is bordered by the Santa Clarita River to the south, the Ventura County line to the west, the Oak Flat Ranger Station to the north, and the Saugus Union Elementary School District to the east.

The district was established March 25, 1889. Its centennial celebration included a dinner dance on June 2, 1989, followed by a pancake breakfast, a parade, and festival the next day.

Some historians have said the name Castaic comes from an Indian word meaning "elbow." Historian Jerry Reynolds, however, notes the name Castaic comes from the Indian word "kashtuk," which means "eyes" or "our eyes." During the time the first school was formed in the area, the name was rendered "Casteca" and the "Chastequike."

The area grew first with the discovery of gold, then with the discovery of oil. Don Antonio Del Valle had been among the settlers of the area, as had Francisco Lopez, who found gold in Placerita Canyon. The Cordova family lived in the upper end of Castaic Canyon, and in 1866 John Babtist Daris settled on 1,200 acres just south of the Cordovas.

Juan Jose Lopez built a home in the area in 1867 and George W. Lechler built a home in Hasley Canyon in 1879. Other family names of the era in which the school district was founded include Billa, Rose, Chronicle, Gardner, Madden, and Tapia. Perhaps the best-remembered person from the era was William W. Jenkins, dubbed the "Baron of Casteca" by the press. Jenkins was involved in a feud in the 1890s that left about 20 people dead.

Oil revenues financed the first school, a one-room building at the corner of Ferguson and the Old Road. It was small enough that when school officials decided to move it to a spot in the San Francisquito Canyon, they were able to haul it on a wagon bed. A second schoolhouse, this one larger, was built on Castaic Creek where the firehouse is now situated on Ridge Route Road.

There was a school in Hasley Canyon that served Hasley Canyon and Val Verde until it was shut down in the early 1950s. The school was administered by the Live Oaks School District, which consolidated with the Castaic District when the school

district's size and rapid growth, we have not been able to offer the students as many classes as we would like," he says.

Johnson says that within 20 years, the district could have four to six elementary schools and a high school. He sees the area gaining more of its own identity, as opposed to just being part of the Santa Clarita Valley. It is possible, he suggests, that the community will even become a city. "We have a good school district," he says. "Even with our growth we have been able to maintain some of the atmosphere that we have always had."

Johnson says the district benefits from the closeness of the community to its

LEFT and BELOW LEFT: Groundbreaking for Live Oak Elementary, 1987.

BELOW: Castaic Elementary, 1979.

was shut down.

There was a day when Castaic was one of the richest school districts in Southern California, thanks in part to oil royalties. The money allowed the district to build a swimming pool and hire a summer lifeguard.

Dr. Brown, superintendent of the district, says the people in Castaic have a strong commitment to do whatever is necessary to improve the course offerings. And, not surprisingly, he says the greatest challenge is to build adequate housing. "The district could easily grow to beyond 5,000 students in the next 20 years," he says. "This increase would facilitate the unification and the acquisition of a high school."

Brown says that while the district remains small, it has many fine teachers as well as a state-of-the-art approach to instruction. "Plans are firmly in place to ensure the orderly expansion of the district and its educational programs," he says.

John W. Johnson, a former long-time member of the school board, says the district has been able to hire and keep good teachers. He says the number-one weakness the district faces has been caused by the growth of the area. "Because of the teachers and students.

With the coming of an industrial center north of Highway 126 just west of Interstate 5, continued growth in the Castaic area is ensured. The area's economy benefits from both an influx of recreationalists coming to Castaic Lake and from the truckers who fuel up at the Giant and S&L truck stops.

The 1990 Census set the population of the area at more than 10,000 people. There are about 1,700 homes in the nucleus of Castaic and more than 1,300 in the other portion of the district, most of which are near the Hasley Canyon exit.

Henry Mayo Newhall Memorial Hospital

As the community of Valencia slowly began to evolve from the sloped terrain in the southwest corner of the Santa Clarita Valley, it became apparent in the late 1960s that growth would also bring the necessity for increased health care facilities in the area. Thus the idea and mission to establish such a facility was born. Spearheaded by Thomas Lowe, former chief executive officer of The Newhall Land and Farming Company, the search for a full service hospital began. Lowe, along with other community leaders of the day, sought out the services of the Lutheran Hospital Society (LHS) of Southern California. The LHS was chosen because of its half-century experience in developing and managing nonprofit hospitals. At the time seven hospitals were being managed by the Society, with an employee base of 5,500.

In December 1970, representatives of Newhall Land, LHS, and the community met and decided that a new medical facility should be formed in the Santa Clarita Valley. From there, the funding, planning, building, and eventual opening of Henry Mayo Newhall Memorial Hospital (HMNMH), quickly took shape. The Newhall name was adopted in recognition of the gifts the Newhall family had donated to the valley through their long-standing history in the area.

One month after the planned hospital was approved, Lowe announced that Newhall Land had authorized a gift of 25 acres along McBean Parkway in Valencia to be used as the site for the hospital. Newhall Land also donated one million dollars toward the early development, along with allocating office space for the HMNMH staff. Lowe sought out several top community leaders to be called the board of trustees for HMNMH. Fund raising became a critical part of the project, with $8 million needed for construction and an additional $2 million for initial operating costs. The Lutheran Hospital Society played a big part in the early financing, securing several million dollars in loans that would otherwise have taken months or years to accumulate in various fund-raising activities.

After entertaining bids from several construction firms from across the country, the San Francisco-based firm of Stone, Marraccini and Patterson was selected to design and construct the hospital. The San Francisco firm had proven itself in a building concept called "fast tracking." Fast tracking was a system that expedited construction in a manner that would save several months in time and millions of dollars.

While the new medical facility was being built, the board of trustees decided to buy an existing hospital in the commu-

nity which it accomplished by purchasing Inter-Valley Community Hospital and renaming it Hillside Community Hospital. The newly acquired hospital served three primary objectives: consolidating medical staff and employee base; serving as an educational pilot for the board of trustees; and acting as a stimulus for additional community support. As HMNMH's pilot hospital, Hillside maintained high census and a good reputation, it was successful enough to pay for its own operational costs plus an additional one million dollars of working capital for the soon to open HMNMH.

On August 3, 1975, the culmination of an intensive community effort was complete. Henry Mayo Newhall Memorial Hospital took its place in the burgeoning Santa Clarita Valley. The 99 bed hospital was staffed with 78 physicians and 287 initial employees. Over the next 15 years, HMNMH continued to grow along with the community: medical staff included more than 200 physicians; 1,000 employees and the bed count increased to 253. The hospital went through extensive expansion over the years, doubling in size by 1990, with the opening of the hospital Pavilion, Medical Office Building, and Ambulatory Care Center.

HMNMH, a state-of-the-art health care facility, offers patients trauma and emergency facilities; inpatient and outpatient medical and surgical services; women's health center; adult day health care; psychiatric programs; post-surgical recovery unit; cardiology; cardiology, pulmonary, and outpatient rehabilitation services; and a cancer center.

The operation of HMNMH remains a local, community responsibility with a volunteer board of directors comprised of people who live and work in the Santa Clarita Valley.

More than 20 years after the conception of an idea, Henry Mayo Newhall Memorial Hospital is a source of pride in a community that continues to reach new heights.

ATC Cablevision

Since 1969, ATC Cablevision, one of Santa Clarita Valley's cable companies, has delivered cable television into area homes. With more than 250 miles of cable in Canyon Country and parts of Newhall and Saugus, ATC Cablevision's preferred service consists of more than three times what was once considered the industry standard of 12 channels.

Without the development of cable, television viewing in the Santa Clarita Valley would be tremendously restricted. ATC Cablevision carries the most successful cable services and also provides commercial-free entertainment options such as HBO, Cinemax, Showtime, and the Disney Channel.

"In our world of satellite communications, cable television has dramatically changed how people send and receive their news and information," Cablevision General Manager Scott Binder relates. "As an example, in the initial hours of Operation Desert Storm, Secretary of Defense, Dick Cheney said, 'The best information I have is coming from CNN ...it would appear, based on comments coming in from the CNN crew in the hotel in Baghdad that the operation was successful.' During the Vietnam War, Americans read the morning paper and had to wait for the evening news to get an update. With CNN, people watch the news unfold."

ATC Cablevision offers the ticket to sports events not aired by broadcast networks with early rounds of Wimbledon and the U.S. Open tennis tournaments on HBO and the USA network. Boxing events, previously available only at closed circuit telecast locations, can now be seen in the comfort of one's home on HBO, Showtime or pay-per-view. With Sunday night football on ESPN and TNT, the NBA on TNT, and Major League Baseball on many cable channels, your favorite professional team is only a wave of the remote control away.

Cablevision employees are sometimes asked to go out on a limb to suit customers needs. Photo by Douglas Ferber

Beginning in the fall of 1992, ATC Cablevision will begin to offer customers four channels of pay-per-view service, including movies and major events such as boxing, wrestling and concerts. Customers will be able to order pay-per-view by phone twenty-four hours a day without leaving their homes.

Today cable offers Valley residents diversified entertainment choices and global news and information around the clock. Cable television has changed dramatically in the last 20 years. By investing millions of dollars into the Santa Clarita Valley, ATC Cablevision has led the way toward an exciting future for cable communications.

Scott Binder, General Manager of ATC Cablevision

Sulphur Springs School District

Nearly everyone would agree that first generating and then maintaining a "family feeling" among hundreds of disparate families in a fast-growing community such as Santa Clarita is not the easiest of tasks. But, judging from the breadth of its programs and its students' high scholastic achievement, it could quite favorably be argued that the Sulphur Springs School District is providing an ideal environment for equal opportunity to all of its family members.

As part of its vision about what the district can and should be, there is unanimous agreement that students should be afforded the opportunity to achieve their full potential through a quality, balanced curriculum. Further, the district is committed to providing students measurable academic achievement and a nurturing, secure climate that prepares them to work and function in the world of tomorrow.

The Sulphur Springs School District got its start in 1872 under the direction of Colonel T.F. Mitchell, who in 1860 was the first permanent settler in the area. The opening of the Sulphur Springs School in a lean-to off Mitchell's adobe home makes it the second-oldest school in Los Angeles County.

Mitchell started the school because he was concerned about the education of his own children. But, with the addition of several other families joining the school, the student body grew to 10 children. By the 1880s school was being held in one of the rooms in Mitchell's home. It was dur-

LEFT and BELOW: The district is committed to providing a secure, nurturing environment so students have the opportunity to achieve their full academic potential.

The Sulphur Springs School District has 3,750 students.

ing the 1880s that a one-room adobe schoolhouse was built on two acres of land donated by Mitchell.

For a time the area was divided into two districts, Honby and Mint Canyon. When fire destroyed the Mint Canyon building in 1943, the two districts consolidated. By the fall of 1944, the Sulphur Springs Union School District had a total enrollment of 83 students. By May 1970, there were 492 pupils, 18 teachers, and 10 classified staff members.

The district today has seven schools; the smallest is Mint Canyon with about 300 students and the largest is Pinetree with about 800 students. The district also includes Leona Cox, Sulphur Springs, Mitchell, Soledad/Honby, and Valley View schools. Combined the district has more than 3,750 students and 145 teachers and specialists.

In order to cope with this growth, the district has embarked on an ambitious undertaking that is being met by positive response. Pinetree is the first school in Santa Clarita to adopt a year-round multi-track, calendar. Students attend classes throughout the year with scheduled breaks. It is a system driven by growth but it allows administrators to obtain 25 percent more space from the schools without sacrificing classroom achievement. It represents only one of the many pioneering and innovative programs at the Sulphur Springs School District.

American Beauty Homes

From its beginning in 1963 and throughout its existence, the image of American Beauty Homes has been carefully molded to become a name synonymous with quality construction, economic value, and consistently well-designed homes for entry-level and move-up buyers at a reasonable price.

Company officials agree that American Beauty Homes' popularity is primarily based on the very simple axiom of value to the home buyer. The use of the most modern building techniques, contemporary materials, and the latest advancements in space planning, guarantee home buyers not only a great price, but an aesthetically pleasing, functional, and solidly built home as well.

With each of its numerous projects, American Beauty Homes has consistently maintained a steadfast commitment to building quality "homes for the people." The success of this concept has been proven each time a new American Beauty Homes' development opens its doors to a crowd of eager home buyers.

Buyer profiles have changed dramatically over the years since the company first began building homes. During the late 1960s and early 1970s, the cost of single-family homes became prohibitive for the first-time buyer. In response to this trend, First Financial Group, American Beauty Homes' parent company, began developing multifamily products such as apartments, condominiums, and townhouses.

At the same time, the company introduced the American Beauty Garden home, a new housing type for the Santa Clarita Valley. The efficient land planning design of these duplex units maintained the same size of a single-family home while allowing the company to keep the price affordable.

Beginning in the late 1970s, American Beauty Homes introduced to the Santa Clarita Valley the idea of a single-family detached unit with common areas, including recreational facilities and a home owners' association responsible for maintaining the common areas.

Previously satisfied with merely owning a house, today's buyer is looking for a life-style in a community that can meet recreational, social, and professional requirements. In order to meet that demand, American Beauty Homes is diversifying and expanding.

One of the most exciting projects planned for the 1990s actually began in 1983, when approximately 1,000 acres of land were purchased in Canyon Country. The specific plan for this area was approved by the county of Los Angeles in 1986 and includes the Canyon Park and Provence communities. The plan allows for the construction of up to 5,400 residential housing units, five commercial properties, two elementary schools, public and private recreational areas, as well as other amenities.

The Canyon Park project lies northwest of the Antelope Valley Freeway at Via Princessa. Sales for this project began in April 1990. When completed, Canyon Park will offer a mix of Townhouses, Villas and Carriage homes totalling approximately 1,000 units.

Even more ambitious is American Beauty Homes' Provence project. Located southeast of the Antelope Valley Freeway, north of Placerita Canyon Road, and south of the Santa Clara River, Provence will blend all of the benefits of a modern-day master-planned community with the classic characteristics of a natural Southern California setting. The name Provence was chosen for the project because of the site's similarity to Provence, France, with respect to terrain, vegetation, and foliage, as well as the style of architecture and landscaping.

The master-planned community involves some 850 acres providing approximately 3,000 residential units as well as commercial and retail development, school sites, and numerous park and recreational facilities. Residents will enjoy a sense of security and community as Provence will be composed of individual neighborhoods, each with its own homeowners' association and private recreational facilities, and a wide variety of prices and styles.

Two other projects by the company are also eagerly anticipated. The Oak Springs Estates project will offer homes from 2,500 to 4,500 square feet. The equestrian-oriented community will be one of Canyon Country's most elite offerings and represents American Beauty Homes' entry into the luxury home market.

The other project, Palmdale Park South, is a specified planned community consisting of 414 home sites of which American Beauty Homes will build 211.

In addition to development, American Beauty Homes is active in the preservation of the character of the Santa Clarita Valley, namely in its participation in the Los Angeles county approved state-of-the-art oak tree program. Among the activities are the preservation of on-site oak trees within parkways, neighborhood parks, and natural open space; the relocation of heritage and specimen oaks into designated oak groves and project landscaping the creation of an on-site 10,000 oak tree nursery to supply trees to Provence and the surrounding communities; and a comprehensive oak tree maintenance program.

The future promises to be an exciting time for American Beauty Homes as it continues to build upon its successes in new and dynamic ways. But, probably more important, is the fact that American Beauty Homes realizes the changing concerns and attitudes of potential home buyers and continues to construct homes that are tailored to their ever-changing needs.

ABOVE: The Meadows
OPPOSITE PAGE: Canyon Park Carriage Homes

Chevron U.S.A. Inc.

Pico Springs, also known as Mentryville, has been called the cradle of the oil industry in the American West. It was there that the first commercially successful oil well west of Pennsylvania was developed. And, it was in nearby Newhall, California, that the first practical oil refinery had its home.

The company behind many of the successes at Mentryville was Standard Oil Company of California, today known as Chevron, a firm in its infancy when Mentryville was in its prime.

In 1880 Mentryville was a town of 100 families. It was not a typical community with streets laid out in block fashion. The homes were scattered; some sites were selected because they were near wells, some because the land was flat. There were boarding and bunk houses for new arrivals and a tent city for single men.

In time, Mentryville had tennis courts, a croquet field, and a horseshoe field. They were perhaps the only such sports facilities in the nation to be lighted by natural gas. Most of the homes were also lighted and heated, thanks to the area's abundant gas resources.

Today, little remains of the industrious community that once existed. Most residents made a practice of hauling away or tearing down homes when they moved away. Of the few buildings surviving this custom, many were subsequently vandalized. Others ultimately collapsed from old age or were torn down when they became hazardous.

Oil in Mentryville was an unusual emerald-green color. It gave Santa Clarita Valley two claims to strange-looking oil. The other was the yellow-colored oil from nearby Placerita Canyon—reportedly so clear a person could read a newspaper while peering through it. John A. Scott, a refinery owner who tested the oil while on a visit to Mentryville, pronounced it as "unsurpassed in quality."

But, whatever its qualities, getting the oil out of the ground and to market posed many problems. One was finding a spot flat enough for a derrick. Another was the geology—subsurface rocks were actually turned over, older ones ending up on top of the younger ones.

Also, drinking water was fouled by sulfur, forcing the oil camp to import water, first on wagons and then through pipelines.

Still, the oil field blossomed. In 1885

Chevron's lineage: Standard Oil Company of California's predecessor was the Pacific Coast Oil Company, operating in Santa Clarita Valley in the 1880s.

the *Los Angeles Times* reported that "C.A. Mentry, superintendent of the Star Oil Works Company and Pacific Coast Oil, has charge of one of the largest industries in Southern California." Mentry was the fledgling oil town's namesake.

Pacific Coast oil's name was later to be changed to Standard Oil Company of California, predecessor of Chevron. The firm's roots in the Santa Clarita Valley can be traced to Frederick B. Taylor, Demetrius G. Scofield, and their California Star Oil Works, a company consisting of four derricks in Pico Canyon.

According to Santa Clarita historian Jerry Reynolds, California Star had the first commercially successful oil well in

LEFT and BELOW: Mentryville, seen here in this circa 1888 photo, is now a California Registered Historical Landmark.

![Pico Canyon photo]

California. Reynolds, who wrote a definitive history of the oil days of Mentryville, notes California Star Oil's No. 4 well was producing 30 barrels a day—an unheard-of rate in California. A steam rig was used to push the well deeper, resulting in a flow of 50 barrels a day on September 26, 1876.

The well eventually became known as the oldest continuously operating oil well in the world, but it lost the title when it was shut down in September 1990.

Small oil producers at the time were always looking for buyers. Taylor solved the problem by merging with a group of oil merchants and investors headed by Scofield, forming Pacific Coast Oil Company.

California Star Oil Company, a subsidiary of Pacific Coast Oil, purchased two existing oil refining stills in late 1875, and moved them to what is now Pine Street in Newhall. By mid-July, 1876, the new Pioneer Oil Refinery was churning out 25 to 40 barrels of refined oil each day, enough to give it claim to being the first practical refinery in California. The long-idle refinery has since become a California Historical Landmark and is now known as the oldest existing refinery in the world.

Pacific Coast Oil was not growing fast enough to keep pace with its competitors. Had it not been for a wealthy investor, John D. Rockefeller, Pacific Coast might have been forced to close. Having operations in the West, Rockefeller's Standard Oil Company of New Jersey purchased Pacific Coast Oil and its subsidiary, California Star Oil, in 1900. For six years Pacific Coast operated as a wholly owned property of Standard Oil of New Jersey. In 1906 Standard Oil Company of California was formed, encompassing what had been Pacific Coast Oil and some smaller firms. Scofield was named president of the Company that would become Chevron.

Today's Chevron no longer produces oil within the Santa Clarita Valley, but continues as a neighbor throughout the area with real estate holdings.

ABOVE: Pico Canyon in November 1910.

LEFT; California's first commercially productive oil well, Pico No. 4, was completed at a depth of 300 feet in 1876 for initial flow of 30 barrels a day. It was later deepened to 600 feet and production increased to 150 barrels daily. In 1975 it was still yielding almost a barrel daily. Photo circa 1877.

Tan Medical Group/Newhall Community Hospital and Clinic

Even today, while still enjoying a full medical career that has spanned five decades, countless surgeries and innumerable diagnoses, Dr. Bienvenido B. Tan, M.D., continues his search for excellence. Tan, founder and chief surgeon of the Tan Medical Group and administrator of the Newhall Community Hospital and Clinic, deeply believes that the search for excellence is an ongoing, never-ending process involving proper preparation and hard work, principles that Tan has applied throughout his career. It is a quest worthy of effort and quite obviously evident throughout both of his medical practices.

Tan came to this country after graduating from the College of Medicine of the University of the Philippines in 1953. He spent his childhood in the hills of the war-ravaged Philippines "where there was little if any proper medical care," which had a significant impact on his life and subsequent career choice. In 1954, after a brief stint at the Toledo Hospital in Ohio, Tan joined Boston City Hospital, one of the largest training facilities for Tufts Medical School. During the five years spent at Boston City Hospital, Tan became a highly trained physician fully capable in all aspects of surgery. In fact, Tan became the first non-Ivy League intern to succeed at Tufts.

Upon completion of his tenure at Tufts, the U.S. Immigration Department wanted to deport Tan back to the Philippines. Then U.S. Senator John F. Kennedy intervened on Tan's behalf and subsequently, as president, granted Tan his U.S. citizenship by executive order.

Tan and his wife moved to California where he received his state license in 1959. Initially, he practiced briefly at a large medical facility in Los Angeles specializing in corrective heart surgery. The experience of working in a large medical facility is not one he cares to repeat.

Says Tan, "The medical facility that I was working for was too large. Everyone became a number—not a person. I personally believe when a patient entrusts you with his confidence to care for him, you should care for that person on an individual basis."

Leaving the safe haven of an established medical practice, Tan opened an office in Pacoima—what is now Lake View Terrace area. One of the reasons he chose this particular community was the fact that there was only one other trained surgeon in the entire northeastern San Fernando Valley. He specialized in vascular work and reconstructive surgery, much of it resulting from industrial accidents.

"During the early 1960s most surgeries were performed by general practitioners with little or no formal training," Tan says. "I was very well trained and the results of my work proved effective, and soon many of the doctors were referring patients to me."

In 1963 Tan purchased the Newhall Community Hospital and Clinic from Dr. Leslie Innis. For many years, Newhall Community Hospital was the only hospital between Los Angeles and Ventura. In those days, before the freeway systems were developed, highway emergency cases were treated at the hospital and some residents of the nearby movie colony were among its patients.

Today, Tan Medical Group and

Newhall Community Hospital receive between 4,000 to 5,000 patient visitations per month. The doctors and staff take pride in their work, a fact which is reflected in their friendly, personalized attitude. Perhaps because the hospital is small—only 14 beds—there is a strong family feeling. In fact, some of the patients are third and fourth generation members of families from the Santa Clarita Valley.

The hospital's surgery suite is equipped with the very latest equipment available. Many of the newer nonsurgical diagnostic procedures are routinely performed by the highly experienced surgical and technical staff. Of course, all the legal requirements for operating a general-acute hospital are the same and equally enforced for all hospitals, large and small. Serving the needs of MediCare patients is of special interest at both Tan Medical Group and Newhall Community Hospital.

The doctor's special skills in medicine and surgery attract patients from surrounding states as well as more distant portions of California.

In addition to Tan, three other full-time physicians work out of the Newhall Community Hospital and the four locations of the Tan Medical Group in Newhall, Sylmar, Frazier Park, and Saugus.

Dr. Clyde W. Johnson, M.D., joined Tan's practice in 1967 and has worked with him ever since. A member of the American Academy of Family Physicians, Johnson received his doctor of medicine degree from Indiana University in 1961.

Dr. Felix M. Barte, M.D., joined Tan Medical Group in 1985. Active in several organizations, including the American Medical Association and the California Medical Association, Barte received his formal medical training in the Philippines.

The newest arrival to the practice is Dr. Jose Pangilinan Mutia, M.D. Like Barte, Mutia attended medical school in the Philippines. Additionally, he worked as a general medical officer for the U.S. Navy and today is a commander in the U.S. Naval Reserve.

These physicians, working in conjunction with more than 100 nurses and support staff, provide a variety of medical services to the community. Included among the many services are cardiac monitoring-holter and stress tests, complete laboratory and X-ray services, physical therapy, spirometry-pulmonary (lung) tests, ultra-sound and echocardiography services, and arterial and venous cardiovascular tests.

Tan's current work and interest lies in endarterectomy, or carotid artery surgery. It is stroke-preventive surgery achieved by cleaning out arteries that have become clotted or damaged. Over the past three years, Tan and his staff have performed more than 280 of these operations resulting in no deaths and only two complications. The national average for complications resulting from this type of surgery runs at about three to five percent. The staff at Tan Medical Group and Newhall Community Hospital and Clinic is running at less than one percent.

The quest for excellence continues. Many of the recent advances in medical technology have been highly publicized and dramatized in the media. It is the standing policy of the Newhall Community Hospital to carefully analyze the medical value of those products and to utilize those that give the most significant benefit to the diagnostic accuracy and treatment of the patient's problems.

In addition to keeping himself and his staff abreast of the latest changes in medical technology, Dr. Tan would also like to expand the existing staff and enlarge the hospital.

Says Tan, "I want to expand but not sacrifice the intimacy we have established over the years. We must incorporate the latest technologies but never at the expense of the patient's individuality. I've seen what happens in those 3,000 bed hospitals. Sometimes you couldn't find your patient for two days."

Tan stops, reflecting for a moment, and then adds, "You see, the way we function around here, our patients aren't just our patients, they're also our friends."

With that kind of humanistic attitude it looks as if Dr. Bienvenido Tan's quest for excellence just took another positive step in the right direction.

AQUAFINE CORPORATION

Ultraviolet disinfection units manufactured by Aquafine Corporation are used to ensure that water is bacteria free before it is added to products made by Pepsi Cola, Coca Cola, 7-Up, Anheuser Busch, Labatts, Corona, Heineken, Johnson & Johnson, Vicks, Eli Lilly, Merck, and others. Aquafine units are used in many of the water vending machines located in front of supermarkets.

These ultraviolet disinfection units are for many purposes: to purify drinking water; prevent the outbreak of disease at fish hatcheries, ensure that rinsing water is bacteria free when it is used during food processing; pharmaceutical and cosmetic manufacturing; and for sanitizing cans, bottles, water lines, and storage tanks.

Aquafine Corporation's ultraviolet disinfection units are also used by IBM, Motorola, Texas Instruments, INTEL, and hundreds of other semiconductor manufacturers to provide bacteria-free water for rinsing chip components. Bacteria on water surfaces can cause short circuiting and can alter electrical values, destroying the value of the chip.

Aquafine Corporation was founded in

RIGHT; Louis P. Veloz, founder, next to custom designed disinfection unit for the City of Long Beach.

BELOW; Aquafine Corporation's facility in Valencia Industrial Park.

1949 by Louis P. Veloz, father of Tom Veloz, the current chairman of the board and chief executive officer. Roberta Veloz is president and chief operating officer.

Louis Veloz was one of the Westinghouse scientists who invented commercial ultraviolet lamps, which were initially used to reduce bacteria in the air and on product surfaces. He was employed by Westinghouse in the late 1930s.

In the late 1940s, Veloz moved to the West Coast, where he purchased and operated the largest Westinghouse ultraviolet light distributorship in the country. From 1949 to 1959 most company sales were related to airborne applications, primarily to reduce airborne disease in poultry farms. Veloz was an inventor, and began manufacturing ultraviolet water disinfection units some 40 years ago, and thus Aquafine was founded.

Fortunately the innovative, resourceful spirit of Louis Veloz was able to meet the challenges of the high-tech market for non-chemical water disinfection, thus ensuring the future of Aquafine.

ACKNOWLEDGMENTS & BIBLIOGRAPHY

A. ORAL HISTORY

Over the years the author has been privileged to know a numberof pioneers, who, unfortunately, are no longer with us except in spirit. These include, first and foremost, Mrs. Anita Ruby Jenkins Kellogg, a delightfully charming lady, the daughter of "The Baron of Castaic." Tall, slender, natty Lloyd Houghton was to the end a true gentleman. Mr. Arthur B. Perkins, feisty and loving nothing better than a good verbal brawl. Charles Outland of Santa Paula contributed much. Tom Mason questioned everything and kept me on the straight and narrow path. Mimi White, the charming librarian, and Art Evans, "Mr. Canyon Country", knew where all of the bodies were buried. Fred Trueblood, Jr. was an eloquent writer and tireless seeker of the truth. George Shaffner of Saugus and Opal Mayhue De Chene, "The Belle of Newhall" eagerly shared the gossip of the good ol' days, as did A.J. Pike of Castaic.

Luckily still with us are Darryl Haskell, with his photographic memory and Mrs. Gladys Laney, who loves to correct my errors. Up in Castaic are Clarence Swanson, Rudy Cordova and Claude Jones (now in Bakersfield). Toward Filmore is Harold Micheal, while Saugus residents Helen wood Cone and Mrs. Fred Cullen are lively sources of information. Thanks, also, to Norman Harris, Dorothy Riley and Alberta Knox. Tom Frew cooks a magnificent meal while telling tales.

Very special thank-yous must go to Scott and Ruth Newhall for their constant encouragements and spelling corrections. Experts on local Indians are Bob Edberg and Dr. Louis J. Tartaglia. Three lovely ladies made history, Bobbie Trueblood Davis, Connie Worden and Jo Anne Darcy. Frenchie and Carol Lagasse are the oil experts. Betty Pember and Melba Fisher deserve medals for their patience.

All of their comments are in the Historical Society archives."

B. UNPUBLISHED MANUSCRIPTS

"The Story of Newhall" by Peggy Brunner, On File at the Newhall Library.
"The Castaic Story"-several authors. Castaic School archives.
"Collected Papers" on file at the Sulphur Springs School.
"Notes On The History Of The Santa Clarita Valley", by Arthur B. Perkins. Documents at the SCV Historical Society Library.
"The Perkins Collection" of books and ms. at the valencia Library.
"Placerita Canyon History", stored at Placerita County Park.¡
"Mentryville and Pico Documents "Pico Cottege," maintained by F.J. and Carol Lagasse.¡
"Incised Petroglyph Sites at Agua Dulce", Linda Barby King. Cal-State Northridge.

C. NEWSPAPERS

"The Acton Rooster" 1891©1915. Microfilm at the Valencia Library. Originals in SCV Historical Society Library.
"The Newhall Signal" 1919©1992. Microfilm at the Valencia Library. Original papers at the Signal office.

D. BOOKS

Bakker, Elna. "Angeles National Forest-Island In the Sky." Big Santa Anita Historical Society, Arcadia. 1991
Bell, Maj. Horace. "Reminiscences of a Ranger." L.A. 1881
Bell, Maj. Horace. "On the Old West Coast." New York. 1930
Cleland, Robert G. "The Cattle on a Thousand Hills." San Marino CA., 1941.¡
Dana, Richard H. "Two Years Before The Mast." Los Angeles 1964
Harrigton, Marie. "A Golden Spike" Mission Hills, CA 1976
Keen, James C. and Emil T. Bunje. "Pre Marshall Gold in California." Volume II, Sacramento, CA 1983.
Greenwood, Robert C. "Vasquez." New York 1968.
Nadeau, Remi. "City Makers." Los Angeles. 1965.
Needham, Henry C. "My First Wild Turkey." Sacramento, CA 1977
Newhall, Ruth W. "The Newhall Ranch." San Marino, CA 1958. Revised and updated in September 1992.
Newmark, Harris. "Sixty Years in Southern California." New York. 1916.
Outland, Charles. "Man Made Disaster." Glendale, CA 1977.
Outland, Charles. "Mines, Murders and Grizzlies." Ventura 1969.
Outland, Charles. "Stagecoaching on El Camino Real." Glendale. 1973.
Perkins, Arthur B. "Rancho San Francisco." Los Angeles, 1957.
Perkins, Arthur B. "History of Eternal Valley:. Newhall. 1958.
Reynolds, Gerald G. "Pico Canyon Chronicles". Glendale. 1985.
Robinson, John W. "Mines of the San Gabriels." Glendale 1990.
Robinson, John W. "The San Gabriels." Arcadia, CA 1991.
Robinson, W.W. "The Story of Valencia." Newhall 1967.
Williamson, R.S. "Pacific Railroad Survey." Washington D.C. 1852.
Young, Walton. "Men of the Tejon." Los Angeles. 1965.

E. GENEOLOGY

Bob Lopez of Los Angeles, especially of early Californias.

F. PERIODICALS

Desert Magazine, August 1981. "A Man and a Mine." Tom McGrath, page 44.

Desert Magazine, January 1952. "Lost Cave of the San Martins." Richard Van Valkenberg, Page 10.

Desert Magazine, March 1957. "Forgotten Mill of the Josuas.")

Evelyn Slack Gist, Page 9.

Real West, July 1978. "Monarch of all he Surveyed." Jerry Reynolds. page 16.

True West, June 1971. "William S. Hart." Pete la Roche. Page 26.

True West, Sept. 1985. "The Baron of Alcatraz." Jerry Reynolds. Page 19.

Westways. March 1981. "Path of the Outlaw." John W. Robinson. Page 53.

INDEX

Italicized numbers indicate illustrations.

A

Abbott, Ed, *88-89*
Acton, 7, 33, 64, 67-68, 74, 106, 117
Acton Community Church, 64, 130
Acton Depot, 47, 67
Acton Hotel, 67, *68*,130
Acton Post Office, 130
Acton Rooster, The, 67, 130
Acton Water Works, 67
Agua Dulce, 7, 16, 77, 117, 118
Agua Dulce Springs, 44
Alexander, David, 29
Ali, Hadji, 30
Aliso Canyon, 106
Allen, Gabriel, 29
Allen, "Greek" George, 30, 45
Alline, Eureka Villa, 92
Alvarado, Juan B., 1
American, The (theater), 108, *109*, 1318
American Express, 31
American Legion Post 107, 109
Anawalt Lumber Company, 55
Andrew's Station, 60, 62
Angeles National Forest, 12, 92, 130
Antelope Valley, 9, 36, 47
Arguello, Santiago, 21
Arrillaga, Jose, 17
Arujo, Pablo, 36
Arujo family, 36
Asistencia de San Francisco Javier, *14, 15*, 17, 18, 19, 32; founding of, 129
Atlantic and Pacific Railroad, 46
Atlantic and Pacific Telegraph, 53
Atwood, M.W., 72
Audubon, John W., 129
Auto racing, 110, *111*. *See also* Saugus Speedway
Autry, Gene, 96, 98, 100, 114, 131; Western Heritage Museum of, 100
Autry, Jackie, 100
Averill, Tom, *94*
Avila, Francisco, 17

B

Bailey, Nell, 87
Baker, Robert S. "Bobby," 39, 40
Baker, Roy, 95
Baker-Hoot Gibson Rodeo Arena, 110, 131
Baldwin, E.J. "Luckey," *52*
Ball, Robert, *88-89*
Bandini, Juan, 25, 29
Banks, Eva, *58*
Banning, Phineas T., 29, 49, *52*, 53, 80, 129
Bard, Thomas R., 46, 129
Bartlett, Governor, 69
Battle of Mad Mountain, 105
Beale, Edward Fitzgerald, 7, 30, 32, *35*, 36, 37, 39, 40, 41, 80, 129
Beale, Mary Edwards, 36
Beale, Truxtun, 36
Beale's Cut, 35, *37*, 95, 96, *97*, 98, 105, 129
Beaudry, Prudent, *52*, 53
Bell, Horace, 29, 31, 58, 59
Bella family, 78
Bercaw, Ore W., *70*; residence of, 70
Bercaw family, 70
Bercaw General Store, 130
Bermite, 104, 116
Bermudez, Domingo, 20, 129
Biscailuz, Valentine, *58*
Bishop, 90
Black community. *See* Val Verde
Bloomfield, Lawrence B., 119
Blum, George, 106, 108
Blum, Magdalena, 106
Boardinghouses: Mentryville, *63*; Mrs. Harper's, 55
Bond, James, 94
Bonelli, William, 95, 109, 110, 111
Booth, Newton, 44, 45, 129
Borax Company of California, 75
Borax Consolidated, 75
Borax mining, 75, 130
Boucher, Minnie, 74
Bouquet Canyon, 21, 36, 49, 100, 129; CCC camp in, 103
Bouquet Dam, 114, 131
Bouquet Junction, 46, 52, 57, 70, 93, 95
Bowers, Stephen, 13
Bower's Cave, 12
Boyd, William, *99*
Boyer, Carl, III, 116, 118, 119
Boynton, D.W., 56
Broome, William, 74; duel with Melrose, *74*
Brough, Ed, *66*
Brown, Edmond G. "Jerry," Jr., 117
Brown, Edmond G. "Pat," 115
Brown, Edward H., 130
Bryant, Edwin, 23
Bryant, Mayor, 53
Bushnell, George, 110
Business and industry, 116; auto repair, 70, 85, 86, 87, 88, 94; banking, 131; borax mining, 75, 130; brick manufacturing, 115, 116; cattle industry, 27-28, 32; chambers of commerce, 112, 118, 131; filmmaking, 95-101, 131; freighting, 7, 31, 33, 34, 62, 67, 78, 80, 129; glassmaking, 108, 115; livery stables, 63, 73; lumberyards, 55; mining, 34, 39, 64, 67, 33-34, 64-66, 106, 108; munitions manufacturing, 104, 116; newspaper publishing, 67, 112, 118-119, 130; oil industry, 39-41, 46, 60-61, 62, 63, 71, 105, 107, 108, 130, 131; real estate development, 47, 55, 58, 69, 108, 110, 112, 114, 119, 122, 130, 131; service stations, 80. *See also* names of individual businesses *and* "Partners in Progress" Index
Butterfield, John, 31
Butterfield Overland Express, 7, 31, 78, 80, 129

C

Cal Arts. *See* California Institute of the Arts
California Aqueduct, 114-115
California Department of Water Resources, 115, 116, 119
California Highway Commission, 80
California Institute of the Arts, 113, 119, 131; student performance at, *126*
California Land Company, 110
California Rangers, 31, 58, 59
California Star Oil Works, 41, 49, 60, 61; No. 4 well of, *41*, 61
Callowhill, H. Gil, 116, 118
Camel Corps, 29-30, 35; officer of, *30*
Camerillo, Adolfo, 92
Cameron, Don, 111
Campton, George, 55, *56*; general store of, 55, 56, *57*; residence of, 55
Campton, Gregeria, 56
Camp Verde, 30
Camulos Ranch, 9, 13, 17, 19, 32, 44, 69, 130; adobe house on, *20*
Canyon Country, 7, 110, 112, 117, 118, 131; post office in, 110
Canyon Country Chamber of Commerce, 112
Canyon Country, 117, 118
Carey, Harry, 95, 96, 103, 105
Carey, Olive Golden, 95, *96*
Carey Ranch, 95
Carmichael family, 59
Carr, Trem, 98
Casey, Ethel, *79*
Cassidy, Hopalong. *See* Boyd, William
Castaic, 7, 16, 21, 70, 78-80, 88, 93, 103, 104, 105, 117, 118, 122; aerial views of, *106-107*, *116*; founding of, 130; State Water Project at, 112
Castaic Brick Yard, 115, 116
Castaic Canyon, 36, 80, 93
Castaic Creek, 14, 19, 58, 59, 115
Castaic Dam, 115, 116, 131
Castaic Depot, *79*, 130
Castaic Field, 105
Castaic Hills, 59
Castaic Junction, 7, 9, 13, 14, 16, 17, 23, 32, 78, 79, 90, 103, 129
Castaic Lake, 115, 116, *117*, 120, *126-127*, 131; Lagoon at, *127*
Castaic Post Office, 130
Castaic School, 130
Castaic School District, 80
Castor, Thomas F., 29
Caswell's, 86
Catalonian Volunteers, *13*
Catholic church, first, 130
Cattle industry, 27-28, 32
Cedar Mining District, 34, 64, 67; stamp mill of, *64*
Chaguayabit, 14, 16, 17
Chaguibit, 9, 13
Chaix, Celina, *89*
Chaix, Emil, 73
Chamber of Commerce. *See* Santa Clarita Valley Chamber of Commerce
Chari, Francisco, *21*, 129; home of, 36
Charley Canyon, 59, 78
Chavez, Cleovaro, 45, 47
Chevalier, Maurice, 84
Chormicle, William C., 78
Chouinard Art Institute, 113
Christian Hill, 62
Churches: Acton Community, 64, 130; first Catholic, 130; First Presbyterian, 72, 96; Newhall Community Presbyterian, 49, 130
Circus Vargas, 110
Cisco Kid, 99, 100
Civic incorporation: attempts at, 116-118. *See also* Santa Clarita, City of
Civilian Conservation Corps, 103
Clark, Alf, 110
Clark, Robert, 66
Clark, Robert E., 59
Clark, W. Lewis, 80
Clubs and organizations, 114
Coast Stage Line, 50; schedule of, *50*
Cochems, Anthony, 62
Coldeway, Tony, 110
College of the Canyons, 112, 131; aerial view of, *113*
Colleges: California Institute of the Arts, 113, 119, 126, 131; College of the Canyons, 112, 113, 131; Los Angeles Baptist College, 113; Los Angeles Baptist Theological Seminary, 113; The Masters College, 113
Collins, King, 86
Colorado River project, 91
Colton, David D., *52*, 69
Cone, Helen Wood, 70
Confusion Hill, 105
Conrad Store, 86
Conservation, environmental, 119
Cook, Dolores, *80*
Cook, Fred, *80*
Cook, Mrs., *80*
Cook, Theodore, *80*
Cook, W.H., 80
Cook Ranch, 115, 116
Cooper, Gary, 99
Cordova, Juan, 36
Cordova, Simon, *80*
Cordova, Virginia, *80*
Cordova family, 78, 80; residence of, *80*
Cordova Ranch, 115, 116
Cota, Manuel, 20, 129
Couts, Cave Johnson, 21 25, 27, *29*
Couts, William Blunt, 24-25, 27, 29
Covarrubias, Jose, 36
Crespi, Juan, 13, 16, 17, 129; journal of, 16
Crime, 44-45, 59, 74, 93-94, 129, 130. *See also* Outlaws
Crocker, Charles, 49, 50, *52*, 53
Crown Valley, 74
Crown Valley Feud, 74
Culver, Mae, *58*
Culver, Marguerite, *58*
Cunio, Captain, 36

D

Darcy, Jo Anne, 117, 118, 119
Daries, John Batist, 78
Daries Ranch, 115, 116
Davenport, 75
Del Valle, Antonio Seferino, 14, 18, 19, 20, 23, 112, 129
Del Valle, Ignacio, 18, *19*, 20, 21, 22, 25, 28, 31; children of, *32*, 44, 58, 129
Del Valle, Ignacio, Jr., *32*
Del Valle, Jacoba Feliz, 18, 19, 20, 21
Del Valle, Josepha, *32*
Del Valle, Juventino, 19
Del Valle, Maria, 18
Del Valle, Maria Concepcion, 19
Del Valle, Maria Josepha Carillo, 18
Del Valle, Maria Los Angeles Carrillo, 19
Del Valle, Reginaldo, *32*, 92, 130
Del Valle, Ulpiano, *32*
Del Valle, Ysabel, *32*
Del Valle family, 46, 92; last annual barbecue given by, 92
Den, Nicholas, 19
Department of Water and Power, City of Los Angeles, 76, 90, 114, 131
Diamond, Milt, 114
Dickason, James E., 114
Disney, Walt, 113, 114, 131
Disney Studios, 98, 99
Dones, Sydney P., 92, 93
Doty, Jesse, 87
Doty's Garage, *85*, 87
Downey, John, *52*, 53, 59
Downtown Newhall Merchant Association, 114
Droughts: (1856), 32, 129; (1862), 32, 129; (1980s-1992), 119
Duehren, John F., 117
Duran, Narcisco, 19

E

Earthquakes: (1857), 32, 129; (1893), 130; (1971) 115, 131
Eaton, Fred, 76
Ebbenger, Louis, 75
Eckles, Joe, *66*
Edison Company, 90
Edmonston, Arthur D., 115
Education, 42, 43, 48, 49, 62, 67, 69, 72, 73, 80, 109, 112-113, 129, 130, 131. *See also* Colleges and names of individual schools
Elizabeth Canyon CCC camp, 103
Elizabeth Creek, 115
Elizabeth Lake, 44
Elizabeth Lake School District, 129
Elizabeth Lake Tunnel, 76
Elsmere Canyon, 13, 17, 22, 23, 39, 60, 119
Emma mine, 64
Entertainment, 126, 131
Ericksen, Frank, *66*
Espinosa, Jose, 21, 92
Eternal Valley, 31, 129
Eureka Villa, 93
Evans, Arthur W., 112, 117
Evergreen Motel, 88
Exploration, Spanish, 7, 13, 16, 129

F

Fages, Pedro, 16
Faulkner, Walt, 111
Feather River Project, 115
Feliz, Maria Jesus Lopez de, 23
Felton, Charles, 61
Felton school, 62
Ferguson, Vern, 103
Ferrier, August, *88-89*
Fields, D.W., 56
Figueroa, Jose, 18
Filmmaking, 95-101, 131
Filmore State Bank, 93
Films, Western, *82*, 83-84, 95-101
Film stars, Western, *82*, 83-84, 95, *97*, *98*, *99*, 122, 130
First Presbyterian Church, 72
Flynn, Errol, 95
Ford Garage, 87
Forester, Francisco, 40
Forester, Juan, 40
Fort Tejon, 7, 29, 30, 31, 35, 36, 37, 43; earthquake, 32; establishment of, 129
49er Saloon, 67, 106
Fraser, Alexander Isaac, 69
Fraser, Christine, 69
Fraser, Margaret Forshner, 69
Frates, Frank, 50
Frazier Park, 75
Fredericks, D.A., 74
Freer, Jim, *58*

Fremont, John C., 7, *22*, 23, 24, 36, 59, 129
Fremont Pass, 22, 23, 29, 31, 35, 129
French Village restaurant/motel, 103
Fritz (horse), 83
Frontier Days celebration, 112, 114, 131
Fustero, Francis, 80, *81*
Fustero, Juan Jose, 9, *12*, 13, 130
Fustero, Lena, 80, *81*

G
Gable, Clark, 95
Gage, Henry T., 64, 65, 66, 67
Garasi, Lou, 118
Garces, Francisco, 16
Garcia, Digna, 80, 81
Gavin, Grace, 61
Gavin, Nellie, 61
Gavin, Pat, 61
Gelcich, Vincent, 39, 40
Gibson, Hoot, 95
Gifford, John T., 39, 50, 52, 55
Gifford, Sarah Beckworth, 55
Gleason, James, 34
Gold: discovery of, 15, 20-21; mining of, 33-34, 64-66, 106, 108. *See also* Gold rushes
Golden Oak Adult School, 113
Golden Oak Ranch, 98, 99
Gold rushes, 7, 15; (1842), 21, 92, 129; (1849) 24, 28, 31, 46, 59, 61; (1854), 29, 92; (1930s), 103
Good Templars Lodge, 72
Gorman, James, 36
Gorman, 7, 36, 80, 117
Governor mine, 64
Grapevine Pass, 29, 43, 80
Grizzly Adams, 43
Grizzly bears, *43*, 44, 49; Monarch of the Mountains, *42*, 43, 129
Gulley, James M., 57, 88, 108; general store of, 88, 108

H
Halifax Powder Company, 104
Hap-A-Land, 108
Happy Valley, 72
Hardison, Wallace, 62
Harnischfeger, Tony, 90
Harry Carey Ranch Store Trading Post, *97*
Harris, Jenks, 93
Harrison, Benjamin, 68, 69, 130
Hart, Mary Ellen, 84
Hart, William, Jr., 84
Hart, William S., *82*, 83-84, *84*, 91, 92, 95, 97, 103, 104, 108, 109, 114, 120, 122, 130, 131
Hart High School, William S., 108, 109, 112
Hart Park, William S., 122, 125, 127; Ramona Chapel in, *128*
Hart School District, William S., 131
Hasley Canyon, 16, 78, 80, 92
Hauser Canyon, 77
Havenstrite, Homer, 105
Havenstrite, Russell, 105
Health care, 130, 131
Heidt, Janice, 117, 118
Hellman, Isaac W., *52*
Henry Mayo Newhall Memorial Hospital, 131
Hickson, Ernie, 98, 99, 100, 103, 131
Hill, Paul, 95
Historic sites, *124*, 125, 127, *128*
Hollandsville, 29
Hon, Daniel, 117
Honby Depot, 47
Hoover, Herbert Clark, 64, 67, 68
Hoover, Lou Henry, 64, *66*, 67
Horseshoe Ranch, 84, 130
Hotels, 52, 53, 55, 56-57, 67, 68, 70, 71, 85, 88, 89, 103, 130
Houghton, Lloyd, 108
Hudson, A.A., 35, 36
Humphrys Depot, 47
Huntington, Collis P., 53
Hydraulic Research, 116

I
Ice House, 70
Indians. *See* Native Americans
Iron Tail, 84, *85*

J
Jaurequi, Andy, 96, 114
Jenkins, Anita Ruby, 58, 59. *See also* Kellogg, Anita Jenkins
Jenkins, June, 58, 59
Jenkins, Olive Rhoades, 58, *59*
Jenkins, William W., 31, 40, 44, 58, *59*, 70, 129
Jenkins family, 78
Jenkins Ranch, 105, 131
Johnson, Hiram W., 77
Jones, Buck, *99*
Jones, Robert Trent, 112

K
Kamulus, 9, 13
Kasababian's Pig Farm, 115, 116
Katzenstein, George B., 71
Kazlinski, Andrew, 60
KBET-1220 AM, 119
Kellogg, Anita Ruby Jenkins, 70, 103
Kellogg, Charles, 70
Kemp, 90
Klijac, Jill, 119
Kline, Alice, 117
Koontz, Dennis, 118, 119
Korean War, 119

L
Lake Elizabeth, 7, 29, 94
Lake Hughes, 7, 21
La Liebre Mountains, 80
La Loma de los Vientos, 84, *122*, 130
Lamkin, Naomi, 89
Lang, John, *42*, 43, 44, 129; family of, *42*; ranch of, 52
Lang, 75
Lang Depot, 47
Lang's Hotel, 52, 53
Lang Station, 42, 43, 52, 75, 131; Golden Spike Ceremony at, *52-53*, 55, 130
Las Palomas Canyon, 21
Lasuen, Fermin Francisco, 16
Law enforcement, 58, *94*
Lazy Z Ranch, 58, 59
Leaming, Christopher, 39, 40
LeBeck, Peter, 43
Lebeck, 7
Lebrun, Frank, 77, 108
Lebrun Ranch, *106*
Lechler, Abbie, 80, *81*
Lechler, Abigail J. Hazzard, 78, *79*
Lechler, George Washington, 78, *79*
Lechler, Hazel, 80, *81*
Lechler, Maudie, 80, *81*
Lee, S. Charles, 109
Leighton, Joe, 71
Leiva, Abdon, 44, 58
Leiva, Rosaria, 44
Levine, Mike, 119
Light, Bill, 117
Lindenfeld and Landell (store), *54*, 55
Live Oak Canyon, 15, 20
Live Oaks School District, 80
Lock, Ed, 90
Lone Pine, 90
Lopez, Chico, 21
Lopez, Juan Francisco, 15, 20, 21, 92, 129
Lopez, Juan Jose, 36
Lopez, Pedro, 21
Lopez family, 78
Los Angeles, 16, 20, 21, 23, 24, 25, 28, 30, 31, 32, 33, 35, 40, 42, 43, 44, 45, 46, 47, 49, 50, 52, 53, 58, 60, 64, 71, 75, 76, 78, 80, 85, 90, 94, 106, 108, 110, 112, 119
Los Angeles Aqueduct, 36, 76-77, 85; opening ceremony for, 77
Los Angeles Asphaltum and Petroleum Mining District, 39, 40
Los Angeles Baptist College, *113*
Los Angeles Baptist Theological Seminary, 113
Los Angeles Board of Supervisors, 31, 35, 47
Los Angeles Conservatory of Music, 113
Los Angeles County, 116, 117, 118
Los Angeles County Sheriff's Department office, 108, *109*
Los Angeles Evening Express, 60
Los Angeles-Owens Valley Aqueduct, 114
Los Angeles Westerners Corral, 100
Los Angeles Petroleum Refining Company, 40
Los Angeles Star, 29, 30, 52
Los Angeles Times, 77, 110
Los Padres National Forest, 92
Lummis, Charles F., 92
Lynch, Ann, 112, 117
Lynch, Ken, 112, 117
Lyon, Annie, 31
Lyon, Cyrus, 7, 31, 42, 58, 71, 129
Lyon, Sanford, 7, *31*, 39, 40, 58, 71, 129
Lyon Ranch, 115, 116
Lyons Bowl, 117
Lyons Canyon, 39
Lyons Refinery, 60
Lyon's Station, 31, 39, 40, 44, 47, 50, 55, 60, 71, 130

M
McBean, Atholl, 110, 114
McDonald, May, *79*
McKeon, Howard "Buck," 118
Magic Mountain, 114, 118, 120, 131; Viper roller coaster at, *121*
Mammoth Claim, 39
Mather, Steven, 75
Mayhue, Lillie Belle, *58*, *106*, 108
Mayhue, Opal, 106, *107*, 108
Mayhue, Pallie, 106, *107*, 108
Mayhue, William, 106, *107*, 108
Maynard, Ken, 99
Melody Ranch, 96, 100, *101*, 131; destruction of by fire, *101*, 131; reconstruction of, 131
Melrose, Flossie A., 74
Melrose, N.H. "Rosy," 74; duel with Broome, *74*
Mentry, Arthur, 61
Mentry, Charles "Alex," *41*, 49, 61, 130; ranch of, 61; residence of, *62*
Mentry, Flora May Lake, 49, 61
Mentry, Guy, 61
Mentry, Irene, 61
Mentry, Ray, 61
Mentry family, 63
Mentryville, 41, 47, 61-63, 71, 105
Mexican War, 23, 129
Miguel, Jose de, 17
Mills, Bonnie, 117
Miners, hard-rock, *66*, 106
Mint Canyon, 33, 104, 110, 112
Mint Canyon Chamber of Commerce, 112
Mint Canyon Elks Lodge, 117
Mitchell, Francis Ann, 34
Mitchell, Frank A., 34
Mitchell, John Wesley, 34
Mitchell, Martha, 42, 43
Mitchell, Mary, 34
Mitchell, Mary Catherine Taylor, 34
Mitchell, Minnie Ivey, 34
Mitchell, Thomas Finley, 33, 34, 42, *43*, 44, 129; cabin of, *33*
Mitchell, Thomas Finley, Jr., 34
Mix, Tom, 84, 95-96, *97*, 114
Mixville, 96
Mojave, 69
Monogram Pictures, 98
Monogram Western Town, 96, 98, 100, 103
Moore, Charley, 78
Moore, Joe, *58*
Moore's Station, 29
Morris Newspaper Corporation, 118
Mulholland, William, *76*, 77, 85, 90, 91
Munoz, Pedro, 17

N
Nadeau, Remi, 36, 43, 110
Native Americans, 8-13, 84, *85*; Chumash, 9; Piute, 33; Tataviam, *8*, 9-13, 16, 129, 130
Needham, Henry Clay, 71, *72*, 108
Newhall, Edwin White, 46
Newhall, George Almer, 46
Newhall, Henry Gregory, 46, 58, 69
Newhall, Henry Mayo, 7, 33, 34, *46*, 47, 55, 56, 58, 67, 69, 112, 130
Newhall, Margaret Jane, 46, 110
Newhall, Ruth, 118-119
Newhall, Sarah Ann White, 46
Newhall, Scott, 112, 118-119
Newhall, Tony, 118-119
Newhall, Walter Scott, 46
Newhall, William Mayo, 46
Newhall, 7, 9, 13, 46, 49, 62, 71, 77, 80, 83, 84, 85, 91, 92, 93, 104, 107, 108, 109, 113, 116, 117, 118, 131; first elementary school in, 129; first service station in, *86*, 87; founding of, 54-58, 130; Fourth of July celebration, 100, 114, 119, *125*, 131; Horseshoe Ranch in, 84; main street of, *56-57*; as movie location, 95, 97, 100; oil industry in, 105; old-timers reunion in, *102*, 103; post office, 89; relocation of, 57, 60; Sheriff's Office in, 108, *109*; Swall Block in, *88-89*
Newhall Community Hospital, 130
Newhall Community Presbyterian Church, 49, 130
Newhall Depot, 47, 55, 125
Newhall Hills, USS, 104
Newhall Land and Farming Company, 47, 58, 69, 108, 110, 114, 119, 130, 131
Newhall Livery Stable, 63,73
Newhall Park, 58, 119
Newhall Pass, 25, 29, 129, 131
Newhall Pharmacy, 88, 89
Newhall Presbyterian Church, 96; as movie set, *96*
Newhall Ranch, 46, 58, 105
Newhall Refinery, *60*, 131. *See also* Pioneer Refinery
Newhall School: (first), *48*, 49, 72, 73; (second), 72, *73*, 103
Newhall Signal, 112, 118, 130
Newhall Tunnel, 103
Newmark, Harris, *52*
Newspapers, 67, 112, 118-119, 130
New York mine, 33, 64
Nickel, Rudolph Eugene, 67, 68, 130
North Oaks, 36, *110*
Nuhubit, 9, 13

O
Oak Canyon, 21
Oak Creek, 98
Oak Flat CCC camp, 103
Oak of the Golden Dream, 15, 98
O'Connell, Margaret, 69, 70
Oil industry, 39-41, 60-61, 62, 63, 71, 105, 130, 131
O'Kane and Brain, 105
Old Orchard Shopping Center, 112
Old Towne Days, 114
Olme, Joe, *80*
O'Reilly, James, 33, 34
Ortega, Manuelita, 19
Osborn family, 70
Otis, Harrison Gray, 77
Outlaws, 44-45, 58, 59, 93, *94*,129, 130
Owens Lake, 90
Owens Valley, 90

P
Pacheco, Romualdo, *52*
Pacific Coast Oil Company, 61, 62
Palmdale, 89
Paper Mill Canyon, 33
Pardee, Charles, *63*
Pardee, Ed, *63*, 71, 72; livery stable of, *73*; residence of, 71
Pardee, Pearl, *71*
Pardee House, 96, *96*
Parnell mine, 33
Parsons, Sam, 80, 88; general store of, 88, 130
Pattee, F.W., 67, 130
Pearl (oil well), 72
Pember, Jack, 93, 94
Perkins, Arthur B., 109
Persian Gulf War, 119, 131
Peters, Dr., 130
Peterson, N. E., 92
Philadelphia and California Petroleum Company, 46
Phillips, Everett, 112
Phillips, Frances Delano, *87*, 88
Phillips, Harry, 88
Pico, Andres, 23, 35, 39, *40*, 129

Pico, Pio, 22
Pico Camp, 60, 71
Pico Canyon, 7, 39, 40, 47, 49, 58, 60, *62*, 63, 71, 89, 105, 129, 130; oil workers, *63*
Pico Springs, 41, 61
Pilcher, Jack, 93, *94*
Pine Canyon, 29, 39
Pioneer Refinery, *60*, 130, 131
Piru, 16, 20, 21, 76, *78-79*, 112; bank robbery in, 93
Piru Canyon, 17, 103
Piru Creek, 9, 16, 17, 19, 46, 47, 92, 114
Piru Dam, 131
Piru Lake, 78, 80, 131
Piru-U-Bit, 9, 13
Placerita Canyon, 21, 39, 41, 87, 92, 95, 103, 112, 113; gold discovered in, 129; as movie location, 95, 98, 99, 100; oil industry in, 105
Placeritos Canyon, 21
Placeritos Ranch, 100
Porter, David D., 30
Portola, Gaspar de, *13*, 129
Portola Expedition, 13, 16
Powell, Dora Lake, *49*, *61*
Powell, Florence, *61*
Powell, Francis, *61*
Powell, Fred *61*
Powell, John F., *47*, *49*, *61*, 130
Powell family, 63
Prall family, 63
Prehistory, 7
Prohibition, 94; enforcement officers, *94*
Provost, Arthur, 92
Puritan mine, 64, 67
Pyle, Everette, 12
Pyle, McCoy, 12
Pyramid Dam, 116
Pyramid Lake, 115, 116, 119

Q

Quail Lake, 29

R

Radio, local, 119
Railroad Canyon, 60
Railroads, 49-53
Ralphs family, 36
Rancheria del Corral, 129
Rancho Castac (Castaic), 35, 36, 129
Rancho del Bouquet, 21, 129
Rancho La Liebre, 32, 35, 36
Rancho Los Alamos y Agua Caliente, 35, 36
Rancho Placeritos, 98
Rancho San Fernando, 39, 40
Rancho San Francisco, 7, 14, 16, 17, 19, 20, 21, 32, 46, 55, 58, 129, 130
Rancho Santa Clarita, 109, 131
Rancho Tejon, 32, 35, 36
Rancho Temescal, 21, 92, 129
Ravenna, Manuel, 33, 34
Ravenna, 33, 34, 129
Ravenna Depot, *34*
Rayburn, Logan K., 67
Reader, William, 31, 58
Reagan, Ronald, 99
Real estate development, residential, 110, 112, 122, 131
Recreation, 114, 120, 121, 125, 127, 131
Red Rover mine, 64; interior of, *66*
Reidel, Roland, 103
Religion, 67, 72, 130. *See also* Churches
Renaldo, Duncan, 99, *100*
Renfro Drugs, 86
Republic Pictures, 98
Reservoir Summit, 88
Reyes, Francisco, 16
Reynolds, Burt, 88
Rice, Dr., 39
Rice Canyon, oil fields of, 107, 108
Ridge Route, 59, 80, 85, 88, 103, 130, 131
Ridge Route Garage, 88
Ritter, Tex, 114
Rivera, Philip, *88-89*
Robbins, Oliver P., 35, 36
Robinson, Alfred, 21
Rodriguez, Maria del Carmen, 19
Rogers, Earl, 74
Rogers, Roy, 98, 114, *115*

Rogers, Will, 77, 84
Roland, Gilbert, 99
Romero, Caesar, 99
Roosevelt, Theodore, 59, 64, *67*, 68, 130
Rose, Billy, 59
Rose, William Blackburn, 78
Rose family, 59
Rowland, William "Billy," 45
Royal Dutch, 105
Ruiz, L., 36
Ruiz family, 36
Russell, Charles M., 84, 92
Ruttman, Troy, 110
Rye Canyon, 112

S

St. Francis Dam, 90, *91*, 108; under construction, *90*
St. Francis Dam disaster, 90-91, *91*, 95, 97, 130
St. John, John, 71
St. John subdivision, 71-72
Salazar, Jose, 20, 21, 22, 23, 32
Saloons: Derrick, 71, *72*, 73; Lifton's, 71; Mike Powell's Palace, 71; Nick Rivera's, 71; Wilson's, 55
Sam's Place, 80
San Blas Company, 18
Sandberg, Herman, 88
Sandberg, 88
Sand Canyon, 36
San Fernando, 31, 40, 62, 89
San Fernando Mining District, 39
San Fernando Mission, 9, 14, 16, 17, 18, 21; dedication of, 129
San Fernando Tunnel, *38*, 39, 50, 51, 52, 55, 130; post office of, *51*
San Fernando Valley, 22, 39, 50, 106, 112
San Francisquito Canyon, 29, 31, 36, 53, 76, 80, 85, 94, 95, 108, *122-123*, 129; gold mining in, 106; Power House Number One, 77; Power House Number Two, 90; St. Francis Dam in, 90, 130; Tunnel Station Camp in, 76
San Gabriel Mountains, 50
San Martin Canyon, 92
Santa Clara Divide Peak, 13
Santa Clara Oil Company, 39, 40
Santa Clara River, 14, 17, 19, 25, 30, 36, 43, 44, 46, 64, 78, 120; basin of, 16; naming of, 129; plain of, 52
Santa Clarita, City of, 7, 118; city council, 118, 119; incorporation of, 118, 131; population statistics for, 119, 131
Santa Clarita National Bank, 131
Santa Clarita Post Office, 131
Santa Clarita Sentinel, 112
Santa Clarita Valley Chamber of Commerce, 118, 131
Santa Clarita Valley Citizen, 119
Santa Clarita Valley Historical Society, 114, 127, 131; headquarters of, *124*, 125
Santa Feliciana Creek, 92
Santa Maria, Vicente de, 16
Santa Monica Mountains Conservancy, 119
Santa Susana Mountains, 40
Sarro, Carmen, 118
Saugus, 7, 11, 69-70, 76, 85, *86-87*, 88, 94, 95, 104, 112, 116, 117, 118, 122, 130
Saugus Air Field, 104
Saugus Cafe, 69, 70, 86, 88, 106, 130
Saugus Elementary School, 103
Saugus Post Office, 70
Saugus Ranger District, 92
Saugus School, *69*
Saugus School District, 69
Saugus Speedway, 95, 110, *111*, 120, 125, *127*, 131
Saugus Swapmeet, 110, 120, *125*, 131
Saugus Train Station, 68, 69, 70, 93, 114, 120, *124*, 125, 130
Schmidt, Helm, 110
Schuyler, Anthony H., 88, 93
Scofield, Demetrius G., 40, 41, 60, 61
Scott, Denton Cyrus, 60
Scott, John A., 41
Scott, Thomas, 129
Seco Canyon, 49; first housing tract in, 108, 109, 131

Serra, Junipero, 13, *16*
Settlement, Spanish, 16-20, 129
Seward, F.D., 130
Shepard, Henry, 75
Sherman, Gene, 105
Shopping centers, 112, 119, 131
Sierra Pelona, 47
Simmons' general store, 110
Sischo, Carl, 86, 87
Six Flags Corporation, 114, 131
Skirvin, Olin, 103
Smith, Babcock, 84, 130
Smith, Francis M. "Borax," 75
Smith, Margie, 87
Smith, Thompson, ranch of, 33
Smith, W.S., 40, 60
Snyder, Jerry, 110
Soledad Canyon, 16, 33, 42, 43, 52, 55, 84, 93, 103, 110, 112, 129; CCC camp in, 103; as movie location, 98; as Vasquez's hide-out, 130
Soledad City, 33, 34, 44, 47, 129
Soledad Judicial District, 47, 130
Soledad Post Office, 67, 129
Soledad School, 67
Soledad Township, 94
Solemint, 110, 112
Solemint Store, 110
Southern Hotel, 55, *56-57*, 71, 130
Southern Pacific Railroad, 42, 46, 49, 52, 53, 55, 67, 69, 71, 78, 79, 94, 125, 130, 131
Standard Oil of California, 41
Stanford, Leland, 49, 50, *52*, 53
Stanwyck, Barbara, 84
Star Oil Company, 40, 60
State Water Project, 112, 115
Stearns, Abel, 21, 22, 27
Steele, Bob, 99
Sterling borax mine, 75
Sterling Borax Works, 75, 130; reduction plant of, *75*
Stewart, Lyman, 62
Stone, Cliffie, 112
Stonegate homes, 59
Sulphur Springs School: (first), 42, 43, 129
Suphur Springs School District, 42, 43
Suraco, Charles, 36
Suraco, Dominga Garla, 36
Suraco, Joseph Antonio, *36*
Suraco, Juan Bautista, *36*, 44
Surrey, 69
Surrey Inn, 70; interior of, *70*
Surrey Post Office, 70, 130
Swall, Albert, 87-88, *88-89*, 108
Swall, Frank, *58*
Swall Hotel, *85*, 88, 89
Sylmar, 77, 115

T

Talmadge, Norma, 84
Talmadge, Richard, 96, 97
Tapia, Jesus, 78
Tapia Canyon, 7, 78
Tapia family, 78
Taylor, Lillie Florence, 71
Taylor, Robert, 84
Tehachapi Mountains, 30, 43, 49, 115
Tejon Route, 80
Telegraph Stage, *33*, 34, 62
Temescal School, 80; students of, *81*
Temple, John (Juan), 22, 25
Thatcher Glass, 115; employee of, *108*
The Masters College, 113
Thompson, Sonia, 119
Thompson's Corner Post Office, 33, 69
Thompson's general store, 110
Thorkildson, Thomas, 75
Tick Canyon, 75
Tip's restaurant, 103, *104*
Tochonanga, 9, 13
Tolefree, James A., 69
Tolefree's Saugus Eating House, 69
Tourist attractions, 114, 120, *124*, *125*
Towsley, Darius, 39, 40
Towsley Canyon, *6*, 7, 9, 39, 119
Train Robbery, Great Saugus, 93-94, 130; aftermath of, *93*
Transportation, 26, 28, 29, 31, 33, 34, 35-36,

37, 38, 39, 43, 49-53, 62, 71, 76, 77, 79, 80, 85, 87, 88, 103, 129, 130, 131
Treaty of Guadalupe-Hidalgo, 129
Triunfo, 16
Trueblood, Fred, Jr., 100, 104
Trueblood Rest Stop, 36
Truman, Benjamin C., *52*
Tumble Inn, 88
Turner, Frank, 117
Turner, Lee, 117

U

U.S. Borax, 75
U.S. Dragoons, Company "A," 29
Union Oil Company, 62
United Water district, 114
Universal Pictures, 104
Urtasun, Mrs., 80

V

Valencia, 7, 107, 108, 110, 112, 113, 115, 116, 117, 118, 131
Valencia Town Center. *See* Shopping centers
Val Verde, 7, 78, 92, 93, 114, 117; black World War I veterans in, *92*, 93; Cinco de Mayo fiesta, 114
Van Norman, Harvey, 77, 90
Vasquez, Claudio, 44
Vasquez, Francisco, 44
Vasquez, Tiburcio, 7, 11, 33, *44*, 45, 47, 58, 59, 93, 129, 130
Vasquez Rocks, *10-11*, 44
Vasquez Rocks County Park, 12
Veluzat, Paul, 100, 131
Ventura, 40, 46, 67, 70, 71, 90, 91
Ventura County, 114, 116
Vernon, "Buffalo" Tom, 93, 94, 130. *See also* Averill, Tom
Victor Gruen Associates, 110
Victoria, Manuel, 18
Vietnam War, 119
Villa Rancho, 92
Vukovich, Bill, 110
Vulcan Company, 75

W

Walker Ranch, 95
Water supply, 114-116, 117, 131
Wayne, John, 95, 96, *98*
Weldon Canyon, 131
Wells, George, 117
Wells Fargo and Co., 31, 78; offices of, 67
Western Development, 55
Western Livestock Yards, 95
Western Walk of Stars, 114, 120
Westover, Winifred, 84
White, Doc, 110
Whitney, Henry M., 75
Whitney, Mary Barnes, *52*
Whitney, Robert M., *52*
Wiley, Henry Clay, 27, 28, 29, 39, 40, 58, 129; windlass of, *26*, 27, 28, 29
Wiley Canyon, 39
Wiley Station, 28, 31
Wilson, B.D., *52*, 53
Wilson, Margaret H., *52*
Wolfskill, William, 22, 32, 46
Wood, Richard, *69*, 70, 88, 130
Wood, Martin, *69*, 70, 88, 130
Wood, Mrs. Martin, *69*
Wood, Mrs. Richard, *69*
Wood's Garage, 70, 86, 88, 94
Worden, Connie, 117
World War I, black veterans of, *92*, 93
World War II, 103-105; end of, 106

Y

Yant, Milford, 105
Yarnell, James, 71
Ye Olde Courthouse, 108
Youle, W.E., 60

Z

Zell, LaVon Harker, *89*
Zenith (oil well), 72